Edward Pennell Elmhirst

The Hunting Countries of England, Their Facilities, Character, and Requirements

A guide to hunting men

Edward Pennell Elmhirst

The Hunting Countries of England, Their Facilities, Character, and Requirements
A guide to hunting men

ISBN/EAN: 9783337427436

Printed in Europe, USA, Canada, Australia, Japan

Cover: Foto ©Lupo / pixelio.de

More available books at **www.hansebooks.com**

THE

HUNTING COUNTRIES

OF

ENGLAND,

THEIR FACILITIES, CHARACTER, AND REQUIREMENTS.

A GUIDE TO HUNTING MEN.

By BROOKSBY.

VOLUME I.
PARTS I., II., AND III.

LONDON:
HORACE COX,
"THE FIELD" OFFICE, 346, STRAND, W.C.

1882.

CONTENTS.

PART I.

	PAGE.
INTRODUCTION	1
THE BELVOIR	5
THE SOUTH WOLD	18
THE BROCKLESBY	33
THE BURTON AND THE BLANKNEY	40
THE FITZWILLIAM	55
THE QUORN	65
THE COTTESMORE	91
THE PUCKERIDGE	107
THE OLD BERKELEY	114

PART II.

THE NORTH WARWICKSHIRE	123
THE PYTCHLEY	130
THE WOODLAND PYTCHLEY	146
THE ATHERSTONE	154
THE BILLESDON OR SOUTH QUORN	165
THE MEYNELL	173
THE BICESTER AND WARDEN HILL HUNT	185
THE HEYTHROP	200
THE OLD BERKSHIRE	208
THE SOUTH OXFORDSHIRE	217
THE SOUTH NOTTINGHAMSHIRE	223
THE EAST KENT	234
THE TICKHAM	241

	PAGE
THE VINE	250
THE SOUTH BERKSHIRE	257
MR. GARTH'S	265
THE H. H.	271
THE TEDWORTH	278
LORD FERRERS'	287
THE WARWICKSHIRE	293

PART III.

THE DULVERTON	305
THE STARS OF THE WEST	316
MR. LUTTRELL'S	325
LORD PORTSMOUTH'S	330
THE ESSEX AND THE ESSEX UNION	340
THE HERTFORDSHIRE	349
THE WHADDON CHASE	356
THE VALE OF WHITE HORSE	365
THE CHESHIRE AND SOUTH CHESHIRE	371
THE BLACKMOOR VALE	384
THE CAMBRIDGESHIRE	392
THE DUKE OF GRAFTON'S	400
THE HOLDERNESS	407
THE OAKLEY	414
THE NORTH HEREFORDSHIRE	422
THE DUKE OF BUCCLEUCH'S	430
THE TYNEDALE	438
LORD PERCY'S	446
THE MORPETH	454
THE RUFFORD	460

THE
HUNTING COUNTRIES
OF
ENGLAND.

INTRODUCTION.

THE object of the series of which this article forms No. 1, will be to afford to hunting men some guide in their choice of country—whether for a visit or a permanence. With this view it will be our endeavour to give, as clearly and concisely as we can, some idea of the characteristics and requirements of each country in turn; so that the reader may learn at a glance under what conditions he will have to open his campaign—should he wish to hunt with a certain pack.

Many men are fond of trying two or three different countries in the same season. Many more would gladly do so, could they but learn at any moment what they must look forward to in the country they propose to visit next. But a work of reference, to aid them in determining their movements, so as best to suit their own peculiar tastes and capabilities, is wanting. In short, a hunting tour would be a much more common undertaking if only a book, and a map, were always at hand—from which to learn where the individual, and his stud, will find themselves most at home.

Army men especially are often puzzled to fix upon the scene of their two or three months' sport. They would frequently prefer to vary their sphere of action; but as their term of leave is limited, they cannot afford the risk of disappointment in trying new ground. Often, too, their stud is weak in numbers; they wish to make the most of it, but do not care to throw their lot in where, if unable to hunt *every* day, they would find themselves left more or less in the lurch. For this reason they must follow the chase either within reach of their own neighbourhood and connections, or within reasonable distance of their Club and the resources of Town.

City men in the same way can seldom afford to devote themselves for long together to the more isolating phases of the sport. They are fain to divide their time, in such proportion as they may, between the two rival divinities whom they serve. The dusty shrine in Lombard-street has as strong a claim upon them as the sylvan grove of Faunus; and for each hour in the merry company of the goat-like deity they must devote two to the golden calf.

It has long been received as an apothegm, that when you are in London you are within reach of everywhere else; and so, in dealing with each country, it will be assumed that London is the base from which the inquirer intends to start. For the route thence to any point is a direct and easy one. To master cross-country travel by groping through the maze of Bradshaw and local map must be left to the

Introduction. 3

ingenuity of the explorer himself; and thus all allusions to the comparative accessibility of different hunting quarters is to be taken with regard to London as the starting point.

Stanford's Large Scale Railway and Station Maps will be taken as illustrating and fixing the topography of the work in question. These are coloured to show the divisions of England into hunts, and will be found as accurate as such frequently-shifting and often indefinite geography can well be. Being on a scale of three miles to an inch, they are of sufficient size to admit of all the principal points and features of a country being shown, and yet are not over-crowded with unnecessary names. They are in twenty-four sheets—each sheet being 28in. by 20in. The price of each sheet is—plain 1s., mounted in case 2s. 6d.; coloured 1s. 6d., in case 3s. The coloured ones, mounted in case, are much to be preferred for our purpose.

As we have inferred before, our object will be to sketch out a *menu*, from which men may choose as their appetite prompts.

It is not every one who enjoys the presence of a crowd, who loves the rush and scramble of three or four hundred people struggling for a start, or who even cares for the thrill of a dashing burst over the grass. Nor, again, is it every one to whom the sight of hounds picking their way over a cold fallow is a thing of joy, nor does every one appreciate the crash of a woodland or the blind plunge down a deep ride. Verily some men hunt to ride, some ride to hunt, and others, thank heaven, double their fun by doing both. *Chacun à son goût.* Let us try and show where each of you can suit his taste, his weight, his nerves, his age and his purse—and yet not go into a barren land.

Most vital contingent and condition of all is the purse. Carry one you must, and always either have a coin in it or imagine you have. This done, its variations need have a less general and arbitrary effect upon your sport than would be imagined. If it be at a low ebb you cannot of course (honestly) buy as many horses as you might otherwise do; and you can't hunt as many days per week. In these ways the ill-filled purse has, it is impossible to deny, a most depressing and confining effect. But beyond these its influence is by no means as strongly felt as the other conditions enumerated—at all events in the main point under consideration—choice of country. If your taste, weight, age and nerves are right, go into a *good* country while you can—and with all confidence. Make yourself other pursuits there to fill up your interim time; or else, as discussed above, let your choice light within reach of your main occupation. Railways have brought good countries enough within reach of London: and almost every other great centre can boast of the same advantage. For, we would argue, a horse eats no more in a *good country* than in a bad one; hotel and stabling charges vary on quite other principles (we know not what) than those of locality; in *no* country are you likely to ride a worse horse if you can afford a better; the best saddlery is everywhere economy; and you ought to have (Why on earth *don't* you?) good leathers, decent boots coat and hat *wherever* you hunt.

THE BELVOIR.*

Our first sketch deals with what is undoubtedly a *good country* in every sense of the term; and one which, perhaps, of all others, admits of an individual enjoying and sharing in hunting of the highest class without necessarily binding him to great extravagance of either time or money. The magnificent Belvoir pack is open, on the one hand, to the Meltonian— with the extensive stud that is almost a *sine quâ non* to the residence in Melton—or is still more constantly and readily available to whoever may choose Grantham as his resting place. Grantham is a neat little town of about 5000 inhabitants, situate in the very midst of the Duke of Rutland's Hunt and replete with every convenience for the hunting man. It lies some six miles from the beautiful Castle of Belvoir, and consequently from the Kennels; while almost all the meets are within a radius of ten or a dozen miles. In two hours and thirty-five minutes from King's Cross the Great Northern Railway (according to Mr. Jorrocks, the best covert hack in England) will land you at Grantham; but unless you are hardy and vigorous enough to leave London at 5 a.m., you will find it more convenient to employ the iron horse to

---

* *Vide* Stanford's " Railway and Hunting Maps," sheet 10.

convey you down to dinner over-night, rather than as a covert hack in the morning.

The Belvoir hounds are quite one of the oldest packs in the kingdom—their kennel books dating back as far as 1756—and certainly they are at the present time the most *striking* pack in England at the covertside. Their beautiful uniformity of colouring, their high class, and their wonderful evenness in appearance are quite unapproached elsewhere. It might be thought that these qualities could not have been brought to such a pitch of excellence, without sacrifice of other more practical attributes, did we not know that nearly a century and a half has been expended in reaching this standard, and that each year as many as a hundred couple of puppies (occasionally even more) are sent out to walk. With such a choice of new material there can be little difficulty in filling up the gaps—or even to maintain a standard so unyielding. It puzzles an outsider to imagine how the kennel men ever learn their hounds by name—so extraordinarily similar are they in marking and *contour*. Every hound has the black "saddle-mark" on his back; every hound has his "Belvoir tan" head; while the groundwork of each skin is purest white. To draw them by name, when standing with their heads all in one direction, would indeed seem an almost hopeless feat. On their pedigrees and history we do not propose to enter here. These have been discussed at length in the columns of *The Field;* and have no immediate connection with our present purpose. But we say it with emphasis, "Who has not seen the Belvoir at the covertside

The Belvoir.

has missed a sight such as no other pack can afford."

With sixty to sixty-five couple of hounds in kennel, they hunt five days a week—which is quite as much as a huntsman can do without over-taxing his strength or destroying his energy. Indeed, in such open seasons as the two last the strain upon the huntsman's physical powers must have been immense—bearing in mind that two months of cubhunting (itself a tiring experience) precede November, and that a huntsman must ever be the last man home.

No country presents a greater variety in itself than the Belvoir. Within its confines you may ride over small grass meadows, broad grazing grounds, light heath and heavy plough. Thus it is impossible to sum up its characteristics in a sentence or two; but they must rather be left to make themselves apparent as we go on to classify the different sections of His Grace's kingdom.

On Mondays and alternate Saturdays the meets are fixed for the neighbourhood of the Castle—and these are Belvoir (for the home woods), Three Queens (whence a gallop over the light plough and easy fences of what they term their "heath country" may generally be looked for), Denton Hall and Harlaxton Hall—the two latter being about midway between Grantham and the kennels. This portion of the country you may well choose for schooling your young horse or for trying your last purchase. But when you get into the Belvoir Vale—a part of which is also comprised in the Monday-and-alternate-Saturday district—you must take out a hunter not only

The Hunting Countries of England.

powerful but well bred; one that can gallop through a deep plough and lift you over a strong fence out of it. For round Plungar, Scrimshaw's Mill, Bottesford, Elton Manor and Staunton—also Allington Hall (all about due north of the Castle) the farmers till their land to the uttermost depths, and gird their fields with stake-and-bounds of the strongest and with ditches dug wide and deep.

On Tuesdays and Fridays hounds are out on their Lincolnshire side—west of Grantham. The best of this is round Folkingham, where there is a wide extent of grass and two capital gorse coverts, called respectively Folkingham Gorse and Heathcote's Gorse. Other famous strongholds in these parts are the Sapperton and Newton Woods, always full of foxes ready to run far and run straight—and the surrounding country being strongly fenced, and carrying a good scent, a bad hunter is of little use here, albeit you have none of the crowd of the Leicestershire side to compete against. A timber jumper is a *sine quâ non* to safe conveyance, as post-and-rails are much in favour for hedge-repair. With a fairly good and fast hunter you may see as much sport hereabouts as anywhere in the Duke's country; for there are no rivers (nor for that matter any *brooks*—so you may save the water jumper of your stable for elsewhere), no canals, and at present no railway to hinder the progress or divert a fox's course. Lenton Village, Weaver's Lodge and Newton Bar are the most likely fixtures.

In the southern portion of this Lincolnshire country are fine large woods, which in former days swarmed with foxes and were thought of in connection with

The Belvoir.

little else. Nowadays there is usually a fox; but the pheasants crowd Reynard out terribly; and the tube of iron gives a more welcome sound to the native ear than the horn of brass. In nearly every other part of the Belvoir country there is a good stock of foxes.

An eastward boundary is formed by the fens of Lincolnshire — an unhuntable tract running up to Boston—but on the north of Folkingham and still in close propinquity of Grantham come Aswarby (Sir Thomas Whichcote's), Culverthorpe, Dembleby Thorns, and Haydor Southards—places full of foxes wild and good. Long runs are the rule rather than the exception; for these foxes travel well, and take some catching over the heavy ploughs which characterise the neighbourhood. And yet, when thoroughly wet, these ploughs maintain a good scent.

Still more to the north we get to Rauceby, where foxes are also well cared for. From Rauceby to Leadenham is again heath land, divided by stone walls into fields of from fifty to one hundred acres. Its scent lies best on it when dry—and with a scent on it hounds can often run clean away from horses. So here your requirements in the matter of horseflesh are again diversified, and blood becomes more an essential than bone.

Leadenham is one of the boundary marks between the Belvoir and the Blankney, and Colonel Reeve finds foxes for both. Dipping into the lower country west of Leadenham we find ourselves in as strong a grass country as it is desirable to ride over; and from Stubton Gorse the Belvoir have scored as many nice gallops of late years as from any covert in the hunt.

Stubton is a favourite meet, as Mr. Neville, though not hunting himself, takes a delight in providing sport for others. From Stubton Gorse to Wellingore is a line of which foxes are fond. Take out a big jumper or you will not ride it!

Other meets between Leadenham and Grantham are Belton Park, Syston Park, Hough-on-the-Hill, Caythorpe Hall, and Fulbeck Hall—and for the last two you want a horse that can travel the Stubton country.

Turning to the Melton district, other conditions have to be considered, other essentials to be borne in mind and other requirements to be set forth. We have spoken hitherto only of what we may designate as the *home country* of the Belvoir—and we use this term by no means in a depreciatory sense, but yet as implying scene and surroundings totally different but to many minds preferable, to that found in the district with which we are now about to deal. Real sport—and nothing but the sport—being the primary object, we are inclined to concede (if only by way of forestalling argument) that such is more likely of attainment on the Lincolnshire than the Leicestershire side of the Belvoir country. For in the former division the ground is, at least here and there, equally favourable; the hounds are the same, while the foxes are undoubtedly *better*. In the one you have a local field, of reasonable dimensions and less ardent aspiration; the huntsman has every chance, hounds every facility, and the unambitious man every opportunity of seeing all that is to be seen. In the latter you have a swollen field, a jealous—no, let us say, a zealous—

The Belvoir.

crowd; your horse should be a little faster, your heart a trifle harder, and your eye a moment quicker, than your neighbour's. Presuming that you possess these advantages, can persuade yourself you have them, or can make up for their want by cunning strategy of movement—then the Gilead of the Melton neighbourhood has indeed balm for you. Without these desiderata or their apology you will never pluck the fruit which hangs so temptingly, except in a second-hand sort of way which *may* content but is more likely to rouse a sense of disappointment and a return to a less exciting and less invidious sphere of action. For here you enter a competition which from its very popularity prevents success to every candidate. There is not room for all in the front, the weak must be crowded out, and only the stouter and swifter can attain a share in the prize. It is not that the country is in itself more difficult to ride over, or that to live with hounds would be a less easy matter here than elsewhere—had you always room to pick your own place, in your own time, and at your own pace. But when hounds fly, with the lightning speed so common to them over this quick-scenting grass, there ensue a rush and a stampede from which only superior quickness, nerve, and decision can extricate a man, and allow him to pass in safety through the whirlpool to sail on over the smoother water beyond. The aim of every rider to hounds is (perhaps we had better say, *should be*) to *see a run* and *every* run if he can (though, again, the question naturally suggests itself—*who can?*), being all the time on such terms with the pack that he may watch and follow all that they do from start to finish. Of three hundred men at the start from a covertside, possibly half are imbued with this desire. Lucky the hounds and the huntsman, if *they* are allowed to get clear—before the thundering mass bursts forward in pursuit, and dashes itself against the first fence. In this fence there may, with luck, be half a dozen practicable openings. Half a dozen men are over in *no* time, two dozen more are over in *fair* time, while ten dozen others—taking their turn, as they can, with courtesy, snatch it—are over by the time hounds are well out of view. The same scene, in a modified or, it may be concentrated, form, repeats itself at the next fence and at others in quick succession—till soon the half dozen are sailing along as near the pack as they can be, or ought to be; and a moiety of the next two dozen are close enough in their wake to obtain an occasional glimpse of a tail hound. Of the eleven dozen, a few have fallen, some have funked, many have taken a false turn, and the rest follow on—either complacently ready to chime in again at a first check, or dismally conscious that they have seen nothing of what they came out to see. How many then of the three hundred can fairly be said to have been with hounds in this fifteen minutes' burst? *Six* are there to pull up when a first check occurs! But the dozens of raging sportsmen in pursuit know nothing of the check, till, in their joy at having caught the leaders, they sweep round and pass the hounds; and unless the huntsman is quick and decided the chances are that these fifteen minutes constitute the whole of the run.

The Belvoir. 13

That this picture is a true and fair sample of what constantly, though by no means invariably, occurs, we could give countless instances to prove. But having sketched it for the double purpose of making the stranger aware of what he must be prepared to meet, and of showing (in all charity towards our neighbours' self-estimate and our own) how impossible it is for the very keenest of us to be always "*with hounds,*" in the thorough sense of the term—we may add that, for men by habit and constitution fitted to take their part in such a scene, there are few things in life more enjoyable than the short sharp scurries of the Belvoir, over the closely fenced meadows of their Melton country.

Take Coston covert, and the grass line (for there are two oft-travelled and widely differing routes) to Woodwell Head! Seventeen more cheery minutes never sweetened existence! Turn from the southern extremity to the northernmost of this the more fashionable section of the Belvoir territory, and ride a twenty minutes from Mr. Sherbrooke's covert to the Curate! Be fortunate enough to pick a plum on either of these occasions; and your palate, once treated to such fruit, will be greedy for a return to the exhilarating food—nor grudge a score of failures in the quest!

To leave generalities and turn to detail. From Grantham, then (for at present we are only considering Melton indirectly, and from such a light as its vicinity and attributes may affect the visitor to Grantham), you will find yourself every Wednesday and each alternate Saturday, wending your way either straight towards the little metropolis, or meeting its contingent at some point a few miles north or south of the road between the two places. On these days Croxton Park, just midway from either town, is the meet nearest to Grantham. Waltham village, being only half a mile away, may be taken as virtually the same fixture—the same coverts being commanded by each. To specify absolutely *which* coverts are drawn from any particular meet of the Belvoir is a thing not to be attempted. Could we do so we might, at the very least, expect a hat sent round for us at Melton alone—in that many a double five-mile trot would be saved to a band of men who have suffered long. A rule, well grounded, is in force with the Belvoir, that their meets never designate any special or foreknown draw. Not many years ago they lost some valuable hounds by poison, laid down in a covert, which we may now leave unnamed, by the fiendish hands of one who took the opportunity of their meeting close by, to wreak his malice thus. Since then they invariably meet wide of the coverts they propose to draw. After this lapse of time there can be no indiscretion in linking with the leading places of rendezvous those coverts which we have more often seen visited in connection. Thus from Croxton Park and Waltham (the adjacent gorse of Croxton Lings and the wood of Bescaby Oaks being, as a rule, left for the afternoon) hounds are generally taken Melton-wards to try Stonesby Gorse, Newman's Gorse, Freeby Wood, and Brentingby Spinneys. Freeby Wood is not more than a fifty-acre stronghold, the others are quite little coverts, and it is not often that more than two have to be searched in succession for a find. Merry spins, pre-eminent for pace, delightful in country, but too often deficient in distance, are constantly witnessed from these spots. Foxes from hence seldom make a wide point; men know this well, and lance themselves forth with a will for a flying race—while the Belvoir pack drive their game with such venom that even a stout fox could scarcely keep his head straight for long.

Or, again, you may hear the word given for Mr. Burbage's Covert or Melton Spinney, which Meltonians would perhaps rather see drawn than any other coverts in his Grace's Hunt—by no means on account of their propinquity to home. Mr. Burbage's famous covert lies close beside the river Wreake, a mile or so from Melton, and from it foxes have the pick of some of the prettiest of the Quorn, Cottesmore, and Belvoir countries—the covert being placed in a loop where the boundaries of the three hunts touch. By crossing the river (at the ford convenient) a fox often pierces by Great Dalby into the Quorn, or by Stapleford or Burrough into the Cottesmore territory. From Melton Spinney a bad fox may lead you a short turn over plough, or a good one take you far afield over good grass right or left of Melton. Either case must be conditional on your not being left behind at the covert, with the hundred or so who invariably are, and on your horse being just bold enough for the Melton brook—a little stream that a polo-pony might jump without difficulty, but yet is often full of the highest-priced horses in England.

16   The Hunting Countries of England.

To return to Bescaby Oaks—an evening fox is always found there when applied for: and in most instances he will carry you towards your Grantham dinner-table. A light soil which is but little worse going than grass, and fences of the easiest, would carry you down to Stoke Pasture, or you may find yourself at Buckminster Park with some fine grass between you and Skillington.

Stonesby is most frequently the meet for Sproxton Thorns and Coston Covert. Goadby Marwood may, or may not, mean Goadby Gorse or Goadby Bullamore and Scalford Bogs. From Piper Hole, the coverts overhanging the Vale of Belvoir are drawn, commencing either with the plantations stretching along the Harby Hills, or with Piper Hole Gorse, or Clawson Thorns. From the last-named, or from Holwell Mouth (neutral with the Quorn), often results a pretty gallop over the Vale—here in its greenest and most tempting form. Saxelby Spinney and Grimston Gorse are also neutral; and when once again relieved from the desolating presence of the swarms of navvies at work on the new railway, will, as before, open the way to the heart of the Quorn Monday country.

In the Vale itself, Hose Grange and Harby are meets leading to the two small coverts that belong to these villages respectively. From these a westerly wind may, literally, treat to the ignominy of sending you to Jericho across a deep and miry tract. To find ourselves in its neighbourhood has usually been sufficient to turn us homewards. But Mr. Sherbrooke's Gorse Covert, situate in the extreme corner of the

The Belvoir.

Vale, has every charm of position. From here to Holwell Mouth, to Dalby Wood, or over the deep and terrifying Smite to the Curate—each of these lines is superb; each should be done, even with slight divergence on the way, in from twenty to thirty minutes; and each and all of them, on a scenting day, demand a horse that is bold and quick and stout.

Indeed, to sum up all we have said on the subject of the horse to carry you with the Belvoir hounds, it may be written that you want a good one to live with them anywhere—but especially *must* you have a good one, and ride him straight and quick, if you would be with them in their Melton country. Moreover, as the Duke of Rutland in his generosity offers you your sport for nothing, you may well afford to give an extra fifty pounds for your Wednesday horse—and, out of gratitude to his Grace, to abstain from riding over his hounds.

THE SOUTH WOLD.*

PROCEEDING with the Hunts of Lincolnshire (a county termed by a good hound-authority the "home of the foxhound") we may next take the South Wold. If not a fashionable country, it is at least a sporting one. Perhaps, too, its fame suffers rather than benefits from the fact of its position being in such close contiguity and comparison with packs like the Brocklesby, Blankney, Belvoir, and Fitzwilliam. In the maintenance of a country, the development of its pack and of its resources generally, an autocracy (and, more than all, an hereditary autocracy) has ever been more successful than any representative style of government. A country that has for generations been a cherished heirloom, is sure to enjoy and retain a reputation, far more distinguished than any "Subscription Pack," however highly supported, may hope to become *permanently* possessed of. Foxhunting *admits* of a republic, where oligarchy cannot be obtained; but it thrives better where the reins of government—and with them pride of possession and system of management—are passed down from father to son. Under a committee *seldom*, under an indi-

---

* "Stanford's Railway and Hunting Map," sheet 10.

The South Wold. 19

vidual vested with temporary authority *often*, it may be brilliant for a time—for a generation, perhaps. But as a Mastership lapses, radical changes of management naturally follow. No traditional and well tried code survives. The newcomer inherits none of the interests of his predecessor; has no object in carrying out his half-completed reforms, follows not his aims, and possibly disagrees *in toto* with his ideas. In all probability he has never been brought up to, or even initiated into, hound-work or the mysteries of kennel; the management of a country is a book into whose pages he has never been called upon to dip (if its very existence ever occurred to him before); while as to the tact and diplomacy required at the hands of an M.F.H., he has at starting neither conception nor natural aptitude. For the Master of a Subscription Pack is, more often than not, one who, by accident of birth or virtue of acquirement, has already wealth (most likely county property) to recommend him to his neighbours, and to whom the further advantage of being looked up to as the Master of their Hounds has an irresistible charm. The distinction is well worth the few hundreds, which a liberal subscription leaves as a yearly deficit; and so, not necessarily with any single better recommendation, he becomes, as opportunity offers, Master of an old-established pack of Fox Hounds. It does not take him a year or two to find that the rosy-looking bed into which he has cast himself is not without thorns many and sharp—while the buzz of disturbed prejudices and the sting of local jealousies show him that there are mosquitoes round his couch of which he never dreamed. So holding up his head bravely, as if unconscious of disappointment, he fulfils his duties with much outward satisfaction, till such time as he can advance a plausible reason for relinquishing them; then shifts his load on to another's shoulders, just as he had begun to learn how it should be carried. The same process is enacted in the person of his successor; and so a Subscription Pack is bandied from hand to hand every few years. Huntsmen seldom remain long to serve a succession of masters; and under the vicissitudes of variety of *régime* and frequent change of system, hounds can scarcely be expected to improve, or even to maintain a fair standard once acquired—still less can each of these short-lived Masterships sustain a fresh pack, of respectable quality, where the country possesses no hounds of its own. Fox-hunting confessedly lives on its traditions and by sufferance. But its traditions are a stronger power, and offer a more solid foothold, where for generations past they have been linked with the fortunes of a leading family, whose name is indigenous to the soil. In *such* case sufferance has been so long and so unhesitatingly granted as to have become a fixed principle, which it would be considered the rankest heresy to call into question—much more to disturb. But the opposite case is open to contingencies so numerous and diversified, that they are beyond our space and present object. Every Master of a Subscription Hunt must have been brought into unpleasant contact with many of them, and will probably find it no difficult task to amplify his list day by day.

The South Wold.

These few remarks should, however, in some degree support the opinion that a Subscription Country has scarcely the same chance of permanent distinction as one whose progress is co-existent with, ruled and supported by, the hereditary leaders of local society.

The South Wold is an instance of an old-established Subscription Pack, which—though long and well-established—has not acquired (or at all events has failed to retain) a name of note comparable with that held by its more eminent neighbours. It can boast of advantages of soil and situation more than equal to theirs (the Belvoir excepted); but while they have gone on steadily flourishing, the South Wold has had many a struggle for bare existence. With the ups and downs of its past career we have nothing to do. In this year of '78 its present is vigorously cared for, and its future promises well. And now we may proceed to tell you how to reach it, if you have a mind to hunt with the South Wold, and convey some notion of what you will find when you get there.

North and north-west of the Belvoir the upper portion of Lincolnshire is hunted in something approaching to a square by the four packs, the Brocklesby, the Burton, the Blankney and the South Wold. Of this square the Brocklesby monopolise nearly the northern half. Of the remaining half the Burton and Blankney take the west between them, the South Wold all the east (as will be seen by Stanford's Map).

The geological features of this square of country

have so direct a bearing on its foxhunting—though the statement sounds neither amusing nor credible—that they must be briefly set down before proceeding further. In fewest words, then—All up the east coast runs the "Marsh"—a wide strip of rich deep land reclaimed from the sea, and whereon grow alike turnips big as pumpkins and sheep that might have been imported from Brobdingnag. Nearest the sea thousands of acres are devoted to development of the latter form of food supply; but the fine turf will never spring to the hunter's hoof—for, like other fen country it is crossed, traversed and cut up by wide open drains which no horse could successfully combat. More inland, where it obtains the name of Middle Marsh, it is chiefly arable (except just above Grimsby), carries a good scent, is in every respect quite rideable, and is much in favour with both Brocklesby and South Wold. Next to the Marsh, and also running north and south, are the Lincolnshire Wolds—high land stretching (approximately speaking) from Brocklesby to Spilsby, and varying from ten to fifteen miles across. A general idea of the extent of the Wolds may be obtained by taking the line of the Great Northern Railway, from Boston to Grimsby, as the eastern boundary, and by then running the eye still along the railway, from Grimsby round by Brocklesby to Market Rasen. For this distance—quite three parts of the whole—the railway will be founded depicted as running immediately beneath the outline of the Wolds.

The soil of the Wolds is strong loam on a substratum of chalk, limestone, or marl. Most of their

The South Wold.

extent is devoted to the plough—with the result that, though fair going enough when not too wet, they are deep and holding when much rain has fallen. And it is, as usual, under the latter condition that they carry the best scent.

Parallel again to the Wolds (though we are for the moment going beyond the South Wold Country in order to finish what we have to say of North Lincolnshire generally) runs another range of hill forming the westward boundary of the county. This is known as the Cliff, and is separated from the Wolds by a narrow plain coming from the Humber southwards. The Cliff is of nothing like the same breadth as the Wolds, varying from three or four miles across in the north (where it touches the Humber near Wintringham) to some twelve or fourteen, where it opens out south of Lincoln to embrace the Lincoln Heath, and stretches down to the neighbourhood of Sleaford and Grantham.

The Cliff, again, is a limestone formation; is lighter going than the Wolds; and does not, as a rule hold so firm a scent. The vale between the two tablelands is flat and of a stiff clay soil: and it is generally considered that hounds can carry a better head across it than horses. It will thus be seen, to sum up our geological sketch, that North Lincolnshire contains four distinct sorts of ground, divided as parallel sections north and south—to wit, Marsh, Wolds, Cliff, and the low Intermediate Plain between the two latter. And, with the map still in front of you, you will observe that the bulk of the South Wold country ¹s situate, as it name implies, on the Wold section.

For, though coloured down to the sea, only a comparatively small part of the Marsh is available for hunting purposes.

Again the members of the Hunt use the term *wold* as distinctly applying by no means to the whole of this high land, but only to the very open and undulating miles of arable that from Louth (the northernmost point of their country proper) is found right and left of the Louth-and-Horncastle-road, to within three miles of the last named town.

Horncastle is quite the most central base of operations from which to hunt with the South Wold Hounds, being near the middle of their country, about four miles from the Kennels, and within easy reach by road of all their meets. It is a town of some 5000 inhabitants, is 130 miles from London, and attainable by the Great Northern Railway in four hours and a half. Hotel and stable accommodation are to be found in full.

Spilsby and Alford (on the east of the Hunt) are almost exactly a similar distance from London by the same line of railway. Louth is another half hour's journey, is a larger town than either of the other three; and is a capital place for anyone wishing to divide his hunting between the Brocklesby and the South Wold.

The kennels (which, with the hounds, are the property of the Hunt) are built beside the Louth and Horncastle Road, opposite the village of Bletchford; and stand there in unsheltered solitude as if to remark to the passer-by how bleak and lonely is this wild

The South Wold.

wold tract. Within them are some five and fifty couple of hounds, with which to hunt four days a week.

These four days we may classify as pertaining to their Louth, Horncastle, Hainton and Spilsby districts respectively; and treat them accordingly.

On Mondays they are in their Louth country (the river Withern being held as separating it from their Saturday, or Spilsby, country)—and some of their chief meets are Tothill, Burwell, Haugham-Guidepost, Belchford, Kenwick and Elkington. Of these Tothill is a meet for the large woods adjacent which overlook the Marsh (and similar woods, it may be remarked, are to be found southwards all along the edge of the wold). Burwell, Haugham, and Maltby here form a chain of woodland from which it is often difficult to drive a fox; though now-and-again hounds get away eastward towards Carlton in the Middle Marsh (over a fair sporting country) or westwards over the open wolds on the Withcall side.

Belchford and Kenwick are for the Wolds pure and simple, where foxes swarm and are to be found even more easily in the pits and turnip fields than in the coverts themselves. For the latter are small plantations and gorses; and foxes, a few times disturbed, are apt to show a preference for the open. The farmers soon discover their haunts; and a large proportion of their good runs have been to the credit of outlying foxes. With hounds running fast over these trying hills, your horse must be able to gallop and stay, even if he cannot jump; and blood is the first desideratum. The same remarks apply to the Wold country all round Louth—that about Elkington being neutral with the Brocklesby, as we shall have to notice farther on. Ploughed fields of many acres, hills of considerable gradient, and fences of little moment are the most prominent characteristics of the true wolds throughout.

To continue with detail which, purely local in its character and necessarily of little interest to the general reader, must yet make up the chief bulk of what is intended as a work of reference—we enter upon the Horncastle district. This is hunted on Tuesdays and has a greater variety and perhaps pleasanter features than the high wold country of which we have just spoken. It touches the latter at the Kennels and Oxcombe, which we may take as the northern points in the Tuesday circle, of which Horncastle is practically the centre. The coverts of Oxcombe, with Manvers' Gorse at Belchford may, likely enough, from the above meets, keep you on the open wolds all day. But, proceeding southward we come to Fulletby, West Ashby (with its gorse and spinnies), Greatham and Winceby—the coverts to be drawn being chiefly small natural plantations and copses, with a gorse here and there. The country immediately round West Ashby and Horncastle is some of the best in the Hunt—all, or nearly all, grass, divided into little fields by strong thorn fences. And here you must have a horse, who can jump big and be quick on his legs to jump again. A long striding horse would be out of place, where a short-backed animal would dip lightly in and out of the narrow meadows, as a fishing smack makes little of a

The South Wold. 27

chopping sea. Below Horncastle we have Moorby and East Kirkby (for Revesby). From Revesby commenced the best day's sport of the season '77-'78—embracing two fair kills in the open, the one after an hour and twenty minutes from Revesby Park *viâ* Enderby and Raithby to Hundleby, the other (with only half an hour's breathing time) after fifty minutes from Keal, *viâ* Eresby Mount, Hundleby, and Sausthorpe round to Enderby. These two runs took place over ground good enough for any shire of higher name: for the line was on grass nearly throughout, the fences were big and fair, and the pace was great. The previous season their best run was also from Keal—being an hour and twenty minutes and a kill, and covering an immense amount of ground in the time. On that occasion they went by Enderby, past Lusby, crossed the Horncastle and Spilsby road between Hackworthingham and Horncastle, and after a wide sweep almost to South Ormsby ran into their fox below Sutterby. The point from find to finish was nearly eight miles and whole line quite thirteen or fourteen. But these runs in reality all took place in their Friday (Spilsby) district, though we have mentioned them incidentally in connection with Revesby which supplied the material for the one first-quoted.

Working round south of Horncastle we may note the meets of Tumby Gate and Martin Railway Bridge —for the woods of Highall Bracken and Waterloo. From Bracken Wood hounds occasionally run across a stretch of moorland and into some better country round Tattershall. From Horsington Mill they draw the same horseshoe-shaped chain of woodlands back to Martin Railway Bridge. These woods are admirably preserved as regards pheasants: and for that matter ground game (with the single exception of Reynard) is thoroughly encouraged. When *he* is to be found, you should be on a hunter; for, though on most days you may afford to lounge about the woods on a pony, if by chance hounds run into the open you will meet with wide ditches and strong fences.

West of Horncastle Thimbleby is a favourite meet, with a view to drawing Edlington Scrubs and the Edlington and Wispington Plantations, which lie in the midst of a very pretty, but limited, range of grass country. The fences hereabouts are mostly of thorn, neatly trimmed and (as is the case over the bulk of Lincolnshire) usually set on a narrow bank, only a foot or two in height—but all that height additional.

Thursday is the day on which they hunt their northern, or Hainton, district—most of the meets being for the neutral woods between Louth and Market Rasen. These great coverts really belong to the Brocklesby; but during the late Lord Yarborough's life, permission was given to the South Wold and Burton to draw them (in some measure to relieve the strain from the Brocklesby due to the wide extent of their country). Of the meets in this district Donnington Brick Yard is in the South Wold proper; but Hainton, Boucherest Arms, Six Hills, Legsby, and Gersby are all for the neutral woods. Hainton Duck Ponds, Legsby Wood and the woods

The South Wold.

of Linwood — North Wood, Bleasby Wood, and Eleanor Wood are the chief of these, and lie on sandy and hilly ground. The neutral zone extends by Gersby, South Elkington, Welton, and North Elkington, the easterly portion consisting, as before-mentioned, altogether of open wold.

On Fridays the South Wold are in their Spilsby district. Owing to fen and marsh they are shut off from hunting at any distance from that town to the south or east: consequently all their Friday meets lie north or west of it. If we commence on the westward, these are Enderby Cross Roads (or more frequently Raithby) for the plantations of Enderby and Keal and Raithby Gorse—and a fox from any of these three should adopt as pleasant a line as in the runs just instanced. Harrington is a meet, and the Harrington and Langton Coverts might hold foxes enough to allow it to be almost a weekly one. Of late years a speedy adjournment has usually been made to Mr. Burton's two coverts at Somersby, known as New England and Burton Gorse, and which have been quite the saving clause of this part of the country. Ormsby is the rendezvous for Ormsby Wood and Dryby Carr, whence hounds generally draw on towards Thoresby and the big woods overlooking the Marsh. Ulceby Cross Roads is chosen as a usual fixture for the woods of Well Vale, Rigsby and Haugh. From Well Vale foxes almost always persist in running into Welton Wood, a covert of 300 acres in extent, from which they may sometimes be persuaded to break on towards Gunby and Boothby. Greenfield and Woodthorpe are for the lower woods of Greenfield and neighbourhood, whence they hunt over the Middle Marsh as far as the dykes will allow.

It was round and about these woods that, towards the end of last season hounds ran uninterruptedly from 5.30 till 8.45—the last hour and a half being of course in complete darkness, and their followers only reaching the hounds when suddenly and inexplicably the music ceased. The pack were found all together a field from Greenfield Wood and reached the kennels at 11.30 that night. Welton Guide Post and Gunby Cross Roads are for Welton Wood and the Gunby coverts just above the Marsh, and for the Boothby plantations on the lower ground. A strong covert at Halton Holgate would utilise a very fine piece of grass country now seldom ridden over; and would often induce foxes to take a line under the hills to, or from, Welton Wood on the one side and Keal on the other. But as there is little likelihood of any man of wealth coming forward to purchase the land for the Hunt (which is itself by no means rich), and as no one has yet discovered a substitute for gorse or blackthorn that in its growth will pay its own rent, Halton New Covert as yet scarcely takes rank as an immediate probability.

This Friday country possesses a great stock of foxes in its woodlands, where the shooting interests might with more reason be expected to clash with those of foxhunting, but which, on the contrary, put to shame certain manors in the centre of the open country, whose proprietors would rather their few acres of covert should hold twenty pheasants and no

The South Wold.

fox, than nineteen pheasants and fun for their neighbours.

It should be concluded from what we have said that the South Wold is, on the whole, a very sporting country. Given a sufficient rainfall, it seldom fails to carry a scent, whether in the open or the woodlands. Though chiefly plough, there is here and there a twenty minutes' patch of grass, over and above the deep drained stretches of the Marsh. And, by the way, that foxes have now and again run for their lives wide over the tracts of fen and marsh, we have proof in a letter now beside us, which takes us back to the days when Sir Richard Sutton hunted both the Burton and South Wold. We learn that "nearly fifty years ago" hounds once ran from Keal straight across the fens and killed their fox at Sibsey within four miles of Boston. Jack Shirley was the huntsman, and was left half way in one of the open drains Only three men rode to the finish. One of these was Mr. Short of Edlington, who jumped every practicable drain in the line—his horse being still fresh enough to bring him home that evening.

In conclusion, a bad horse will neither do for the South Wold nor for any other part of Lincolnshire; for, though you may see a certain amount of sport on an indifferent one—fences, as a rule, being easy, and the field not big enough for individuals to get much in each other's way—yet when hounds really run, you ought to have both blood and bone under you to live with them. The farmers are fully alive to this—and though, apparently, they breed nothing like the number of horses *for sale* that they used to, they still take care, in most instances, to keep thoroughbred ones for their own riding. In twenty minutes over the Wolds your steed will surely tell you, in unmistakable language, if his grandsire's name was Smiler (as Custance so aptly put it); for only a clean, or nearly-clean bred one can climb the hills or breast the plough till hounds run into their fox.

THE BROCKLESBY.*

So many of the previous remarks as to conformation and requirements of country apply equally to the Brocklesby as to the South Wold, that, instead of repeating them, it will merely be necessary to point out *en passant* those to which we refer. It will be remembered that we described the Marsh and the Wolds as running side by side up to the Humber. The Brocklesby country includes also the other two parallel sections in the formation of North Lincolnshire, to wit, the Cliff and the Intermediate Vale. But wide as is its extent on paper, its hunting area is in practice virtually narrowed to little more than the Wold and the Marsh. For down the centre of this Intermediate Valley, between the Wold and the Cliff, runs the Ankholm River or New Navigation Canal; and westward of this hounds are seldom advertised to meet — Kirton Station and Grayingham being among the exceptions. Again, the North East portion of the vale—near the mouth of the canal, is rendered unserviceable by the presence of large open drains.

What has already been said regarding the character

---

* *Vide* "Stanford's Railway and Hunting Map," sheet 10.

of the wold and marsh country farther south, applies equally to this Hunt as to the South Wold; and on these points description would be but repetition. But, as ranking highest in historical fame and pride of position—not only in Lincolnshire but among all England—the Brocklesby tower over their neighbours. Longer even than the Belvoir have they been the care and cherished property of one family; and each Lord Yarborough in turn has done his utmost to keep the famous Brocklesby blood from losing anything of caste or high degree. History has to do with our present subject only in its results: and so we may limit allusion to the past to the fact that this constant hereditary care has produced a pack of hounds, worthy of a journey twice as long as to North Lincolnshire—if only to look upon them in the Kennel. To hunt with them go to Louth; or better still, secure stabling at Limber Magna, which is quite close to the Kennels.

Louth is some five hours from London (by Great Northern Railway), and, though at first glance it would scarcely appear to recommend itself as an accessible hunting quarter, the journey is really no more difficult or tedious than to Melton Mowbray —man and beasts being conveyed almost without stoppage to their journey's end. Once there, you are in a position to command a choice of hunting and a very first-class pack, without any of the inconveniences incidental to a more fashionable centre.

By road and easy rail, the Brocklesby and South Wold offer five or even six days a week between them —their respective days being as follows: On Mondays

The Brocklesby. 35

the two packs will often embarrass you by both meeting in the neighbourhood of Louth—under which circumstances you must just "gang yer ain gait" and follow your inclination. On Tuesday you have the South Wold in their Horncastle district. On Wednesdays you may take train to Grimsby and hunt with the Brocklesby in their country between the kennels and that town. On Thursday you may ride the glades of the neutral woods about Hainton with the South Wold. On Friday you may possibly find yourself in the same merry woods with the Brocklesby, or be following them over their West Wold country—or, again, you may, if you wish, start from home an hour earlier to jog your hunter (half an hour to gallop your hack) towards Spilsby to hunt with the South Wold. On Saturdays you must either take train up to Brocklesby, or stay at home to make up your accounts.

Should you fix your headquarters at Limber Magna (on most maps anglicised to our comprehensions as Great Limber) you will have to confine your operations altogether to the Brocklesby, save when now and again you take the ferry over the Humber and throw in your luck with the Holderness. Great Limber is four miles from Stallingborough Station—about $5\frac{1}{2}$ hours from London, by way of Grimsby and the Great Northern Railway. From here you would follow hounds to covert four days a week without having to make use of the train. Take with you the same class of horse already noted as suitable to carry you with the South Wold; be quick at getting away when the Brocklesby are once on to their fox; and, if you *mean business*, you will see a great deal of sport without having to ride desperately. The country is mostly plough—a great part of it wold (in the full sense of our previous definition). There are few woods of any size, except the neutral ones between Louth and Market Rasen; but the coverts generally are small and foxes seldom hang long in them. The number of resident gentry in the Brocklesby country is curiously small, and the bulk of the field is made up of farmers well-to-do, well mounted and thoroughly fond of the sport. Some seventy couples of puppies are every year sent out to walk, all or nearly all of which are taken by the tenants of Lady Yarboro'. Never, it should here be remarked, have the pack and the country been an object of greater solicitude than to Her Ladyship—their present ruler; who, besides always riding well to the front and watching her hounds in the field, has made them a study in the kennel, and so gains a double pleasure from being able to discern each individual of the pack as he developes at his work and in appearance.

Proceeding now to specify some of their meets and consequent draws—we have to repeat that on Mondays the Brocklesby are usually in the southern part of their country, between Louth and Grimsby, which is all either wold or Middle Marsh. On the wold they meet at Elkington, Wyham, Cadeby, Binbrook, Thorganby, Wold Newton, &c. All these are within half a dozen miles of Louth, and all have good coverts handy—Elkington being for the plantations surrounding and Agthorpe Wood; Cadeby and Wyham for Wyham Gorse and Hell Furze; while Binbrook,

The Brocklesby. 37

Thorganby and Wold Newton have Wold Newton Gorse, Thorganby Covert, Croxby Pond and Gorse, &c. In the Middle Marsh (which is much heavier going than the wolds, and is here almost entirely plough) there is Brackenbury and its covert, Utterby, Grainsby, and, farther north, Bradley and its woods.

On Wednesdays hounds are out in the upper part of the Middle Marsh—in fact, their country on this day is included within the points of New Holland (on the Humber), Brocklesby, Swallow, Barnetby, Grimsby, and the sea coast. And the Middle Marsh here developes itself into their best country, in the form of rich pasturage and stiff fences—over which a hunter of high class, and only such an one, will carry you.

Grimsby, by the way, is another base you might choose for your sport with the Brocklesby—though, unless you happen to be much interested in docks, or wish to follow a second pursuit in the shape of sea fishing, it is scarcely a quarter we should recommend to a hunting man. New Holland, Thornton College, Newsam Lodge, Aylesby Mill, Immingham, Weelsby House, Laceby, and Barnetby Beck, are included in this day's meets; and the coverts are chiefly small (such as Houlton Covert near Immingham), though exceptions, such as Raxton Wood, are to be found.

On Fridays they more often hunt on the west of their wold country, or work the southern woods which as above-mentioned, have been thrown open also to the South Wold and the Burton. Moortown, Normanby, and Stainton-le-Hole are meets on the edge of the wolds, and Swallow is a village on the centre of the high ground which is often named as a rendezvous. From the former places a choice is had of either drawing the upland coverts of Stainton (plantations), Swinhope Gorse, Rothwell, &c., or of dipping into the lower country for Normanby Clump, Claxby Wood, and the Usselby and Osgodby Plantations. On the flat below are Owersby, Kingerby, &c., with a wood near the latter place; while Linwood Warren and Gersby Manor are among the most common fixtures for the big neutral woods. The pleasures of woodland hunting are measured entirely by the accident of individual taste; and call for no comment at our hands. Supposing you to possess a fondness for this, the wilder and more classic phase of foxhunting, you may here indulge your predilections to the full—leading an almost forest life under the joint auspices of the Brocklesby, South Wold and Burton. With foxes enough for all, these glades and dells are ringing every other day to the stirring sounds of hound and horn.

Farther westward, and beyond the New Navigation Canal, hounds are taken occasionally to the neighbourhood of Kirton and Grayingham—for Grayingham Gorse and Blyborough Covert, &c. North of these places are various woods; but the fixture-card seldom points in their direction. The lower country is of a rather deep character (being stiff clay); and carries a good scent. Above Kirton you get on to the Cliff—an inferior scenting tract, and lighter going.

Saturdays are generally employed in working the country round, and to the north of Brocklesby. In

The Brocklesby.

the neighbourhood of the Park are numerous plantations, and Hendel Wood, close by, is of considerable size. Wootton Hall is a favourable meet some four miles northward, and all up the wold to the Humber they have a great deal of sport. By no means one of the least merits of the Brocklesby country is that it is well stocked with foxes almost throughout. The foxes are wild and ready to travel, and there are few parts of the country which do not carry at least a fair scent.

THE BURTON AND THE BLANKNEY.*

Not only may Lincoln be set down as their common centre; but we may go so far as to add that no other available base offers itself, from which to hunt in either country. Again, the area of each being limited, all the meets of both are within reach of the cathedral town; and you will find excellent hunting on all sides. Both possess hounds of high repute; both are well stocked with foxes; and both are well and liberally managed. The Burton hounds claim a strong relationship with the Grove while taking their foundation from a pack brought from Mr. Chaplin some half dozen years ago. The Blankney, with a variety of blue blood in their veins, have been bred to a type which stands quite alone. For fashion and class Mr. Chaplin's present hounds shine out as distinctly apart from ordinary packs, as racehorses among hunters. Blood and breeding are relied upon as the root and source of all needful qualities; and it is claimed on their behalf that in the field they are wanting in none of the virtues possessed by coarser bred hounds. Moreover, that when a more plebeian class begins to tire in the late afternoon, these are

---

* *Vide* " Stanford's Railway and Hunting Map," sheet 10.

only at their best. It is argued, in fact, that to the hound as much as to the horse applies the aphorism that an ounce of blood is worth a pound of bone. To what extent this may be successfully carried, we do not pretend to say. Certain it is that the experiment is here a high one: and so far from any failure being recorded, the theory is maintained to be proved. It is asserted that no virtue has been lost, no power of wear and tear sacrificed; but that, like a thoroughbred horse, a hound of this type has twice the endurance of one of meaner blood and more cumbrous build. Bone, *bone down to the feet*, has been the common kennel cry of late years; and every hound-show has seen the judges more exacting than before on this point. But you would go to the Blankney kennels rather to look upon beautiful heads and necks, to fill your eye with clean-cut shoulders, and to see high breeding typified. Drive and dash are, perhaps, their most conspicuous characteristics in the field; though, that selection has not induced these qualities only, to the extinction of others equally important, may quickly be gathered by watching them on a cold-scenting afternoon. That is the time to which their admirers point, as proving the truth of the principles on which the pack has been built. "That is the time," they say, "which shows how blood can stay!"

Both kennels are within easy riding distance of Lincoln—the Burton at Reepham, a station on the Manchester, Sheffield and Lincoln line, four miles to the north-east; the other ten miles to the south-east, at Mr. Chaplin's seat at Blankney. The two countries were long hunted as one: and, while this was the case Lincoln was almost always chosen as the headquarters of the master. Sir Richard Sutton lived there during his term of office; so did Lord Henry Bentinck; and so did Mr. Chaplin, when he kept two packs and found eight days sport in the week for the country. Indeed, whether as master, or as one independent of all ties of place or position, it would be difficult to point to any other spot to pitch your tent with a view to hunting with the two packs.

Lincoln is less than three hours and a half from King's Cross. Be careful how you handle Bradshaw when you meditate a first visit there: or the Great Northern may entice you an hour further round by Spalding and Boston. Your way is by Peterboro and Grantham, and by this route you may practise your eye all the while over a hunting country, before coming once again into more active contact with the half-forgotten fences. Thus may you brush off much of the six months' rust that have accumulated on your perception, sharpen again the instinct that was before so keen, revive your memory, and reanimate the spirit that for months has lain dormant.

The Burton and Blankney countries are in many respects very similar. The high tableland known as the Cliff runs north and south through both of them; and so does the stiff clay valley between it and the wolds. Light plough, divided by stone walls into fields of many acres, covers the limestone of the Cliff, which is much narrower in the Burton country (in parts only three or four miles across) than where it

The Burton and the Blankney. 43

opens out in the Blankney country into the Lincoln Heath. As a rule the lower ground carries a better scent than the Cliff. Both countries have also a fair sprinkling of grass, especially (as we may have to notice by and bye) the Blankney, where west of the Cliff they border on the Belvoir.

The map will show you at a glance that the Burton hunt north of Lincoln, the Blankney to the south—the River Witham being more or less the boundary between the two, and the Trent limiting both on the west. The map, however, as at present issued, fails to show that the Wragby woodlands are virtually neutral ground—forming a great stand-by to both Hunts. They always contain a supply of the material, generally carry a hot scent, and their rides, as a rule, are quite as good as big woods can be expected to contain.

The whole chain of the Wragby woodlands and the country as far west as the river Langworth and as far north as the Lincoln and Horncastle road, is hunted at the present time by both packs (with the exception of Vyner's Gorse and the few coverts in the neighbourhood of Gautby). There are Southery, New Park, Austacre, Hatton, Chambers', Stainfield, West, Keyes, and Bullingdon Woods, and Newbold Common. The Blankney hunt them one day a week (usually Wednesday), the Burton sometimes two (Mondays and Tuesdays). Keyes Wood and West Wood are often deep after rain and when well trodden; but on the whole, every care is taken that riding through these woods should be a feasible and, as much as possible, a pleasant matter—which, as hounds ever go through them with a determined head, is of some importance.

Friday is the only day in the week on which neither pack is out. For the others, the Burton hunt Monday, Tuesday, Thursday and Saturday; the Blankney Monday, Wednesday, Thursday and Saturday.

The Burton are on Mondays, as we have said, often in the Wragby woodlands. Often, however, they advertise for the extreme north of their country, where Magin Moor and Caenby Corner are two of their favourite meets. From the former they have Yawthorpe, Harpswell, and Glentworth Coverts, whilst from the latter they have Caenby Wood, Toft Newton, Spridlington Thorns, and Lord Brownlow's Covert. From this last, in Mr. Chaplin's first year of mastership, they had a great run, which ended in the field being entirely beaten off and the pack remaining out all night. This was on a Tuesday, and the last hound came in on Saturday morning. They killed their fox by themselves in a covert called Doglands, where at eleven o'clock a keeper found them sleeping round the remains of their quarry—an intrusion they resented by driving him and his lantern away. The 5th milestone on the Spital Road is not an uncommon fixture. From it they can draw eastward to Hackthorn and Dunholme Gorse, or westward for Carlton Gorse, Brattleby Thorns or Scampton. Brattleby and Fillingham are also often included in Monday's meets; though no hard and fast rule is laid down for this day or Tuesday; and Wickenby Station, for the famous covert of Wickenby Wood and Holton and Torrington Gorse, occur on the former day. From

Wickenby Wood some years ago they had, on successive Saturdays, two of the best days on record in the annals of Lincolnshire. The one contained a run with a point of eighteen miles, nearly up to Caistor. On the second they had a gallop of extraordinary pace: and it is said that hounds covered an eight-mile point in thirty-two minutes! And it is further related as a fact that, in the last field their fox turned back stone-blind from exhaustion, and cantered right in among the hounds. Some of the trysting places in the woods of the Wragby neighbourhood are (on either Monday and Tuesday) Clay Bridge, for Stainton Wood and so on; Stainfield Hall, Apley, Langworth Bridge, Newbold Common, &c. On Tuesdays, too, they often meet quite near Lincoln. Greetwell is frequently chosen; as from it they can either draw Fiskerton Long Wood or northwards to Barlings, Sudbrooke and Dunholme Gorse. At Stainton is a wood celebrated for the stoutness of its foxes. From it the Burton had, last season, some of their longest and best runs ; and not unfrequently found themselves carried to the far extremity of the Wragby woodlands. In fact, they had nothing better than on one snowy day, when the ground appeared barred against hunting, and only one or two men attended the meet. Yet, with scarcely a check, they ran from Stainton Wood, past Wragby, just clear of the big woods, and killed at Edlington—only the second whip and one other rider accomplishing the line taken by hounds.

North of the Wragby woods is a fine wild open country, including a good deal of grass, chiefly in the neighbourhood of Holton and Torrington—a rich grass vale stretching from Stainton Wood by Holton and Torrington, to Hainton in the South Wold; and this, although a narrow strip, is a line often taken by foxes. Torrington Gorse is a never-failing find. In the season '76-'77 it was drawn not less than thirteen or fourteen times, and always held a fox. It forms, moreover, a link between the Wragby and Linwood woodlands; from one to the other of which both the Burton and the Blankney are constantly running. If they hit off the Torrington valley they may be on grass most of the way; otherwise the journey is over deep plough. But the whole is a wild sporting country; foxes must make a good point; and hounds can go a great pace over it.

On Thursdays the Burton are almost always on the west of their country—in or near the valley of the Trent. This district was at one time entirely grass—little of which, however, has been allowed to survive. Some little remains all along under the western edge of the Cliff; but the bulk of it has been sacrificed to the plough—and, worse than all, to the *steam plough*. To make it more difficult, too, the great thorn fences and wide ditches of the old pastures still exist; so your horse must combine great jumping power with ability to make his way quickly through dirt. And this, indeed, holds good with regard to your mounts for the Burton country throughout. You must ride strong horses, clever horses, and well-bred horses—horses that can travel fast and yet are temperate and powerful withal at their jumps. The country is essentially a deep one—being nearly all stiff clay except the narrow stretch of heath on the Cliff. It is in parts strongly fenced; and, being a good scenting soil, puts a severe test on a horse as compared with hounds. Among their Thursday meets are Torksey Station, for Brampton Holt and the Fox Covert; Thonock and Lea Hall for the Gainsborough Woods. It should be remarked that the drain running from Torksey to Saxilby is here the boundary between the Burton and the Blankney — leaving Kettlethorpe in the latter country, and not as shown in Stanford's map.

Saturday is generally on the east of the country— Wickenby Station, Linwood, Torrington, and Panton being frequent meets. When at Wickenby they have the above-mentioned celebrated covert, of that name. When at Linwood, they usually draw the big wood in the morning, falling back on Holton and Torrington Gorse for their afternoon fox. From Panton they have the coverts round the house, the Hatton Plantations, &c.—all certain finds. Hungram Gorse, drawn by both Burton and Blankney, gives a very good instance of the merits of an artificial earth. The latter pack had many runs from it last season. If the gorse was drawn blank, a terrier was put into the earth, and without fail there issued a fox—often two, and sometimes three.

The woods of Linwood, though neutral between the Burton, Brocklesby and South Wold, and frequently rattled three times in a week, never fail to show foxes and sport. With a wild country all round, hounds huntsmen and foxes have here a fair field, and are pitted on their merits. Saturdays are thus frequently marked by long runs into the South Wold country; and Mr. Foljambe had, during last season, a great deal of sport on this side—though his field, never of great dimensions, is by no means at its fullest when the woodlands are to be drawn.

The Blankney country presents a much greater variety than the Burton—embracing, as it does, a less amount of deep plough, a much wider tract of heath, and a more liberal allowance of grass. It will be noticed that few runs round the north and east of the country. Near this there is solid arable till the vicinity of Blankney is reached. Then comes, conveying its own character, the Heath (or, as we have designated it, the Cliff); while further westward your taste for grass may often be indulged to the full and your love of jumping more than fairly tried.

The days selected for these various conditions, and the places of meeting for each, are much as follows. On Mondays they are out on their Newark side, in which term is comprehended all their country north and north-west of the River Witham as it runs up to Lincoln. Kettlethorpe, Thorney, Doddington (for Skellingthorpe Big Wood and Mr. Jarvis' coverts), are among their most frequent meets: as is also the seventh milestone Newark Road, for Tunman's Wood and Eagle Wood. The last-named was one of the late Sir Richard Sutton's favourite coverts, and is equally valued nowadays. For the same wood they meet at Eagle Hall; the preference however, if anything, being for the Seventh Milestone as entailing a less journey for hounds. Occasionally too, on a Monday, they go to Aubourn Moor, for an afternoon

The Burton and the Blankney. 49

fox on their way back to kennels. Stapleford Moor is another fixture, and this brings hounds among the large fir coverts and high heather which mark Lord Middleton's property in this neighbourhood. From here, too, they draw the Norton-Disney woods, to both of which the Hunt are very partial, on account of the likelihood of crossing the river into the Broughton district and getting upon the grass towards Wellingore. Very valuable also might these woods be for cub-hunting—but that hounds are not allowed to enter them till late in the season.

Between this point (Norton, &c.) and the River Trent is an apparently nice sporting country (chiefly small grass enclosures); but, owing to the unfriendly disposition of various petty freeholders, there has of late years been much difficulty with regard to foxes, and in consequence hounds are seldom seen there.

The surface soil of the Monday country in the main consists of gravel or sand, which often holds a scent when hounds cannot run a yard over the clay of the lower ground. Such an inconsistency may now and again be noticed, when, on an otherwise perfect hunting day, a loaded or frosty surface causes the heavy plough to "carry," and scent to be completely annulled—when a change to the lighter soil perhaps sets hounds running furiously. Wide ditches, small hedges, and rotten banks, are the leading features of the fences; varied often by a wide dug drain.

The Blankney Wednesdays may be set down as belonging to the Wragby Woodlands. Of these Key's Wood, West Wood, and Chambers' Wood are perhaps the most popular, as being on the borders of

E

the fine open country to the north: and Tile House Beck, Southery, New Park Wood and Chambers' Wood are the leading meets. These woodlands are so regularly worked by both the packs under notice that the foxes from Wragby are always on the stir, and finding no peace in the Burton coverts at Wickenby are always ready to fly between one quarter and the other. Consequently either seldom fail to give out at least one good fox per diem when called upon: and from the Wragby Woods he always runs northwards, and away from the Blankney Kennels—never crossing the Witham to the south. Stainfield Wood is almost always drawn by the Blankney on Ash Wednesday: and in Lord Henry Bentinck's day was noted as having, several years in succession, commemorated that day with a run of high merit.

Their Thursdays, are generally somewhere in the immediate neighbourhood, or to the east, of Blankney. The chief meets on this day are Blankney itself, Scopwick, Ashby, Nocton—these lying in the deep country between the Heath and the fens (which will be noticed as here stretching down to Boston). Occasional meets on the Heath itself are Temple Bruer (a former possession of the Knights Templar), the Green Man, or now and again Canwick. The Nocton and Blankney Woods are fine coverts; while working southwards we come to the gorses of Blankney, Kirkby Green, Digby, and Bloxholm—all trusty places and almost certain finds. The Bloxholm Coverts are neutral with the Belvoir, which pack also draw Mr. Chaplin's thorn covert at Temple Bruer (known as Crow Bottom). On the Heath days they

The Burton and the Blankney.   51

have the Green Man Coverts, Bartholomew's Gorse, and the Ashby Coverts (the latter being on the borders of the low ground); while, further west, are the coverts of Temple Bruer and Griffin's (in the centre of the Heath).

In the eastern vale you will ride for the most part over plough, with here and there some grass to stretch your horse. Round Digby is steam plough, and much of it. Round Blankney the farmers have been content to keep the grass intact (and this year, if ever, they should believe that the shorthorn will repay them rather than the ploughshare). As is right, they build their fences frequent, stiff, and honest, and they like to see hounds leading quickly over them.

Below Lincoln the Heath spreads out fan-shaped, till at Temple Bruer it is about its widest. Light plough, stone walls, and no ditches are among its characteristics, to which may be added the fact that, *with a real scent,* hounds can beat horses over it. This is more likely to happen when after rain the ground has become holding even here. In such case horses are hampered, while hounds can go their best, flying the walls as they come, without a moment's stoppage. Then indeed you want blood under you—as you have highest blood racing before you. Yet, taking months and years throughout, the Heath is *not* a great scenting country.

But Saturday is *par excellence the* day of the Blankney. Keep your best horse for it; and smoke one less cigar over night than is your rule. For the meet will surely be for the Wellingore Vale; and your head must be clear, your heart must be bold, and your horse worthy of the task, if you would cross it in comfort. For a *fair* country there can be no stiffer in England; though to compare it with Mr. Tailby's Vale of Skeffington or with the Pytchley district of Oxenden, would be inapt, inasmuch as a good man and a good horse can ride over Wellingore, while no combinations of virtue will carry a rider systematically to hounds over the other two. A big and determined jumper you want here, and a galloper too; for the Wellingore Vale (all excellent scenting ground) is still mostly grass—at all events towards Leadenham and Broughton, and along under the Cliff. The most common meets are Wellingore, Coleby, Aubourn, Carlton-le-Moorland, and Brant Broughton (which in Lincolnshire they pronounce as Bruton, not as we hear it at the Leicestershire end of the Vale of Belvoir). Wellingore Gorse is perhaps the most famous covert in the Vale; but there are also good thorn coverts at Broughton and Aubourn, and two good gorses at Coleby and Harmston). From Coleby Gorse two years ago hounds scored an extraordinary performance. In twenty-two minutes they covered a five-mile point (their actual course being nearer seven)—then dashing over their fox as he lay down, they went on with a fresh one, and, running him some miles beyond Leadenham, got clean away from huntsman, master, and field, who were scouring the country for hours before coming upon them again. Boothby Park (belonging to Mr. Marfleet) is a certain find, though its sole pretence at covert consists of the laurels round the house, two or

The Burton and the Blankney. 53

three miniature copses, and an artificial earth. In most of these vale coverts Mr. Chaplin has instituted artificial earths with the greatest success. The system is further continued by having a "fox keeper" (as he is termed), and his terriers, always out with hounds — then if the covert be drawn blank, the grating of the earth is removed, the terriers put in, and a fox usually bolted. This plan has been found to work admirably. A line frequently taken by the Wellingore foxes, and much in favour with the field, is along under the Cliff to Leadenham and then across to Broughton or Stubton (the latter in the Duke's country). Of very grand character is this Saturday country—the only drawback to it being its limited size. Foxes, consequently, are easily driven out of it, generally to mount the less favoured Heath above. The vale is intersected by the well-known Brant—a stream which, though jumpable in a few places, has usually to be forded. Men have learned to recognise the fact fully, and now seldom ride at it. The fords, too, have been put in order; and getting through the water is no longer the difficult task of days gone by.

The only addenda that occur to us are that the Blankney owed what was perhaps their best run of last season to Tunman's Wood. Hounds had much of it to themselves, and killed their fox in the open in an hour and twenty-six minutes—a thirteen-mile point. And, on the subject of the Burton, we ought to have mentioned, in speaking of Hackthorn Gorse and Carlton, that these beautiful coverts were as the apple of his eye to Lord Henry Bentinck—who was wont to speak of the latter as "the fox's model lodging house." It is made of blackthorn—laid and plashed as level as a bed of verbenas.

We should now have shown how five days a week are to be had from Lincoln, with the Burton and Blankney—each day's meet being within an extreme radius of fourteen or fifteen miles. It should also have been gathered that *much* sport is to be met with, and that, though essentially good horses are wanted, a hunting man's establishment need not be on the exaggerated scale necessary for the requirements of the more crowded shires.

THE FITZWILLIAM.*

THAT this great pack has been a hundred and five years the property of the Fitzwilliam family is no little to say of it. But present merit has more to do with our subject than past history; and it is more to the point to be able to add that, in the field or on the flags, none of its younger rivals can give it the go-by. Witness the Hound Show at Peterborough (July 1878) —when none but an even older kennel, the Brocklesby, had any chance with it—endorsing what we have always held, that *confirmed excellence* must belong ever to private than to subscription packs. The Fitzwilliam or (as it is even better known in kennel parlance) the Milton blood, has—like the Belvoir and Brocklesby — built many a pack, but suffered no deterioration in the process. Refreshing itself now and again with a slight infusion from other sources— chiefly from the two just named—it has ever kept itself not only vigorous but steadily improving. And that good looks and good work should—and with them *do*—go together, is proved by their system of breeding only from the best working hounds. Indeed,

---

* *Vide* "Stanford's Railway and Hunting Map," sheets 10 and 16.

their winners at the show were all the progeny of famous workers. With them, a hound faulty in the chase is not good enough to keep, still less to breed from—a summary system upon which a younger kennel can seldom afford to act rigidly.

Their country is essentially one for bringing hounds out to advantage; and, while offering them every opportunity and encouragement, will quickly make patent any radical failing. There are large tracts of woodland for cubhunting, schooling, and practising—wild straight foxes and an open country elsewhere—the scent seldom strong enough to carry hounds out of reach—and few difficulties to part them from the huntsman and his attendant lictors. There was a time, the natives say, when *all* the Fitzwilliam country was grass—and wild wet grass on which scent hovered naturally. Now the bulk of its broad acres are condemned to grow wheat that does not pay for sowing—and, easy though it is to root up pasturage, farmers cannot afford the lengthy process of restoring it. And so is it, in more or less degree, all over England. Farmers cannot compete in the corn market against importation; their crops scarcely cover the needed outlay; and thousands of arable farms are consequently going begging. But if tenants have seldom either capital or inclination to lay down herbage in place of the unremunerative ploughland, landlords must do it soon—or be content to see their farms unoccupied. Then will grazing resume its sway—we shall ride over grass everywhere—and *Ware wheat* will be a cry unknown! That such a consummation would be desirable in the Fitzwilliam

The Fitzwilliam.

country its most ardent admirers would find it difficult to deny. They don't trouble themselves much about *ware wheat* there—or they would never go a-hunting at all—but they would be glad, no doubt, to ride on a sounder surface. The fences, in much of the best of the country, fully bear out the theory that they were grown to separate cattle, rather than to mark the boundary between one field of cereal and another; for they are of blackthorn of high rank growth, often quite impervious and impracticable. The only way to combat them, then, is to "go round." There is usually a comfortable hole in one corner, which the old hands know as readily as a hare does a smeuse. This kind of fence is especially the rule all over the south and south-west of the Fitzwilliam country—a district into which you must take a horse as strong and well-bred as you can afford yourself. Before purchasing, just give him five minutes at his best pace through a deep fallow *with the reins laid on his neck*, and you will know pretty well if he is suited to carry you from Barnwell Wold.

It is much to be wondered at that more hunting-men do not run down—if only for an occasional day—to these hounds. The kennels are at Milton Park, only three miles from Peterborough; and Peterborough, where the best of accommodation may be had, is only about one hour and three quarters from King's Cross. Indeed, for a man whose occupation only allows him two or three days of liberty in the week (and who aspires to something a little wilder than one of Her Majesty's bucks) a much better position at which to station a few horses could not be chosen. Once, or sometimes twice, a week he might even leave London at nine o'clock, and be in time for the meet of this, one of the greatest packs in England. Or, again, with the railway at the door of his hotel, he may at any time throw in his luck for the day with the Cottesmore, or even run down for an occasional gallop with the Quorn or the Belvoir.

Huntingdon, twenty minutes nearer London on the same line, is another place from which to hunt with the Fitzwilliam, and from here the other days of the week may be filled in with the Cambridgeshire and the Oakley. But Peterborough, as being the point from which hounds start in the morning to return in the evening, may be taken as the special base of operation with a view to the pack in question.

It is rather a severe country for horses — the distances being long, the ground deep, and the woods very trying. It sometimes happens that hounds have as much as thirty miles to journey back to kennels; and, though you may occasionally find your way home by train, your lot may at any time be the same as theirs. So, start with sound horses and strong ones; and be prepared to fill up a gap in the stable should a casualty demand it.

The meets of the Fitzwilliam are regulated as follows—on a system that would appear not only to have been adopted by the present Master, the Marquis of Huntly, but to have been in vogue for many years past. Wednesday and Saturday, being market days at Peterborough, are chosen for the more distant meets in the south of the country—while Monday and Thursday are reserved for the north, which is all within easy ride of Peterborough. Friday is very frequently a bye-day; and is generally at no great distance from kennels.

Monday is more essentially a Peterborough day; and no effort is spared to render it as good as possible. It will be observed that the river Nene, after running all down the south-west boundary of the country, works across from Oundle to Peterborough. In so doing, it divides the Monday from the Thursday district—the meets of the former being all to the south of the river, those of the latter to the north and north-west.

Some of the chief fixtures for Monday are Alwalton, Chesterton, Ashton Wold, Elton Hall, Washingley, Shark's Lodge, and sometimes as far south as Holme Station. As regards coverts, the nearest to Peterborough are those of Orton and Thompson's Thorns, Jones's Covert, Chesterton, and Alwalton Hills. Haddon Nursery is a very thick newly-planted covert, part of which at one time lay near the North Road, and was much exposed to disturbance. This objection was got over by grubbing up a certain portion, and planting three or four acres more remote from the road—with the best result. Lord Carysford's Coverts, Elton-New-Close, Stock Hill, and Elton Firs lie next —with Lord Huntly's beautiful new gorse at Water Newton, which has already proved very attractive to foxes. There is some fine grass country to the east of Elton, when foxes can be persuaded to take it: and all the Monday district, though much of it is plough, is pleasant riding ground.

Turning to the Thursdays, we find ourselves on

the other side of the Nene, either in what is known as the Soke (as the land just beyond the river is termed), in the Forest, or in the vicinity of Stamford. Some thirty years ago an unbroken line of woodland existed from Milton right across to Deene (the residence of the Cardigan family) and Bulwick, and formed a continuation of the Rockingham Forest. Much of this woodland has been cleared away; but large woods still exist to the west of the Nene; and here the chief part of the cub-hunting, and hound education generally, is carried on. The two greatest strongholds in the Soke—among others too numerous to enumerate—are the Bedford Purlieus (as its name would imply, the property of the Duke of Bedford) and Castor Hanglands. This large covert belongs to the Ecclesiastical Commissioners, who for years have let it to the Fitzwilliam family—sufficient guarantee that all desiderata for a schooling ground for hounds are duly forthcoming. In drawing these woods—as indeed may be said of hunting the whole country—the rule is observed of working homewards from the most distant coverts. Near Stamford the country becomes lighter and more open. Lord Exeter has considerable coverts; but foxes apparently find their welcome at Burghley a colder one than they were accustomed to under a previous generation. Lord Kesteven's little coverts are better favoured, Lawn Wood and Hilly Wood, and, before the Great Northern Railway pushed across here, there were other coverts down towards Burrough Fen. Now, however, under the multiplied dangers of the railways this part is not regularly hunted. Walcot Hall

The Fitzwilliam.

and Stamford Racecourse are two of their most northerly meets; while, moving on to the woods, we have Thornhaugh, Wansford, Nassington, and Cotterstock Hall (the hunting residence of the Marquis of Huntly). If the supply of foxes appears to admit of it, Friday generally supplies a second day in the woods.

To the widest meets of Wednesday and Saturday hounds have to be carried by rail—no slight yearly addition to the expenditure of the master. With a railway, however, running southward on either side of the country—to Higham Ferrars and Huntingdon, the inconvenience of the journey is minimised as much as possible; and, under the system of always drawing in the direction of the kennels, hounds always return on foot.

Wednesday is in what is decidedly the best of the Fitzwilliam territory—their Thrapston country, as applied to include their south-west border, touching upon the Pytchley and the Oakley. As neither the last-named pack nor the Cambridgeshire are out on a Wednesday, large contingents gladly lend their strength to the Fitzwilliam. Accordingly the train brings numbers from Cambridge, and even Newmarket, when hounds are advertised for Lilford, Clapton, Thrapston Bridge, Bythorne Tollbar, or Catworth Guide Post. From Lord Lilford's park, they invariably get a strong good fox and a run, either over the grass along the riverside, or far over the wild open country by Barnwell and Weston—sometimes even down to Kimbolton. For the other meets mentioned above there are Barnwell Wold, a splendid wood of the Duke of Buccleugh's, wherein a few years ago half a dozen foxes might be seen to cross a ride in succession, and where it is promised that the same shall be seen again; Thorpe Gorse, Titchmarsh Warren (from which foxes *must* take a good line), George's Thorns, Denford Ash, Raunds-Old-Meadow, Stanwick Pastures, with Catworth Gorse and Hunt's Closes at the extremity of the country. All these, except Barnwell Wold, are comparatively small thorn or gorse coverts—where a fox is glad to lie but not to stay when found. To the north again, Oundle belongs more to the Thursday country, as from it all Lord Westmorland's woods and Cotterstock Wood (forming the extremity of the Soke country) are often drawn—though in the other direction it has Baron Rothschild's excellent covert Ashton Wold to depend upon.

Saturday is more especially for the Huntingdon side, and its meets are, as a rule, to the east of the Oundle and Thrapston Road—though Wednesday and Saturday are looked upon as belonging so much to one district that the rule is anything but an absolute one, and such fixtures as Barnwell Castle, Alconbury Hill, Abbott's Ripton, and Buckworth Village are as often told off for one day as the other. Very little hunting is to be done on the east of the Peterborough and Huntingdon Railway (coloured though it is on Stanford's Map—Sheet 16); for you are in the Fens almost immediately. And it may here be noted that the Fitzwilliam southern boundary line runs from Kimbolton to Graffham and from Graffham straight across to Huntingdon, instead of along the river Ouse, west of Huntingdon—as shown on that map. Holmewood House, Gidding Windmill, Sawtry Tollbar, Aversley Wood and Luton Village are other meets in Saturday's country; and from Barnwell Wold westward there are excellent gorses and coverts of every description, such as Gidding Grove, Hemmington Spinneys, Little Gidding Gorse, Gidding Cow Pasture, and Sawtrey Gorse. They had a great evening run from the first-named covert about the middle of February last. Rather than score a bad day's sport, the Master decided on putting hounds into covert once more at 4.20 p.m. Fortunately, their fox put, and kept, his head straight for kennels. They ran right to Alwalton; and at six o'clock were glad to whip the hounds off—though one of the field, only a short distance away down wind, was striving in vain to signal them to where their fox was barely crawling across a road. Washingley Coverts too, are very good; but belong more to the Orton, or Monday country. More to the south are Solom Wood, Flittermere Gorse and Buckworth Woods. Nearest to Huntingdon are Ellington Gorse and the large coverts belonging to Lord Chesham— Monk's Wood (over 1000 acres), Archer's, Coppingford, Upton, and Aversley Woods, where foxes are wild and good. Game is not allowed to shoulder them out; and, towards the end of the season especially, good runs from here are frequent. Holme Wood (Mr. Well's) deserves special mention as a stronghold. Foxes from this covert have of late taken a great fancy for running down into the fens, where it is next to impossible to follow them for any distance.

The great feature of all the southern portion of the Fitzwilliam country is the strength and distance apart of its coverts. Take, for instance, Aversley Wood, Barnwell Wold, and Ashton Wold. Foxes are almost always on the spot; and, once disturbed, they must travel long distances to reach a second refuge. With the Fitzwilliam you will always see sport, and see foxes well hunted—AND KILLED.

THE QUORN.*

HONOURED and renowned in history, and with its prestige never higher than at the present time, the Quorn takes first rank among subscription packs. It derives most of its support from Melton Mowbray, which is, *par excellence*, the fashionable hunting centre of England; and apart from its time-honoured and intimate association with that place, and beyond the fact that its maintenance and well-being has ever been the foremost care of Meltonians, it has such advantages of position and country as few other Hunts can claim.

To hunt with the Quorn, "there are three courses open to you." If Melton seems suited to you, *by all means go there*. 'Tis a hunting man's paradise. BUT, we would add, before labelling yourself and your belongings for Melton, take stock of yourself, your proclivities, your capabilities, and above all, the sphere which you have hitherto chosen—or which has chosen you. Melton is not intolerant of the outer world; neither is it rigorous towards its own. Installed and accepted there, no stern censorship will

---

* *Vide* " Stanford's Railway and Hunting Map," sheet 9.

note your tastes or pounce upon your shortcomings; your horsemanship or your nerve will not be harshly judged, nor even your adaptation of ethics be roughly criticised. But (*verbum sap.*) do not go to Melton to be a fish out of water—even to find yourself not the only one gasping on the bank.

As a quarter the Metropolis of Hunting (as it has long been justly termed) is unrivalled; but though, if at Melton, you would naturally become a member of the Quorn Hunt (and probably give the price of a horse towards its funds), yet your sport would by no means be restricted to that pack. The Quorn country is but limited. The best of it—viz., the Melton side, and generally termed the *grass country*, in contradistinction to the Forest—is only sufficient for two advertised days a week (Mondays and Fridays), to which the master usually adds a Thursday byeday. Tuesdays and Saturdays are held on the west of the country (totally different ground, and but little worthy of a place in the Shires)—Tuesday in Charnwood Forest and its neighbourhood, and Saturday in a well-tilled wilderness north of Loughborough. These two days are better reached from the latter town, or from Leicester: the Melton men preferring a more favourable scene, nearer home, with the Cottesmore and Belvoir, even to hunting with their own pack.

It is by no means one of the least advantages of Melton Mowbray that hounds are close at hand every day in the week. With the variety offered by three, or even four, packs, it seldom happens that the ride to covert is more than ten miles—and the average may be taken as nearer six. Better still, hounds almost always leave off equally near at home—and so, from every point of view, hunting may be done as comfortably from Melton as from any place in the world. Standing, as it does, a central point in a sea of grass, in a country where foxhunting is all in all, and where squires, farmers, and even keepers, have been reared to worship the little red animal, the best meets of each pack are those in the neighbourhood of Melton. The Quorn, Cottesmore, and Belvoir countries all run up to a common apex in the town of Melton Mowbray; and arrange their meets so that each day one or other of them shall be in its neighbourhood. To breakfast each morning at 9.30 (with still a marginal half hour for the sluggard), and yet be in good time at the covert-side, is not given to many hunting quarters—and might well encourage the late hours which, whether devoted to society or to tobacco, seldom fail in the end to make their mark on the hardest and the boldest. But men who belong to the latter class know this too well. They know, too, that they have come to Leicestershire to hunt and to ride; and that, if their power and zest to do this once fails, the land will be but a desert to them —and so they go to bed early, leaving those to sit up to whom the chase offers nothing more sterling than another school for scandal, another field for small talk. The canter to covert, too! That "it is better fun riding to covert in Leicestershire than hunting elsewhere" is as solemnly true as ever, albeit the gallant author has been beguiled into another county. Mile upon mile of swinging turf—if only you know your way, and how to avoid the muddy, fresh granited roads. Geography is not—may we be pardoned for saying?—the strong point of the Meltonian. Each has his own way to covert; but it by no means always happens that he has one to take him home. It does not chime in with his creed to know the country— and the creed is not altogether an unsound one. When hounds are running, *he* will ride best to them who can attend solely to what they are doing, and blind himself to the direction the fox may be taking. Thus will novelty never be wanting, and enjoyment reaped where others are grumbling because they have ridden this line before.

Melton, then, commands the Quorn on Mondays and Fridays, and on Thursday there is either a byeday with that pack, or the Cottesmore are in reach, or else Mr. Tailby is in the north of his country. On Tuesdays the Cottesmore, and on Wednesdays the Belvoir, are always at hand; while on alternate Saturdays these packs take it in turn to be close to Melton. Thus, it will be seen, the six days are pretty well occupied; and, unless you wish to have Melton all to yourself for a day, you must have horses enough to carry you on all six. Half a dozen thoroughly seasoned, and conditioned, hunters will see you through the winter, *with luck*; especially if a fortnight's frost comes at the time you could best do with it. But with this number, and with everything in your favour, you will often have to come home early in the day and miss many an afternoon gallop. Two horses a day (besides the hack who, from some extraordinary combination of virtues, is able to come out nearly *every* day) are almost indispensable to the thorough enjoyment of hunting in Leicestershire. In the crowd and confusion of the morning you are not so likely to see sport; but it is all one horse's work to keep moving on with the ruck. In the afternoon there is generally a run—and for this you want a fresh horse. The crowd have gone home; hounds have a fair chance, and the master has kept his best covert for the evening draw. The sun has disappeared; the wind, maybe, has fallen; the glass is rising, and scent is a moral certainty. Your fox is only too ready to go; hounds get away at his brush; all the choicest spirits are there, *full of ride;* and the country is the Twyford Vale. To be on a tired horse is misery—and perhaps grief to you both. You *ought* not to ride bad ones at all (at least within hail of Melton); but we all get them occasionally, and have to make the best of them—wrapping the secret of their vileness in our own breasts. If obliged to bring such an one to the covert side, ride him in the morning. If necessary, trot the brute about the roads, keeping your own counsel, and letting the world think, if it chooses, that you are not so keen and hard as you used to be. The world—at all events the morning world—will not take half as much note of you as you fancy. But, as you value your pleasure (and your reputation), don't ride the said brute in the afternoon. Send him home with a thanksgiving; and get on your trusty one with a chuckle. He is bold, and swift, and stout. Your heart bounds; your blood warms; you feel you are as good as your neighbours; you mutter something in his ear that you would not for a thousand should be overheard—and, if hounds run, you will ride none the worse for that morning's abstinence.

The first of the three courses by which you may hunt with the Quorn being to take a six-days a-week stud to Melton; the second is to establish yourself at Leicester or Loughborough, the third is to take a hunting box in the country. We have already made some allusion to the first-named plan; and further, in treating of the grass side of the Quorn, shall consider that part of the country in connection with Melton. On the merits of the other plans we shall have something to say as we continue.

As regards its position from London, Melton Mowbray is a little more than three hours' journey from St. Pancras, by way of Leicester. Leaving London at 3.30 p.m., you are landed anywhere in Melton before 7. But it is only attainable on the morning of hunting by taking the mail train at 5.15 a.m.—with all the miseries consequent on such an hour in December or January.

Monday and Friday being, as we have said, the two days on which the Quorn are out on their Melton, or *grass*, side, we will take them first in order. A glance at the map (sheet 9 of Stanford's series) will show the river Wreake running from Melton to Syston, where it joins the river Soar on its way from Leicester. North of the Wreake, then, is the Monday country of the Quorn, while south and south-east of the two rivers is the Friday country. The Midland Railway has cunningly chosen the valleys of these rivers for its course; and close parallel to them runs the

Leicester and Melton turnpike road—whereof the story has been told for a century that two Meltonians of coaching fame, wagering to name the best fifteen miles of coach road against each other, handed their respective judgments on paper to a referee; the papers being opened, the one had written "from Leicester to Melton," the other "from Melton to Leicester."

Once a year the Quorn meet at Melton Mowbray itself—usually at Egerton Lodge, the hunting-box of the Father of the Hunt, Lord Wilton. This, however, is generally a sequence to the races of Croxton Park or the Steeplechases of Burrough Hill, and an immediate prelude to the break up of the season. The nearest covert to Melton is Welby Fishponds, planted by Lord Wilton for the Hunt—an excellent little covert of gorse and osiers, and in ordinary times fruitful of fine runs. For it is too small for foxes to dwell; and beyond a couple of ploughed fields immediately adjoining, there is a wide area of strong scenting grass in every direction. *In ordinary times*, we said advisedly—for look at those strings of red dotted lines festooning the map on every side of Melton! What are these but *railways in progress?* Railways *in being* are hateful and sport-spoiling enough; but railways in progress are to a hunting country as the Colorado beetle to the potato. To the iron rails and the puffing engines foxes get used. To the indignity of galloping a mile round to a bridge (where we were wont to strike a free bee line as we chose) we can become blunted. But not only are railways in course of construction bristling all day with gangs of shouting workmen; but the honest navvy cares not to work more than three or four days in the week, preferring to take his pleasure in snaring in solitude, in rabbit digging with a chum after his own heart, or in openly beating the fox-coverts in force. If the hounds are out they have mustered, a noisy hundred, at the covertside, an hour or so before the pack is thrown in. Yes, lamentable and disfiguring as those red lines will still look on the face of this fair country, they will be welcome when drawn continuous and finished, in comparison with the state of progress and devastation conveyed by their present dotted length.

Asfordby is another meet for Welby Fishponds and the useful little copse of Cant's Thorns adjoining. Hounds are also sometimes brought to Ab Kettleby for the same; but more often for the coverts neutral with the Belvoir, to which we shall come immediately. Ragdale is for Shoby Scholes and Lord Aylesford's—two splendid coverts almost touching each other. The former is a thickly wooded dell, overlooking which the field have to stand on the grass hills on either side the wide hollow. Their fox, likely enough, breaks down the valley; then, with a rare country, and a quick scenting one, all round, it is a ride to be with hounds. Over the brow is Lord Aylesford's—a grand gorse and broom covert of twenty or thirty acres, where more foxes were found last season than anywhere in the Monday country. A free loan it is, too—and a loan right well appreciated.

Further to the left along the roadside is Ratcliff-on-the-Wreake, the widest Monday meet in this direction.

Cossington Gorse from here (more of thorn than gorse in its composition, by the way) is a covert of happy memory and glorious connection. It stands by the side of the old Roman Fosse Road, which (well cared for to Six Hills, afterwards a deep wild track such as would do credit to the New Forest) runs from Leicester to Newark, as any map will plainly tell. A Cossington fox must either break westwards into a country whose style is more befitting a Saturday draw; or he puts a very different colouring on the proceedings by crossing the road and embarking on ground almost sacred in its associations—the Hoby and Thrussington lordships, to wit. That is the country to test the best of men, and the best of horses; even of Melton; for the fields are forty acres apiece, and the fences are to be jumped—but *nothing more*. Hounds, on fair terms with their fox, can fly over them on anything like a scenting day; and we maintain it is a pleasanter country to cross quick than to crane over—for the fences will not bear too much looking at. From Cossington Gorse past Thrussington and Hoby villages to Shoby Scholes is a twenty-five minutes' enjoyment not to be surpassed even in the Shires—provided always that you are riding a horse fit for the journey. A good horse is essential to comfort anywhere—but a *superlatively good horse* is needed for Leicestershire, not only to accomplish the country, but to combat the crowd. He should be as nearly thoroughbred as you can get him, or he will not live the pace or *jump when he is half beat*. He must be bold, and yet be tractable. Believe not what is often broadly stated, that riding over Leicestershire is no more difficult for horse or man than a practice gallop over a training course, and that the fences may be taken as they come, like hurdles. *Many* men have we seen come down imbued with this idea (perhaps we once held it ourselves), and one and all were quickly in grief in consequence—with the result that they either benefited by the experience to do themselves and their horses justice, or retired hurt and mortified. No, Leicestershire is the last county over which to ride haphazard; and a Leicestershire horse should possess no common combination of qualities. He must be able to gallop, and he must be ready to jump; but he must be handy to turn, and easy to stop—willing to creep a bottom, to drop his hind legs at a double, to brush a bullfinch, or to fly an oxer. It may be argued that a four-year-old has often been known to carry a man successfully to hounds over the grass. True, but the credit belongs rather to the man than the horse. The colt has blood and courage; the man has coolness and cleverness sufficient to help him through his difficulties; and the line has probably been all plain sailing. Depend upon it, four-year-olds (and a four-year-old of high class is far better in the Shires than an older horse of inferior stamp) will not carry the best men to the front every day and all day; and to live with hounds regularly, you must ride horses of superior stamp, of thorough training, and, if possible, over your weight.

Six Hills is a kind of Croydon Junction to the best coverts of the Monday country; and, consequently, seldom remains unadvertised two weeks in succession. It is little more than half a dozen miles from Melton,

The Quorn.

and constitutes almost a central spot for the whole of the Quorn country. With hounds at Six Hills it is useless for the most practised sinner to attempt the vice of speculating on the draw. Thrussington Wolds is a couple of hundred yards away, Thrussington Gorse half a mile, Walton Thorns the same, Mr. Cradock's Spinney still less, Shoby Scholes and Lord Aylesford's a mile and a half, and Cossington Gorse two miles—and any of them may be chosen as first draw. Of these coverts Thrussington Wolds is a snug little wood of about thirty acres; the Gorse (or New Covert) is sound, and thick, and well favoured, and both overlook the fine bullock-pastures that stretch down to the Wreake—offering every temptation to a good fox to try his luck across the open. Walton Thorns and Mr. Cradock's spinney are the property of the same good fox preserver; and, in spite of neighbouring difficulties the Thorns are seldom untenanted, no matter how often appealed to. Great runs are on record, and great runs are recent, from Walton Thorns. Did they not kill THE *bobtail* from there—fifty-three minutes without a check, the death at Sysonby (by Melton) and nearly every field grass? Twelve years ago; but three times twelve will not wipe it from the memories of the few who rode that November gallop. And it was last November again that the Quorn bitches, never lifted or touched, ran into an old fox " as big as a wolf," in Bunny Park—fifty-five minutes from the Thorns, and *very few* fields grass. Just beyond Walton Thorns is Burton Park. It is a matter of regret that Lord Archibald Seymour no longer hunts.

For years he kept twenty horses at Melton. But he has many nice little coverts at Burton—and of course he is pleased to think they are full of foxes for his old friends, and, in all the generous feeling evolved by foxhunting and its memories, delights in seeing hounds drawing his plantations as often as they can come. As a stuttering friend of mine responded to one who would fain have helped him through his half completed sentence—" N . . . nothing of the sort, sir! *Damme, sir, nothing of the sort!!*" He has forgotten the past.

Plunging northwards up the unkempt Fosse Road from Six Hills (which after Christmas, by the way, no one thinks of doing if they can possibly go round), a three-mile journey brings us to a point opposite Willoughby Village, and about midway between the covert of that name and Curate's Gorse. Willoughby Village is a frequent, and—so long as the Widmerpool country beyond was well cared for—was a favourite meet. The covert (which is blackthorn and gorse) is rather too close to the village, but the inhabitants are vastly fond of foxhunting—so they leave it undisturbed and many a pretty gallop accrues. If the line should be towards Bunny or Widmerpool, you soon find yourself on a light plough district; but immediately round Willoughby, on every side but one, are small grass enclosures, with neat nice fences worthy of a good horse. Once well away from here, the country will either be still made up of these pleasant green fields (as is the case round Wimeswould), or degenerate into plough, with fences of no size, but trappy and blind. Your fox must determine which variety you shall encounter; for both phases are to be found in any direction. A common, and, it may be, a good line is to Ellar's Gorse—a covert that has, however, scarcely paid its rent of late years—and thence over the Fosse to the Curate. The last named famous gorse, with its companion Parson's Thorns, are just over, and on, the summit of the high ground above the Belvoir Vale—the village of Hickling being a mile or so beneath the Parson's. Indeed, the chief charm of these time-honoured coverts is the chance of dropping into the Vale (in its very best part) and attaining a sharp sweet burst to Old Dalby Wood, to Sherbrooke's Covert (of the Duke's), or to the neutral covert of Holwell Mouth. A pleasanter line cannot be ridden than to either of these three points—save when the Smite is encountered in an intractable form. As we move on to Widmerpool all again depends on the direction taken by foxes—when there are any. It may be accepted as a general statement (not without its exceptions) that all the country to the west of the Fosse Road is very inferior to that on the east, the Melton side. At and near Widmerpool are extensive coverts (as Leicestershire coverts go)—Roehoe Wood and Kinoulton Gorse being instances. Beyond these are Owthorpe Borders, Wynstay Gorse, and many plantations, all which are just above the Vale —and if a fox will run thither 'tis all you want. But should he take you down towards Costock, Bunny, Plumptre, &c., your fate will be a less stirring one, and your career less exciting.

Turning now to the part that is neutral with the

Belvoir, we have the meets of Wartnaby (sometimes at the Stonepits, or, better in every sense, at the Hall) and Ab Kettleby, each about four miles from Melton. After drawing the Long Plantation of Wartnaby, hounds are taken, generally by their fox, along the hill side to Holwell Mouth. Holwell Mouth is the warmest of basin copses, and foxes delight in it. From here a fox will more often cross the brow to Clawson Thorns, half a mile into the Duke's country; and from there he will probably come back again, repeating the operation *ad lib.* But frequently he slips away into the tempting Vale, which lies mapped out like a green chessboard below; and in this case he invariably leaves nine-tenths of his scarlet-coated followers behind. The Quorn have no covert in their slip of the Belvoir Vale; so a Holwell Mouth fox taking the lower ground will either lead them to Sherbrooke's Covert of the Duke's, or mount the Hill again to the Curate, or round to, and through, Old Dalby Wood. The latter is a thin, but well-placed brake; but foxes have not favoured it, or else have been but little favoured, of late years; for though they will run through it they decline to reside there. After Holwell Mouth the next neutral covert is Saxelby Spinney, and then Grimston Gorse—the last named a fine covert, but with a railway cutting in course of formation through it. All round Grimston and Saxelby is a grand stiff grass country, as fine as can be ridden over, and generally carrying a rich scent.

Having now completed our brief sketch of the geography of the Monday country, we may carry our

The Quorn.   79

pen across the Wreake for a few topographical jottings anent the Quorn Fridays. Kirby Gate (or rather, the site of the old tollbar) is the first, and nearest, meet of the season. Custom says they ought to come there for the opening day; and so, as is right, they do. Later on, they save three miles by making Great Dalby the rendezvous before proceeding to draw Gartree Hill. This famous thorn covert of Mr. Hartopp's (adjoining the Punchbowl and others which he provides, all equally stocked, for the Cottesmore) is situated quite in an extreme corner of the Quorn territory. The Burton Flat stretches out at its feet, with Stapleford Park, the Whissendine, and many miles of grass beyond; just to the right is the hill of Little Dalby, with the Punchbowl, Burrough Hill, and the cream of the Cottesmore behind these. At the back of Gartree Hill again are the great ox-fenced pastures of Great Dalby. Little wonder, then, that, with every advantage of preservation and situation, such great and frequent runs should have been booked to this covert, and the adjacent one of Sir Francis Burdett's —another thick thorn fastness below Dalby Hill. After a morning here, hounds may be taken on to draw Adams' Gorse, a little covert near Thorpe Satchville, close to the Melton Steeplechase Course, and with the best country in the hunt within hail. Or, without stopping here, they will be thrown into one of the great trio of coverts—Thorpe Trussels, Ashby Pastures, and Cream Gorse. When these are required for morning work, the meets will probably be Thorpe Satchville Hall, Ashby Folville, and

Gaddesby Hall, respectively. A narrow chain of plough (some two or three fields broad) embraces all three coverts; but once clear, either to the north or south, you will ride, in the best of company, over a grass country that has no superior. Thorpe Trussels is composed of some six or eight acres of dense thorn growth, Cream Gorse is a trifle bigger, with Ashby Pastures in between, a tangled wood of about fifty acres—each being about a mile from the other. To run down by Ashby and Twyford, perhaps to Baggrave, John o' Gaunt, or the Cottesmore Woods, with a good scent and a start, is only so much short of Elysium as your disposition is phlegmatic and yourself out of place.

Another meet, with an ulterior view to Cream Gorse, &c., is Brooksby Hall. It is also very frequently fixed upon for the Thursday byedays; and it has many little spinneys in its neighbourhood, to which the smaller field of such days are often taken for a find and a gallop. There are two or three similar spinnies belonging to Rearsby, besides the well sheltered little covert of Bleakmore by the side of the Wreake. Beyond Gaddesby there is Mr. Cheney's new little covert; then Queniboro' Spinney, a well frequented plantation by the roadside; and beyond it we find ourselves at the great good covert of Barkby Holt, and the newly grown gorse attached—the village of Queniboro' and Barkby Hall being the places of meeting. When Barkby Hall is advertised, the spinnies of Barkby Thorpe, and perhaps those of Humberston, may be drawn before proceeding to the Holt; and, in the early part of the

The Quorn. 81

season especially, they are more than likely to hold foxes. Barkby Holt has for fifty years or more been one of the tightest strongholds of the Friday country. It is, like Ashby Pasture, a wood of perhaps fifty acres, with great density of undergrowth, and, when looked after as it has been during Mr. Brooks' time, is a nursery and never failing reservoir of foxes. It stands in a district peculiarly known as the Barkby-and-Scraptoft-country; and is perhaps more generally popular among the Quornites than any ground in the Hunt. The greater proportion of farms in the neighbourhood are grass in its purest and simplest form; and the fences, not set very far from each other, are all not only jumpable, but "cry out to be jumped"—so fair and clean and negotiable are they. From Barkby Holt to Scraptoft Gorse is a twenty minutes that will teach a four-year-old, or make an octogenarian think himself as young as ever. Next to Barkby is Baggrave—whose energetic owner is never content with *one* fox in six acres. By some magic he tempts them, till we have seen five in succession break *in February*, from the Prince of Wales' Covert. Hounds away in a moment with the last, their original choice—the brook at the bottom of the valley, only to be jumped here and there — five hundred horsemen and the devil to pay—for they hate that brook and three are in already! 'Tis as quick a scenting country as any in the Hunt, and in five minutes you are in the Twyford country. A long pair of spurs, the best horse in your stable (perhaps a luncheon at the Hall), and it will come easy to you. Such is Baggrave. The meet at Lowesby Hall, the

G

find John o'Gaunt, used to be much the same thing—
only the disagreeable element was in the ascendant,
for the Marfield Brook couldn't be jumped. Happily
they have changed that, bridged the chasm, and left
the road open for the line that has made John
o'Gaunt immortal—if only the new railway does not
spoil all. We are getting into a country now that
requires control over pen and pencil. The quill
jumps as to the spur, and comment and description
fling against the bit—remembering that often of late
they have been curbed to write the clumsiness of
plough as " good sporting country," and to title slow
scenting fallows as "honest hunting ground."
Honest forsooth! Is not every foot of soil turned by
the ploughshare *suppressio veri* in its wickedest form?
In front of John o' Gaunt are thousands of acres
which never grew a quartern loaf or brought grist to
any mill save the grazier's and the butcher's. Hounds
can run, and horses must gallop, if a fox will cross
the Twyford Brook to Burrough Hill, or thread the
brookside to Owston Wood. There is other country
as good in the Shires—for you can't go beyond
perfection; but we have yet to ride over, or learn of,
better. No, not even from the Coplow of Billesdon,
or from Lord Moreton's covert at Cold Newton on the
way thither, superlative as is the ride across the
nullah-broken plains to Tilton Wood, or over the
smoother acres to Norton Gorse and Kibworth.
Billesdon Coplow is, perhaps, the best memorialised
landmark in the whole Quorn country. It has had
its deserts in song and say during each era of mastership for generations past, and is still as prominent a

The Quorn.

feature in the sport—and the scenery—of the Hunt as ever. Botany Bay, as the covert at its base is called, gives forth foxes and runs as freely as in years gone by. A mile or so away is Scraptoft, with its hall of hospitality, and its sterling gorse—another point from which the Billesdon country is frequently pierced. But whichever line foxes take from the Coplow or from Scraptoft Gorse, they have strong good grass over which to lead a Friday field. And this Quorn Friday field is of numbers such as would horrify—or even crush—any other hunt. Of course every man who wears a Q. H. button on his coat, or lives on Quorn soil, is there. So is everyone from the Cottesmore who is within reach, and who has a horse to bring out. Mr. Tailby's followers all join in; and even some of the Belvoir for the nearer meets. It is the great day for Leicester; and Rugby sends a contingent by train. Of such a multitude of course only a small minority ever catch a glimpse of hounds at work. But all do not care about that. The country is so wide, there are so many places where they can jump, and so many gates that they can go through, that it is easy enough for all to get about — and so they do, enjoying themselves each in his own way. But a Quorn Friday for the man who loves hounds is pleasanter at four o'clock than at twelve.

Adding that Mr. Warner has given the Hunt a very promising young covert near Willoughby (in the Monday country); that Beeby, Keyham, and Quenby Hall are frequent Friday meets (Beeby for Barkby Holt or Scraptoft Gorse, Keyham for Foxholes, and

Quenby for the Coplow)—and we have done with the grass country of the Quorn.

Of the three alternative plans for hunting with the Quorn, we have hitherto considered only that of a stud at Melton, and written only of that part of the Quorn country of which Melton is the principal and legitimate base. But from Leicester or Loughborough you may be just as staunch a Quornite, and stick even more closely to your colours—for you will not have the same temptation or opportunity of leaving them, to go elsewhere. Leicester will give you a Thursday with Mr. Tailby (if you prefer it to a bye-day with the pack in question), and an occasional day with the Atherstone. From Loughborough you may go out (if you think it good enough to abandon the grass on Monday or Friday) with Lord Ferrers, in the slip of country that has been lent him by the Quorn. But from both towns you will in all probability attend all the four, or five, Quorn meets; and as few people, nowadays, go to either place with horses for six days a week, you are most likely to limit yourself altogether to the home pack. A quarter of a century ago the Bell at Leicester was a great resort of hunting-men. Lord Gardner, for instance, made it his head quarters for years, and so did many other leading Leicestershire men. But Leicester in those days was a small market town, knew nothing of cotton hose, and had no chimneys higher than that of the hotel. Now it is like a great ever-growing octopus—stretching its brick and mortar limbs in every direction and daily gathering more of the sacred soil into its unhallowed grasp, while its black breath is wafted over half the country. But you may still get your hunting from it, and the accommodation is no less complete than ever. And yet, to settle down in the midst of a manufacturing town, with a view to foxhunting, has something incongruous about it. It doesn't seem natural that the first mile or two of your journey to covert should be past factories, workshops and trams; still less that the last stage of your return home should be enlivened by narrow escapes from hansom cabs, while, perhaps, your muddy pink and broken hat provide jest and jibe for unsympathising "factory hands." Loughborough is less than three miles from the kennels; so as regards distances and journeys you are no worse off than the huntsman (besides having the pull over him of being able to choose your own pace). Loughborough is a quiet little town—though yearning to swell itself out after the manner of its big brother. Both are on the main line of the Midland Railway—Leicester about two hours and a quarter, Loughborough some three hours, from St. Pancras.

The third alternative—viz., to take a hunting box, away from the towns—recommends itself to many people, especially such as, while wishing to spend their season in a good country, are unwilling to bind themselves down to hunting every day in the week. A man must live somewhere; so must his wife—and children. And setting aside the mere accident of his taste, surely the green lanes of Leicestershire are to be preferred, for these others, even to the "salubrisome" vicinity of Great Coram Street—still more to the unhealthy miasma of upturned arable. He puts it to himself (with the most satisfactory results) whether his other half will not find an unlimited source of enjoyment in the Shires. She does not ride much, it is true; but then she can drive to the meets, and see as much society there in a morning as she could elsewhere in a week. The advantage is so evident, that he does not hesitate to appeal to his *cara sposa* to endorse his conclusion, and is rather startled to find that her delight somewhat hangs fire. So he probably remembers that this is the very moment he ought to have been out of doors with a cigar; and a week afterwards has learned from his agents that they cannot possibly find him a house elsewhere, and that it would be madness to lose such an opportunity as the "bijou residence within a few miles of the Quorn kennels," &c. So of necessity he moves down to Leicestershire for better—or for worse, if, a stranger to the country, he has been beguiled by his agents into the depths of Charnwood Forest, as being "in the heart of the Quorn country." If he has avoided the latter fate, he is now on the spot, to hunt according to his means—or beyond them. The measure of horses he allows himself, eat no more here than in an inferior country, while they give him infinitely more fun. As for the days he stops at home, he is to be pitied if he cannot find occupation in the resources at his command. At Melton, on the other hand (at all events as an unprotected bachelor), a day's absence from the hunting field—the weather being open—will not only be prolonged agony in itself, but an evening among more fortunate comrades cannot but oppress and mortify the spirit—kindly though they may strive to ignore the happy burst, with which they are glowing still.

Tuesday and Saturday are essentially and respectively the days for Leicester and Loughborough *only*. Leicester often sends out a strong representative body—chiefly citizens, for Leicester has comparatively few visitors now; and these citizens are of various degree, the variety being more broadly marked as the meet is nearer the burgh. The *haute noblesse* of the city is well mounted, fairly caparisoned, and anxious to be "High Leicestershire" in all its prowess and appointment. The middle ten, and squires of lower degree, make up a field that will challenge comparison unabashed with that of the other side of the county—and, doubtless, when meeting near the town, Tom Firr has instituted more than one happy comparison, under his breath. It is at one or two of the best Tuesday fixtures that Leicester is most fully represented. A wedge of country runs southward from Leicester, cutting in between the Atherstone and Mr. Tailby; and with excellent grass on either side. Narborough Cross Roads is the best meet in this outlying strip; and from the osier bed of Narborough Bogs, whenever a fox can escape the joint difficulties of road, river, and railway, a capital gallop is to be had. From Cosby Spinnies, too (the southernmost point of the Quorn country), many a good line has been struck into the neighbouring countries; and the same may be said of the Enderby Spinnies. After drawing these they have no choice but to move on by Braunston towards the Forest. In this direction (west of Leicester and bordering on the Atherstone) are meets at Kirby Muxloe, Ratby Burrows, &c., from which they draw Martinshaw Wood and a chain of woods northwards—the best result that can ensue being a trip into the Atherstone kingdom. Failing this they probably find themselves amid the ruins, rocks, and rabbit holes of Bradgate Park, or the woods and quarries of Swithland. If Charnwood Forest now exists only in name, its former whereabouts is unmistakeable. Nothing but forest has a right to occupy those wild rugged hills that run from Bradgate nearly to Gracedieu. Clearly they must have been a landslip from far Derbyshire into Leicestershire, for they have no place in a county that the world generally believes to consist of flat grass. Rather we expect to see Charnwood Forest again when we hunt with the wild stag in Somersetshire. And yet Firr's horn sounds not less merrily here than in the open; nor do hounds dash after their game with diminished vigour. Foxes are killed here more certainly than under the baffling presence of a crowd. The same good hounds and the same good horses take their turn as on the grass; for Mr. Coupland hunts the better country and the inferior with impartial hearty earnestness. And yet in advising the stranger, we shall not err much in saying that fifty pounds will carry him nearly as well in the Forest as a hundred and fifty—except that, if hounds slip over the border to the Atherstone, twenty minutes may possibly put that hundred pounds difference them and him. The Forest is a fine scenting ground, and invaluable for educating hounds—at least in such parts as are available for the early

The Quorn. 89

hunting. Bradgate Ruins, Newtown Linford, Ansty and Grooby Pool are three meets all with one intent; then we have Swithland Slate Quarries, Woodhouse Eaves, Ulverscroft, &c.—all in the Forest. Copt Oak is for Bardon Wood and Charley Wood, and thence on into the Outwoods—Lord Ferrers' holding beginning where the Forest ends. Beaumanor is the meet nearest to home, except the kennels themselves, which have Quorn Wood as a standing dish close by.

The Quorn Saturdays range from immediately round Loughborough northwards to the Nottingham end of the country. The scene is laid on ground that, though apart from the Forest is on the other hand blessed with but little of the Leicestershire specialty, turf. Here and there a smattering is to be found, but on the whole this district is very Nottingham-like in character and appearance. It contains many good coverts, is well preserved and vigorously hunted, but as a country to ride over it's uninteresting —dull, in fact, as dry bread on a thirsty morning. Hounds travel well over many parts; but the chief merit of its cold ploughs lies in the necessity of their putting their heads down—thus eradicating any ill effects consequent on a previous day's temptation on the grass. Down the valley of the Soar there are indeed some very pretty meadows, over which, when meeting at Cotes Tollbar (just outside Loughborough) a fox may possibly travel from the spinney between river and railway. If they do not find there, Stanford Park is usually the next order—and here they are sure to find game. On the other side of Loughborough they have Hathern Turn and Dishley Grange, for Oakley Wood and Piper Wood; Garendon Park, too, with Burleigh Wood close handy. Prestwold Park generally has foxes in it; while the meets of Rempstone and Wymeswould refer to Hoton Spinney and the New Coverts for their first fox. Wysall on the cards means Bunny Park and the wooded ridge adjoining—and a prayer that the wind will not blow you over the Leak Hills. Widmerpool, though we have included it in Monday's meets has frequently been named for Saturday—in which case more than one Meltonian will forsake the Belvoir, on the chance of "the Curate" in the afternoon.

THE COTTESMORE.*

For the truest sport, the straightest foxes, for perfection of country, for long runs and fast runs, commend us to the wild pastures of the Cottesmore. A wide spread region scarcely inhabited; ground that carries a scent in all weathers; woodlands which breed a travelling race; and mile upon mile of untracked grass, where a fox will meet nothing more terrifying than a bullock — no wonder, then, the finest runs of the season are with the Cottesmore; that more hard riders and grand horses are present when Ranksboro' is drawn than are ever mustered elsewhere; or that the Punchbowl and Stapleford are names to make us stir in our chairs, even in this listless early August. Surely, if the hunting field can ever claim comparison with the field of chivalry, if ever the doings of the chase can be reckoned with the daring deeds of tournament or joust, it is when three hundred of the best men of the present day sit down to keep the Cottesmore bitches in sight on a scenting morning. Head and hand, heart and horseflesh, are the first requisites. Some practice, and

---

* "Stanford's Railway and Hunting Map," sheets 9, 10, 15, 16.

much self-confidence, are almost as necessary. Depend upon it, the leaders have all these; with a keen eye, a quick pulse, and no little enthusiasm (perhaps a shade of ambition) besides. But the present articles are meant to form a matter-of-fact, and doubtless dry, directory; so our sketch of the Cottesmore must be cut in as clear and naked outline as we can.

First of all, it is necessary to tell you that, if you are to look at the country through the medium of Stanford's maps, you must provide yourself with no less than four sheets (Nos. 9, 10, 15, and 16), as the Cottesmore have the misfortune to fall at the junction of the four. Another shilling will give you one of W. H. Smith's Reduced Ordnance Maps of Leicester, or Peterboro', and its environs; and five minutes work will suffice for inking off the boundaries of the Cottesmore as pourtrayed (more, or less, correctly) by Mr. Stanford's draughtsman. The gentleman in question, it will be noticed, after getting safely over the Whissendine, stopped short at the little stream under Leesthorpe, and declined to include even Stapleford Park, Berry Gorse, and Mr. Hartopp's riverside plantations. If we mistake not, the River Eye (lower down being the Wreake) carries the boundary of the Cottesmore to Melton Mowbray, to meet the Belvoir and the Quorn. At any rate in the corner between the Melton and Oakham Road and the River Eye you will go with no other hounds, unless on a marauding expedition.

The Cottesmore country is not exactly easy to describe and classify. Perhaps we may best divide it as follows, viz., into three longitudinal sections, terming them respectively the Melton country, the Oakham or middle country, and the woods. For two days and the best two days in their week Melton is an admirable base. Oakham is in the very middle of the country and commands every meet; while if some vagary of fancy should prompt you to take stabling at Stamford you are on the spot for the woodlands. Concerning Melton we have already spoken. Oakham is held by its patrons to be *facile princeps* as a centre for sport; for, besides holding good all the Cottesmore meets, it is within reach of a Quorn Friday, an occasional Belvoir Saturday, and a day once a fortnight with Mr. Tailby. But it is, of course, essentially in connection with the Cottesmore that Oakham recommends itself—offering such a fill of wild and varied hunting that a man need go no farther afield, in quest of change. The Cottesmore country, indeed, is the one of all others where a hard riding well mounted lover of foxhunting may best enjoy himself. It is here that foxhunting is to be seen in its wildest truest form; but to see it a man *must* ride hard, and to ride hard (and successfully) he must, as we have said, be more than fairly mounted. As regards Stamford, we doubt if any one ever fixes upon it as a hunting quarter, though it is about as near London as either Melton or Oakham, and commands as much of the Fitzwilliam as it does of the Cottesmore. All three places are situate on the line between Leicester and Peterboro', and can thus be reached either by the Midland or Great Northern, in three to three and a half hours. All three, also, are quiet market towns. Apart from hunting, they were evidently of more importance in coaching days than now; and all are replete with accommodation for man, and for beasts to any number.

The western half of the Cottesmore territory (including what we shall term the Melton, and most of the Oakham country) is not only the better moiety, but in our opinion reaches a higher standard than any tract of ground we know. There are woods of manageable size providing the stoutest of foxes in fullest abundance, while, on every side alike, hill and plain offer the same staunch scenting grass, and a bold fox cannot choose a bad line. Exception is sometimes taken to the severity of the hills in certain parts, such as the neighbourhood of Tilton, Launde, Lodington, and Tugby. They certainly test a horse; but we have never seen hounds run over them so quickly, but that well bred horses could live with them. And, again, foxes seldom cling long to the higher and rougher ground—preferring rather to go for their lives over the smoother country. Then it is that the grand flying runs of the Cottesmore take place. It seldom happens that there is not scent enough to carry hounds along; and so, once in the open, on fair terms with their fox, they are pretty sure to make a run, of merit more or less. 'An old and well established pack, they have had great attention paid to them of late years. Quick, determined, and persevering, they can burst a fox or work him to death, as scent and circumstance allow. And theirs is a country in which they have scope to do it.

It is on Tuesdays and Saturdays that they are in

The Cottesmore.

what we have denominated their Melton country, being the westernmost strip, running down from Melton and Stapleford till it joins Mr. Tailby's at Skeffington and Allexton. (Curiously enough, the river Eye marks for a short distance this northern boundary, while the Eye Brook marks the southern, from Allexton to the Welland.)

On Thursdays, too, they are often attainable from Melton in their middle country, from Market Overton southwards.

In treating of the geography of the country, we will take the meets and coverts in order, more in regard to their distance from Melton and Oakham, than in connection with the day of the week to which they belong. For Tuesdays and Saturdays often point to a similar district, while the Saturdays alternate between the extreme south and north of this Melton country—the Cottesmore and the Belvoir taking it in turn to hold their Saturday close to the metropolis.

It has to be noted, too, that Mr. Stanford's topographer painted his boundaries previous to the reclaiming by the Cottesmore of their loan to Mr. Tailby, whose country may now be described as coming no further north than Skeffington, Allexton and Stockerston.

The nearest meets, and almost always chosen for this last-named day, are Wyld's Lodge, Stapleford Bedehouses, and Leesthorpe. Wyld's Lodge has the little covert of Berry Gorse close at hand, with Mr. Hartopp's plantations to follow, and Stapleford Park as the *pièce de resistance*; and Stapleford Bedehouses may be said to offer the same *menu* in inverted order. The former meet is between two and three miles from Melton; while Stapleford Bedehouses and Park is about four. In the Park is the Pond Plantation, fertile of good runs, but requiring every sense on the watch for a start. A minute's delay in hitting off the nearest gateway in the ring fence; and you may not see hounds again till you learn that they have had "a screaming forty minutes and a kill." Just outside the Park is Laxton's covert, with a famous stream flowing just below—jumpable in most places, but varying deceptively. By the way, there are two brooks running parallel to each other hereabouts. They cannot both be *the* Whissendine, though they have been made one by confusion, and termed the Whissendine indiscriminately. Belonging to adjacent valleys, they have generally been taken for a single twisting watercourse; and the Whissendine accordingly jumped twice as often. In truth, the stream below Laxton's Covert is *not* the veritable brook of history and song; which, on the contrary, runs through the village of Whissendine, before it, also, joins the Eye. In the splendid line from Laxton's Covert to Ranksboro'—which, in part or whole, forms a frequent happy feature in a season in the Melton country—you will cross both streams, if you are lucky enough, and good enough, to achieve the feat. The Whissendine, indeed, is in few places half as terrible as it is painted. Yet have we often seen its turgid waters dammed (Printer, play us not false with the spelling) by struggling men and horses; and its very reputation makes the ordinary

The Cottesmore.

rider look round for a lead as he approaches its banks.

Leesthorpe (five miles on the Oakham road) for the meet, leaves it open to proceed to Stapleford Park, or to turn towards Little Dalby and the Punchbowl. If the plantations (Wheathills, &c.) round Dalby Hall do not hold, the Punchbowl's snug nest is sure to be full of foxes. Then away over Burrough Hill to Twyford, Somerby, Owston, or where you will—sharp descents and steep ascents at first, then all smooth sailing and a perfect country. If your morning fox does not carry you to the woods of Owston, you will probably seek one for the afternoon at Ranksboro' Gorse—of which you have heard if ever you have heard of hunting. Below the sloping hill the level plain stretches across to the woods of Burley. To the left equally fine grass leads to Whissendine or Ashwell. To the right are Orton Park and Owston Woods, with their surroundings of turf unlimited; while behind are Somerby, Pickwell and the Punchbowl, with all that is inviting on the way. To make Ranksboro' a morning draw, Langham is the usual fixture. And now we move on to more extensive coverts—the chain of medium-sized woods, which, if in themselves not altogether without their drawbacks, yet in our humble opinion are the making of the Cottesmore country. You may not be fond of slushing through rides that occasionally take you in to the girths, and now and again cost you even an extra horse; and you may have a still greater objection to discovering that for the last half hour you have been straining every nerve to keep at least in hearing of what turn out to be but two odd couple, while the body of the pack is miles away. But you forget all this when at last your turn comes to be with hounds as they issue forth for one of the long straight runs that belong only to a wild country and woodland bred foxes. Orton Park Wood (some fifty acres at the most) is one of the fairest samples of the Hunt. It is generally called upon in immediate sequence to an appeal to the hospitable precincts of Knossington Hall. There are always foxes at Orton Park Wood, and nearly always a run from it— whether over the half drained pastures towards Braunston or Barleythorpe, or on to Prior's Coppice or its neighbours, or by Ranksboro' to any other good point. Lady Wood forms a link with the larger woods of Owston, distant a smart five minutes' gallop. Owston Great Wood and Little Wood together are a couple of miles in length; but nowhere much more than a quarter of a mile in breadth. There is little undergrowth, but a hearty welcome has ever made the fastness sweet in vulpine eyes; and foxes are more often found by the half dozen. Hounds rattle through it like wildfire, slip away from it at the most unexpected point, and to make *sure* of a start with them is looked upon in the Hunt as a problem little short of squaring the circle. Owston Wood is often advertised as a meet; but from one point or another it is seldom left undrawn for a week. With a fox breaking back to Launde Wood there need not necessarily be a run, though there often will be. But let him go for the Quorn covert of John o' Gaunt, for the Twyford or Burrough lordships, and there *must* be a gallop, passing fair and fast. Some two miles east of Owston Wood is another hundred-acre brake known as Prior's Coppice, for which Brook Hall or Leigh Lodge may be the meet, and round which a grand country circles to Oakham, Manton, and Belton. From here too the smaller copse of Oakham Pasture, and Manton Gorse, form either a second draw, or tempting points to fix a fox's course.

At the back of Owston Wood, and running parallel with it a couple of miles away, are Launde Wood and Launde Park Wood—each being deep rided, extensive, and well stored with foxes. Rough hills contain, and surround, these great coverts; and to post yourself at one spot with a view to getting away with hounds is merely accepting a hundred to one chance. You must wade the rides, or scramble through the thin undergrowth with hounds and huntsman. Then will you break into the open with them; and follow a fox that will hang nowhere till he is lost, or his mask is at the saddle. For the foxes of these *grass woodlands* (as we may term them, in contradistinction to the still bigger coverts of their eastern ploughs) love the open hills; and it is seldom their fault if they do not give a gallop. Round the parishes of Tugby, Belton, and Allexton there is a great grass country; or your line may be struck in the Melton direction. In the latter case you either run on towards the Quorn country (perhaps John O'Gaunt), or find yourself cutting through (seldom dwelling in) another cluster of woods—to wit Skeffington and Tilton Woods, Tugby Bushes, Loddington Redditch, and several of minor growth. Deep dells, and lofty hills, hard climbing, continual energy and increasing movement, are the characteristics of this rough region and the cue for your conduct. A pony might show you all that takes place till the woods are suddenly quitted. *Then* you need the best horse your banker will find you, the best years of your youth, and a belief that most fences are to be jumped when the pace is good. For the Skeffington neighbourhood requires a dash and determination, a fling and a devilment, that are not called for in a more sober sphere—though that sphere be grass as quick scenting and one whereon hounds can fly as quick as here, For the fences of this district are *just* to be done—if the horse has all the best and boldest qualities of a true Leicestershire hunter, and the man is the pick of Melton or Market Harborough. Even then, he will have to turn aside now and again; for the bottoms which thread the valleys are not to be taken as they offer themselves; and the wide-built oxers are not to be trifled with, when twenty minutes up-and-down these green hills has taken the steel out of even a thoroughbred. Launde Abbey will be the meet for the good Launde Woods, and Loddington Hall and Tilton Wood will generally be named for the woods adjacent. Still further south we have Beaumont Chase as a fixture for Wardley Wood and Stoke End. A sixteen or seventeen miles' ride to covert recommends itself but indifferently to Meltonian taste; and, were Wardley Wood anything but what it is, the journey would seldom be made. But such a covert, whose wide turf rides are almost as carefully preserved as its breed of strong wild foxes,

The Cottesmore.

may well draw men from a distance—when a reward may await them like the run of last season, to Leesthorpe and halfway back (a three hours' gallop, and of course a change of foxes). All round Wardley is a strong country; and the best line, perhaps, is one that will land you at Prior's Coppice.

Turning now to their Oakham, or middle country, by which term we have denominated the centre strip, running north and south past Oakham, we find that hounds are usually in it on Thursdays; and that it embraces such a variety of feature, as to include light easy grass, small gorse coverts, big woodlands and a wide extent of plough. The Bull at Witham Common and Crown Point are the northernmost meets; and may probably mean Gunby Gorse, whence a fox may come westwards for the grass, but is more likely to travel the light plough into the big woods of Witham or Morkery, and land you therein for the afternoon. If, however, a fair wind blows him to Woodwell Head, you may forthwith be embarked on quite a different campaign. Some of the prettiest ground in the Hunt is the timber-fenced vale that stretches below Woodwell Head (which, by the way, is a neat small wood of great attraction to foxes). The land here would seem to be more suited to the placid Leicester ewe, or, at most, the heavy milch cow—rather than to the restless shorthorn bullock—for the rails which go to make up the greater proportion of the fences are thin as hurdles and brittle as touchwood. So the faintest heart may travel in confidence till the Vale of Catmose changes its mood, as it is sure to do in a few miles to south or west. Then let him be sure of himself, and of his mount—or a sudden reaction may take the place of the lately acquired boldness. Stocken Hall is another Thursday meet; and apropos of Morkery Wood it may be instanced that the four litters with which it is this year credited, are no more than its usual complement. Witham Wood is, like Morkery, a splendid covert for teaching young hounds: and it has, moreover, the character of being one of the best scenting coverts in the Cottesmore country—hounds being able to run hard through it in any weather. Market Overton, Teigh and Ashwell are also often named for Woodwell Head and Cottesmore Gorse, and a run over the valley to Ranksboro' is again the thing to wish for. From Market Overton a string of plantations are found under the hill running down to Burley, and likely to carry a fox on to that stronghold. The big wood of Burley is, like Wardley, celebrated for its sound open rides, and its store of foxes. The latter when disturbed are most likely to move forward to Barnsdale Wood, Hambleton Wood, and perhaps on to Normanton Park or to Exton Park. At Exton are the two good coverts of Cottesmore Wood and Tunby Wood. At Normanton the coverts are small, and after Christmas so open that foxes are apt to move elsewhere. At Greetham Inn are drawn other woodland coverts of Mr. Finch's, stretching up to the Pickwell and Holywell Woods, which, again, belong to Mr. Birch Reynardson, another staunch fox preserver. These are especially valuable for cubhunting —as, while holding plenty of cubs, there is always other game afoot, and every opportunity afforded of impressing discrimination on the young entry. At the extreme south of this middle country are the meets of Luffenham and Ketton Hall. Luffenham Heath is another great stronghold for foxes, and right well cared for; but is held to be a curiously bad-scenting covert. Wakerly Woods, which adjoin, are the property of the Marquis of Exeter, and neutral with the Fitzwilliam, and they enjoy the reputation of being usually short of foxes. At Ketton is a range of old workings known as The Pitts, wherein foxes can get to ground at any time. Of the Thursday country (and applying to the Cottesmore territory *in toto*) it may be added that very little grass will be found to the east of Woodwell Head: while east of Luffenham we get on to light stony plough, whereon stone walls in a great measure supplant the blackthorn.

The eastern woodlands of the Cottesmore are very extensive, and occupy almost entirely their Mondays and Wednesdays. On these days they hunt as far eastward as the fens of Lincolnshire will allow, their country in this direction being limited only by the impracticable form (as far as hunting is concerned) into which it here lapses. Thus the great Car Dyke, passing through Bourn, may be said to be the boundary of operations on this side. Without dwelling at great length on the features of their woodlands, we may mention that among the more distant meets is Manthorpe, for Dikey Wood and Thurlby Park Wood—two sure finds. The foxes of this neighbourhood are well taken care of by the sporting farmers of the district. On the other side of the town we have

Bourn Wood, one of the largest coverts in the hunt, and in great favour during cubhunting. Part of this, including Oscar Wood, belongs to Lady Willoughby, and the remainder to Lord Exeter. From here, in fact, runs a great range of woodland to the north, and, passing through Elsthorpe Springs, we get to Dunsby Wood, which is neutral between the Cottesmore and the Belvoir. Grimsthorpe Castle is another Wednesday meet (the extreme east of the country being more often hunted on that day); the coverts in the park are a sure find; the park itself is four miles in length, and hounds often race along it from end to end—delighting in the oasis of grass. For all this portion of the Cottesmore country a stout, short-legged horse is to be recommended; and he must be able to *jump*, or he will certainly fathom some of the wide drains which he will have to encounter. Heavy plough is the prevailing feature of the soil; and in a wet season hounds can carry a good head over it and account for their foxes; but in a dry winter it is difficult ground to work over with success. Corby Bircholm for the Witham Woods and the other big coverts just below (and to most of which we have already alluded) is usually a Monday meet. Castle Bytham and Little Bytham Kennels are for the woods of Morkery and the coverts running south to Clipsham, which place—together with Holywell Hall and Greetham Inn—is for the Holywell Woods, Pickworth Wood, the Twin Woods, and the coverts round Exton Park; while Tickencote Hall is, perhaps, their southernmost Monday fixture. Uffington and Casewick (for Lord Kesteven's and Lord Lindsay's coverts

The Cottesmore.

near Stamford) take them to the most distant of their Wednesday ground.

The following "official" document may be of interest, as setting forth the limits, and something of the history of the Hunt:

Boundaries of the COTTESMORE HUNT, 1842, when the Earl of Lonsdale gave up the country:

To the EAST, as far as practicable.

To the SOUTH, it is bounded by the River Welland as far as Duddington, it then extends to the Wakerley Woods, joining the Welland and Harringworth, which again divides the country as far as Rockingham.

To the WEST, the Brook that runs from Rockingham to Allexton is the division; Allexton Wood is neutral; the remaining part of the West side of the country is marked by the boundaries of the Lordships of East Norton, Tugby, Skeffington, Tilton Newton, Marefield and Quorn (?). These Lordships are all in the Cottesmore country with the exception of the coverts on Newton Hills which are neutral.

The NORTH, the Lordships of Little Dalby, Burton Lazars, Stapleford, Wymondham, Sewstern, Gunby, Stainby, Colsterworth, are in the Cottesmore; the road that runs between Easton and Witham Woods to Irnham village divides the country; the Burton Woods, Easton Wood and Pasture, Bitchfield, Osgaby Coppice, Irnham Old Park Wood, *Stoke Park Wood*, Butley Hall, *Kaisby*, *Kirkby*, *Aslackby*, and Dunsby Wood being neutral.

In 1807, Lord Sherard made a covert in Stainby conditionally, that it should be hunted alternately by the Cottesmore and Belvoir Packs.

On the 11th March, 1822, it was agreed by Lord Forester on he part of the Duke of Rutland and Colonel Lowther on the part of Lord Lonsdale, that Stoke Park Wood, Kirkby and Aslackby Woods, should be given up to the Belvoir Hunt.

Sir William Lowther (afterwards 1st Earl of Lonsdale) lived

at Uffington, when married in 1781, resided there three or four years, and then took Stocken, where the present Lord was born, he remained there till 1796. The late Earl kept harriers when at Uffington, and at the Duke of Ancaster's death converted them into foxhounds; and made rides which still exist in Bourn, Kirkby, Aslackby, Grimsthorpe, Bulby Hall, and Dunsby Wood; when Lord Lonsdale's hounds were sold, the Pedigree of his Pack went back 130 years.

Mr. Smith, of Edmondthorpe, kept a Pack of Foxhounds (no date to this memorandum.)

THE PUCKERIDGE.*

ACCESSIBILITY from London is a point that we have endeavoured to keep in mind in referring to each of the countries hitherto considered. Our sphere has, however, so far, lain beyond the scope of a day's hunting from Town: and accordingly can only have had interest for men desirous of planting themselves where at least a month of hunting may be attained, to the oblivion of all minor, or (may we say it?) more sordid pursuits. But there exists a large body of ardent sportsmen, who can only take their recreation by the day; who can only break in upon their week of labour by extra work on five days, that they may secure the sixth for a holiday; and who have also, by nature or by effort of will, the power to absorb themselves for a few short hours in the thrilling incidents of fox-hunting, and yet afterwards to recover mind and thought from the thraldom, the moment they return to office or re-enter chambers. The faculty is begotten, of course, of necessity: and the credit is due to circumstances, and to the sporting spirit which makes the best of a situation. The man is fond of

---

* *Vide* " Stanford's Railway and Hunting Map," sheet 16.

hunting and he must have it—yet must subordinate his passion to a mainer object. So only a day can be stolen here and there—while stocks and shares, briefs and patients, demand all his existence before the world. To such a man a country recommends itself, that will give him honest sport between breakfast and dinner, and allow him a steam covert hack for his morning and evening ride. He may keep a couple of horses on the spot; but he himself must snatch an early breakfast, finish the bows of his leathers in a hansom, and with a cigarette, the *Times*, and a heart full of hope, work out the next hour not altogether uncomfortably in a soft-cushioned railway carriage.

Within easy morning's rail of London is the Puckeridge Hunt—with an old-established and excellent pack, and a sporting, if not a brilliant country. Here a man may see a great deal of genuine hunting, without any great primary outlay in horseflesh, and without having to encounter greater risk to life and limb than is consistent with steady business habits and an increasing family. The Puckeridge country is, generally speaking, plough. A grass field may be seen here and there, but has a foreign look amid the many miles of tillage. Like most other arable, the soil will carry a scent best when wet; and when wet it is, of course, less pleasant riding. But a fox generally leaves sign enough to ensure himself a hard pressed journey; and the Puckeridge are not behind their neighbours in accounting for their game. A horse that can move steadily on, through dirt and difficulty, is the animal to ride here—one that will trot and canter all day, that will squeeze through a

The Puckeridge.

hole in a thick dark bullfinch without dashing your face into the thorns, that will crawl over a bank and scramble in and out of the wide ditch beyond—and at all times take the office from his master. A rash impetuous horse will quickly break his own back, and possibly his confiding owner's neck—except, it may be, in the eastern strip of the country, or in a foray into the Ruthins of the Essex, where the fences are low and unbanked, and may be taken in a fly by a vigorous jumper.

Bishop's Stortford and Buntingford are the two quarters where horses can best be stationed, to hunt with the Puckeridge. Buntingford is more in the centre of the country; but Bishop's Stortford is easier reached from Town, and is nearer to the present kennels. Furneuse Pelham is the actual centre spot of the Hunt, and nearly a century ago was chosen by Mr. Calvert for his kennels; but it would nowadays scarcely answer the purpose of a base for the hunting-man running down from London. Mr. Parry kept his hounds at Albury; and Mr. Gosling, the present Master, has built kennels at Manewden, between three and four miles from Bishop's Stortford. From Liverpool Street Station it is but an hour's journey by the Great Eastern to Bishop's Stortford; and, according to present arrangements, a train leaving London at 9.10 slips a carriage at the latter place at 10.8—which should allow you time to reach all the nearer meets. For the wider fixtures you will, of course, have to break your fast sooner, and take an earlier train.

The Puckeridge hunt three days a week, Monday,

Wednesday, and Saturday : and Mr. Gosling adds a frequent bye day—indeed, after Christmas, Friday is almost always included in the programme of the week.

Monday is taken up essentially with the home country; and its limits may be said to be marked (though not imperatively)—on the *west* by the road leading from Ware to Barkway, on the *east* by the old London-and-Cambridge turnpike road, which runs almost alongside the railway.

Some of the chief Monday draws (and all very sure finds) are Maddams, Hadham Park coverts, Patmore Hall, Hormead Park, Turks, and The Hammels. Maunden Mill or Thorley Wash will be the meet for Maddams; The Angel Inn, Little Hadham, or Patmore Heath for Hadham Park; Barkway or the Pelhams for Hormead, and often Standon for The Hammels (which coverts, again, consisting of park plantations and copses, are not unfrequently drawn on a Saturday). All this Monday country is of a very cramped character; and to creep your fences slowly must be the order of your going, if you would cross it at all successfully. And the Hadham district especially merits the description.

On Wednesdays they move over to the east of this London-and-Cambridge road for their Widdington country and the neutral Forest; or else work the extreme north of their territory, above a line drawn from, say, Barkway to Saffron Walden. In the former district they meet at Debden Cross, Peverelle and Widdington, for Rowney and Widdington Woods, two fine coverts bordering on the Thaxted country

—which (though within the boundaries of the Essex) presents a tempting arena for Puckeridge foxes, when these woods do themselves justice. Of late years, however, 'tis said, the pheasants have taking to crowing so loud that they have somewhat interfered with bold Reynard's comfort; and he is not so often found at home as is to be wished. For the Thaxted district, though plough, has all the good qualities of "the Ruthins"—to wit, good scenting soil, low thorn fences which may be charged anywhere (the faster the better, if you would clear the wide deep ditches beyond), and which nowhere obstruct the rider's view of hounds as they run over the broad open fields.

Takeley Forest, on the contrary, is a splendid instance of hearty and unselfish fox-preserving. It is neutral between the Puckeridge and the Essex, and yet there is always game enough for both—as may be gathered from the fact that the former pack killed four brace of foxes from it last season. Mr. J. Archer-Houblon no longer hunts himself, though he was formerly co-partner with Messrs. Parry and W. Wigram: for some years they had the pack between them, till Mr. Parry bought the shares of the other two gentlemen. From Takeley you will expect, or rather hope, to run into the Essex Ruthins. Sir Richard Sutton (no mean authority) gave it as his opinion that the Ruthins were "the best plough land in England;" and, in our humble way, we are far from wishing to contradict him. In the Ruthins you can always see hounds at their work, and you may always ride to them, fast and freely and wide of their backs. If you drop into the ditches, you should have a sovereign in your pocket for the assistance of a plough team; but with the pace well on, and the spurs well in to a sticky one, Providence will generally help you over the Ruthins. Elsdenham is another capital meet on a Wednesday; for East End, a fine holding covert of Mr. Gilby's, who, while renting the shooting, does ample duty by foxhunting. "Birchanger" gives Birchanger Wood: and other coverts yet to be named are Quendon, Broom Wood, Ugley (or Oakley) Park, and Alsa Wood. To the north are various woodlands—among them Langley High Wood, Roughway, Clavering Park, Scales Park, Cheshall Wood, and Earl's Wood. In the extreme south Stanstead is more often chosen for a Wednesday, though often included also in a Saturday's bill of fare.

The Saturday or western country may be said to extend from Wade's Mill northwards to Royston, going westward (as will be seen from the map) as far as Watton, and, higher up, a little beyond Walkern and Wallington. Its leading coverts are Sacombe, Coombe Wood, Bennington High Wood, St. John's Wood (an excellent stand-by), Broadfield and Friars Woods, and the small coverts at Clothall — also Sandon Row, Reed Wood, and Capons Wood (this last seldom without a fox). From Friar's Wood, some thirty years ago, Mr. Parry (to whom, by the way, the high standard of the Puckeridge pack is entirely owing) had his most celebrated hunt. To this day he calls it "my run." It ended in his fox getting to ground, in view, at Sandy Warren, between Cambridge and Woburn. Some of the Saturday

The Puckeridge.

meets are Nuthampstead, Old Hall Green, Layston Church (a favourite fixture, with the Capons in view), Throcken (for Friar's Broadfield, &c.), Munden, and Bennington, with occasionally Watton for the Ware district. Box Wood and Aston Bury in the extreme west are neutral coverts with the Hertfordshire, for which Walkern is a frequent meet.

For a byeday, Hunsdon, Great Hadham (or Much Hadham, as it is called in the language of the county), and occasionally Standon, are usually chosen—with coverts at Eastwick, Plashes, Blake's Bushes (small but well favoured), Buckney, and Culvers.

To sum up, the best scent for the last three seasons has been found in the Monday country, though in Mr. Parry's time the Saturday ground had the best reputation. The Monday country has, as we have said, the disadvantage of being extremely cramped, while on Saturdays you find yourself with more room to ride. Round Royston, for instance, the country is very open, and the coverts only small plantations. The greater part of the Puckeridge territory is well stored with foxes, though, as we have hinted, there are certain parts (east and south) where foxes might have rather more chance given them, without buying the goodwill of neighbours too dearly.

THE OLD BERKELEY.*

ANOTHER country of old tradition and honoured name, existing close to London, is the Old Berkeley. As its title almost implies, it was at one time part of the original Berkeley country, and to this day its hunt servants wear the Fitzhardinge livery of yellow plush. In the days we allude to the then Lord Berkeley hunted a vast territory stretching from Berkeley Castle to London, bringing his hounds into what is now the Old Berkeley country for the spring and autumn, and remaining at home for the winter months.

The fact that the Old Berkeley no longer advertise their meets would point to a desire on their part to exclude strangers. If such were absolutely the case, it would render our task of facilitating acquaintance with their hounds and country a somewhat delicate—or even ungracious—one. But this apparent objection to intrusion by no means points to the hunting man proper, though he, too, often finds himself

---

* Stanford's map, sheet 16, will illustrate, more or less satisfactorily, the geography of the O. B. H.; though it will be noticed that it fails to colour the neutral territory.

The Old Berkeley. 115

inconvenienced by a reticence which forbids approach. It has been called into existence by the pressure of a swarm of nondescripts, who, starting from every suburb in London, were glad to make a meet of foxhounds their excuse for a holiday on hackney or in waggonette—overwhelming the whole procedure of the chase by their presence, and irritating farmers and landowners to the great injury of the hunt. Thus it was found necessary to make known the places of meeting only to subscribers, and even to take the additional precaution of substituting Tuesday for Saturday in the Watford country—so to escape the " Saturday-outers," as they are termed with the Surrey Union. But a subscription (it need not be a heavy one) will always procure a weekly card of the fixtures; and the man for whom foxhunting is really a pursuit will always find a welcome with the Old Berkeley. It is not a superlatively good country—even its best friends will not assign to it more than comparative merit. But it has its advantages—of being within the easiest possible reach of London, and so immediately available to the man who can only steal away from business for an occasional single day; of being thoroughly hunted, and by no means deficient of sport.

Though its chief features are included in the terms *wood and plough*, there yet remains in the Watford and Harrow district a small stretch of as good grass as is to be ridden over in England. Year by year the advancing wave of brick and mortar is narrowing this chosen area. But, over and above the encroachments of building, there is an inner cause militating against the full vigour of the chase within what might indeed be a charmed circle. As London grows farther westward, the land it nears becomes daily more and more valuable; and more and more do the occupants begrudge any damage that might accrue to the remaining acres of their rich pasturage. The soil being a deep clay, the passage of horses is, when the ground is wet, not only an eyesore, but an almost ineradicable source of mortification to those who hold the land. It is difficult to see how tangible harm can be done by galloping over grass, however wet; for what nature will not do in the way of "welling up" the footprints, a roller should easily put to rights in good time for the scythe—while as for the passage of a field of horses availing to *destroy* grass, the "poaching" of four times the number of hoofs likely to accompany the Old Berkeley could not do it, except by trampling ever on the same spot. However, the fact remains that, as soon as the Harrow Vale becomes deep, it is forthwith almost forbidden ground.

No less than three lines of railway will land you in the Old Berkeley country, viz., the Midland, the London-and-North-Western, and the Great Western; and your journey by either will not amount to an hour. The Midland is nowadays of use for but few meets—Newberries being one of them, and close to Radlett Station. In former days this was a rendezvous very highly thought of; and many and oft were the good gallops from Newberries Gorse over the grass to Mimms Wood and Scratch Wood (near Elstree). The latter covert is within eight miles, as the crow flies, from Hyde Park Corner. But of late years foxes from Newberries have declined this line. Efforts, however, are being made to re-establish the reputation of the other two coverts; and so to bring this, the best piece of the country, again into favour.

The London and North-Western commands nearly the whole of the country, and a man wishing to join the O.B.H. cannot do better than keep his horses at Watford or Tring, at both of which places he will find the best of loose boxes at his call. At Watford he will get both the O.B.H. and the Hertfordshire; while at Tring he will have these two packs, with Mr. Selby Lowndes' pack and the Baron's Staghounds besides. Near Watford are the neutral coverts of Newberries and Bricket; and the Hertfordshire also claim the right of drawing Scratch Wood. Newberries is still counted as offering as good a chance of a run as anything in the hunt; for, if a fox from it will only choose his direction aright, he must give a pretty gallop. (They have been known to kill a fox from here in the middle of Watford.) Bricket Wood is an immense place, pretty sure find, but difficult to get away from, and the rides are of deep clay. But for all this it is a covert of a great value to the hunt. Other meets near Watford (which we may consider as on the whole the most convenient base for the O.B.H., and which is only half an hour from Euston-square Station) are Hamper Mill, Hunton Bridge (for Mr. Jones Lloyd's coverts at Langley Bury), Croxley Green, Chenies (for Lord Chesham's good coverts), Cassiobury (for Lord Essex's), Grove Park (a pretty meet for Lord Clarendon's), Moor Park (for

Lord Ebury's), Chandler's, and Chorley Wood Common. The Duke of Bedford owns a good deal of property near the last-named place and Chenies; and one of his tenants generally has a fox in Weedon's Gorse and Fox Wood. Mr. Gilliatt's Gorse is also a valuable covert, and so is Bottom Wood.

The stations of King's Langley, Boxmoor, Berkhampstead, and Tring (L. & N. W. R.) all command meets of the O.B.H. Mr. Longman has built new kennels at his place at Shendish (midway between the two first-named stations); and within a small radius from the kennels are the meets of Chipperfield Common, Bovingdon Green, Layhill Common, Whelpley Hill, Ashley Green, Haresfoot and Wiggington Common. The master has good coverts of his own; and Scatterell's and Woodman's Wood do credit to the same neighbourhood, with good foxes. Near Layhill Common, Lord Chesham provides the very useful covert of Cowcroft; and Haresfoot, though not quite so productive of late, has generally furnished the needful animal. And this part of their country is rather more open than most of the O.B.H.

A little more apart from the lines of railway, but within easy riding reach of Watford, is the Amersham district—in which Mr. T. Drake, of Shardeloes, and Lord Chelsham are the principal covert owners. About Missenden and Wendover the country is hilly, flinty, and wild, but generally affords sport. Among the meets hereabouts are the Black Horse Amersham, Penn Street Church, Tyler's Green Penn, Peterley Manor, Chesham Poor's-Common, Charteridge, Little Missenden, Missenden Abbey, and Nag's Head Great

Missenden, Hyde Heath, Hampden Church, Wendover Hall, Chequers Court and Saunderton.

In the extreme north of their country is included a small corner of the Vale of Aylesbury; and hounds are taken there a few times during the season. But in the days when the Earl of Lonsdale hunted the country, it was the regular custom of the " Old Lord " to meet in the Vale once a week with his "harriers" as he called them. These were nothing more or less than a pack of dwarf foxhounds; and in front of them he was wont to turn down a bag fox that had been regularly *conditioned and trained in a yard at home*. In this way, with both Jim and Goddard Morgan successively as huntsmen, there was many a merry gallop over the Vale: and familiar to every Hertfordshire man are the lines of the late Mr. Wm. Reid (so well known at that time with Lord Dacre's hounds), beginning

> There's a noble Earl of antient name;
> He hunts the fox, but he likes it tame.

And that there was no deception about the proceeding, but that it was carried on in the frankest fashion, may be gathered from the dialogue described as taking place before the assembled field—culminating in

> Says the noble earl to the elder Brown—
> "Open the box and turn him down!"

The Uxbridge neighbourhood is attainable by the Great Western Railway; and is nearest of all to the actual Harrow Vale. In fact, from Ruislip Wood or Oxley Wood is nowadays the only chance of a spurt over the Vale proper; and is looked for as eagerly as a scurry over the Bushey and Elstree country is waited for from Newberries. Ruislip and Oxley are both big deep woods: generally holding foxes. Indeed, this part of the O.B.H. country, though thickly wooded, and not altogether good riding ground (being often deep and boggy), is better stocked with foxes than any in the hunt—and especially round Hedgerley and Fulmer. The following is a list of meets that will probably anticipate anything on the fixture-card. We have given them thus fully throughout this article that the names may be found connected with one or other of the points mentioned as accessible, by train or otherwise—Denham Place, Denham Court, Harefield, West Hyde, Maple Cross, Newlands, Gott's Monument, The Pheasant at Chalfont, Chalfont Potteries, Gerrard's Cross Common, Longbottom Walton Park, Fulmer Hall, Hedgerley, Hall Barn, and The Feathers Taplow. The leading covert owners of the district are the Duke of Somerset, Sir Robert Harvey, Messrs. Hibbert, W. Thompson, Du Pré, and Allen. Hodgemoor (a first-rate covert for foxes, though not altogether easy to ride through) is, we believe, the property of Lord Denbigh.

In conclusion, it may be said that the O.B.H. is a country where, as long as anywhere, foxhunting has been made the most of. There are, it is true, here and there resident landowners who try and excuse themselves for their lukewarmedness in the cause by the plea that the country is not naturally well suited for the sport. But in spite of cold scenting ground and other difficulties many foxes are killed; and the

The Old Berkeley.

hounds are right well-cared for in their present hands.

With the O.B.H. you will find the fences that most often tempt you to jump are light stake-and-bounds, with small ditches—though in the Elstree neighbourhood more leaping power will be wanted, and a timber jumper is everywhere useful. But only the angels' visits to the vales of Harrow and Aylesbury demand a flying horse.

Yet the visitor will often, if he be fond of hounds and hunting for their own sake, be well rewarded in a trip to the O.B.H. He may hunt with them with less labour, and as little expense, as he will anywhere. Lastly, as to the class of horse he should take with him, we should advise him to buy as good a one as he can get—for a little money.

PART II.

THE NORTH WARWICKSHIRE.*

A COUNTRY of which much less is heard than it deserves is the North Warwickshire. Parts of it are superlatively good; and all of it is worth hunting in. Two hours of railway will bring you to it from London; and set you down either at Leamington or Rugby—its two most fashionable commanding points. Leamington has many attractions, varied by hunting. Rugby offers hunting, undiluted. At Leamington you may wear out as many pumps as tops; you must be as carefully got up as at Melton—but it is not by any means incumbent on you to ride as hard, that you may be a worthy citizen. At Rugby you may get up a quiet rubber after hunting; but to arrange your route, by road or rail, for next day's hunting will be your usual after-dinner occupation—for hunt you must, though often at a distance. At Leamington you have the choice of two packs, the one under discussion, and the Warwickshire. Rugby stands in a nook whereat the North Warwickshire, Atherstone, and Pitchley

* *Vide* "Stanford's Large Scale Map," Sheet 15; also "Hobson's Foxhunting Atlas."

touch each other—with the Warwickshire close at hand, Mr. Tailby's within riding distance, and the Quorn and Duke of Grafton's easily available by train.

Coventry, too, commands the North Warwickshire, and also the Atherstone. But it is scarcely a popular hunting quarter—except with soldiers, who are not consulted in the matter, but glad enough that Her Majesty should require their services not altogether away from good fox-hunting.

Birmingham, again, forms a fourth point marking the boundary line of the North Warwickshire Hunt. But, though there are many sporting men in Birmingham, your primary object in acquiring a residence in Birmingham would scarcely be participation in the sport of kings.

In a word, then, Leamington is the place whence to ally yourself altogether with the North Warwickshire; for, while Rugby has one day a fortnight in its creamy corner, and Birmingham has (after Christmas) a weekly hunt over some desirable ground, Leamington overlooks the whole country, and has other advantages to which Coventry can lay no claim.

Looking at it as a whole, it may be stated roughly, and not unfairly, that the bulk of the North Warwickshire country is taken up to grow either wood or wheat—the latter preponderating. Near Birmingham is a fair sprinkling of grass, and often you are there given a run, through which you may skim, quick and sharp, from one green field into another. But the chief exception lies in the Rugby neighbourhood, where a corner of their domain can throw down the glove to any half dozen parishes in England. In my humble opinion there is no covert in the Shires to compare with Hillmorton Gorse—when (as it always has of late) it holds a fox that will go, no matter where. Let him choose what direction he please, he *must* give a run over a smooth grass country, such as they would be glad of even in Meath. Bunker's Hill is another splendid starting point, when (as has *not* happened of late) there is a fox to face the vale below, and to fill the Leame, as it and the Hillmorton Brook ever consider their due. [Mr. Stanford's colouring brush, by the way, has carried the North Warwickshire no farther than Hillmorton Village, instead of to the Old Watling-street-road, near which the covert lies, and near which the men of the Hunt are so prone to bathe in their own waters.]

Rough, but very sporting, is the character of all the interior of the North-W. country — carrying an excellent scent, not overburdened with foxes, yet blessed with fair and consistent sport.

The North Warwickshire first took the position of a separate hunt about the beginning of the century, under Lord Anson. After again reverting to the parent establishment (the Warwickshire), it once more became a distinct country, till, having passed through various hands, it at length came under the mastership of Mr. Lant—who still holds the reins. The present Kennels are at Milverton, a mile or two out of Leamington; but the lease having expired, it is in contemplation to erect new ones near Kenilworth; and it is said that the requisite land has already been purchased from Lord Clarendon.

Their days of meeting are arranged thus. The

Master undertakes to hunt the country three days a week; but after Christmas it has for some time been the custom to give an extra day in the vicinity of Birmingham—the sportsmen of that town on their part providing horses for the hunt servants, and sending them to meet the hounds at whatever railway station may be fixed upon by the huntsman. This day is Monday; and their regular hunting days are Tuesday, Wednesday *or* Thursday (in alternate weeks), and Friday. Few rigid rules being observed as to the area told off for each especial day, it is difficult to write specifically beyond that Tuesday is generally passed in the country immediately round home, *i.e.*, between Coventry on the north and Leamington on the south—that Thursday is for the Rugby district (usually by train to Rugby Station)—and that Wednesday and Friday are more often passed in the west-centre of their territory.

The after-Christmas Mondays near Birmingham are, as we have said before, by no means on their worst ground. There is a good deal of grass, and the foxes (what there are) are stout and straight. That they exist in even their present numbers is mainly due to the exertions of a very well-known character, Mr. W. Williams (who wrote and composed the most popular of the hunting songs of to-day—The Hunting Day). But, besides bringing his talents to the shrine of Diana in votive offering of poesy and music, he labours in her cause in a more practical and no less earnest form. As Hon. Secretary for the Birmingham district, he works day, *and night,* to induce the preservation of foxes; and on many a moonlight night he will order his dog-

The North Warwickshire. 127

cart round, and drive off to where a litter of cubs is laid up—that he may spend an hour or two in watching their gambols. Mr. Joseph Page (father of John Page, the steeplechase jockey) used to find the servant's horses for these Mondays. Now, we believe, it is entrusted to Mr. Robert Hunt, of Edgbaston. A very fair horse is required—and, it should be added, has generally been forthcoming. For, though most of this part of the country is plain sailing, it often happens that you have to jump on and off a high bank. The inclosures are small, and the fences accordingly come quick and frequent. The hounds are brought, as a rule, to Solihull or Knowle stations, and some of the more frequent meets are there, or at the Clock at Bickenhill, Elmdon, Castle Bromwich, Hall Green, the Lion Portway, Hockley House, Inkford, Brook, and Umberslade. Tanworth, too, may almost be included in the Birmingham country. The coverts are not large but numerous. Earl's Wood, Forshaw Park, and Hampton Coppice are among the most important. At the last-named place many a good fox has been found; and the same may be said of Coleshill Pool. The smaller coverts round Knowle and Solihull also show quite their share of sport.

The Tuesday country embraces a great deal of wood, but there are some nice little strips of land between Coventry and Kenilworth. To the eastward we get into the forest of Arden, and the landscape is rather picturesque than sporting.

Tile Hill is one of the meets nearest to Coventry—for Tile Hill Wood and coverts, and sometimes on to the Master's covert at Frogmore. Stoneleigh is, of course, for Lord Leigh's coverts (Bericote Wood, the Grove, and Thickthorn being great strongholds), with Chase Wood and Long Meadow Wood in close proximity. Woodcote leads to the Woodcote coverts and Warwick Old Park. Cubbington Gate will take you into Waverley Wood, and on into the great chain of woods reaching as far east as Stretton upon Duusmore—for which the latter place, Princethorpe and Bubbenhall are all constantly named as rendezvous. To the north of these, again, we have the fixture of the Bull and Butcher, Ryton, for Ryton and the big woods below. All these woodlands form, of course, capital ground for cub-hunting; and hounds are there made very handy.

Turning to the west centre of their country (Wednesday's, or it may be Friday's) we have Berkswell, whence after trying its small spinnies you may get to the Tile Hill woods, or perhaps to Frogmore. Wroxall has near it Hay Wood, often chosen by a good fox. The Boot, Honily, has a great number of small woods within reach. Indeed, such like coverts are scattered freely over all this portion of the North Warwickshire kingdom; and foxes naturally run a great deal from one to another. Hatton has the very improving covert of Newlands not far from it. Claverdon is for Ansty Wood and Claverdon Woods—the former neutral with the Warwickshire. And that the two packs may not clash, an excellent arrangement has been made, whereby it is hunted by the one or the other for alternate months. Wootton Wawen, Henley-in-Arden are for the neighbouring small woods. Tanworth and Beoley are in the farther west; and a good covert is found at Packwood. A rough country for riding; but not altogether difficult to cross, is this: and hounds do well in it.

The Thursday meets are not numerous; but point to an area that we have already designated as well-nigh perfect. Rugby Station or Hillmorton generally mean the famous Hillmorton Gorse. But to get to fresh ground in the afternoon calls for a long jog—for Mr. Chirnside's little gorse near Clifton is altogether too small, and the new covert to break the journey to Bilton Grange is not yet completed. Bilton Grange is also a meet, and often has foxes. Leicester's Piece is the next covert (of inconsiderable size). Dunchurch is generally named for Bunker's Hill—a beautifully situated covert, looking over the lovely green vale to Shuckburgh, but which has not done its duty of late years. Cawston takes us on into a different country, where the land is plough, the hedges straggling, and the ditches wide—and so we merge again into the big woodlands beyond Stretton.

THE PYTCHLEY.*

No pack in England, certainly no Subscription Pack, has had older associations or more honoured names than the Pytchley. And their fame never stood higher than now.

Their country embraces some of the fairest of the Midlands, covering, as it does, the best part of Northamptonshire, and dove-tailed into Leicestershire between the Atherstone and Mr. Tailby's. Its easy accessibility from London is not the smallest of its attractions (at least in the eyes of readers for whom these sketches are chiefly intended); and cannot but commend it to them as the most desirable of all hunting grounds.

At the same time it necessarily follows that he who would hunt with the Pytchley must not be shy of a crowd. In that crowd he will be free to move as he thinks fit, without cavil and without criticism—to throw in his luck with the hard riders, to follow steadily with the main body, or to trot the roads and gates that by their felicitous help render such a country as delectable for sober old age as for hot-blooded youth.

---

* *Vide* "Stanford's Large Scale Map," Sheets 15 and 16; also "Hobson's Foxhunting Atlas."

The Pytchley. 131

The Pytchley country, without having any absolute centre, is commanded by four or five points in its circumference—all easily attainable from London, and all offering variety for intermediate days, when the pack under notice happens to be in kennel or out of distance. Rugby, Weedon, Northampton, and Market Harboro' are the chief of these. Daventry and Lutterworth may be pointed out as easy excellent quarters, less familiar by name and less within the scope of the flying visitor. Rugby and Harboro' are best known; and Rugby is the most fully patronised. All the four former are within two hours' distance of Euston or St. Pancras; and (what is not given to the more remote grandeur of Melton, Oakham, and Upper Leicestershire) it is feasible to reach them by a 7.30 train, in time for an eleven o'clock meet.

Rugby is most in favour with those who would run and hunt. For not only does it link itself with the Pytchley, and give a choice of packs besides; but it has a wide society of its own, and has express trains to Town almost every hour. Thus, to keep two or three horses at Rugby, and run down from London for such days as one feels oneself at liberty, is a common and easy plan on the part of men who, while unable to separate themselves for any length of time from more serious occupation, are yet anxious to obtain hunting of the highest class. With the further advantage of a club, with good and almost unlimited accommodation to be had for horses, with a good hotel, and hunting residences galore, no wonder that Rugby also attracts many to take up permanent quarters for the winter. For these—if they would make the most of their week—the many lines of railway radiating from Rugby Junction are of no little use. At least once a week, often more, the horsebox must be resorted to, if the sportsman is unwilling to stay at home. For, with all its choice of packs (and it forms a point of junction for almost as many countries as railroads), Rugby is distant from every kennel. Consequently, not only do hounds draw away from it every afternoon, but on certain days it happens that there is no meet within riding distance. On Mondays Rugby is within reach of Mr. Tailby. On Tuesdays, the Quorn are to be attained by rail to Leicester, or the Oakley may be reached by train. On Wednesdays the Pytchley are always tolerably near; and on Thursdays either the Warwickshire or North Warwickshire. On Fridays the Atherstone are never far away; and on Saturdays the Pytchley are to be got at by road or rail. Mr. Selby Lowndes sometimes tempts a travel, and the Baron often draws a party to the Vale. So it will be seen that no day need be spent idly at Rugby, for want of hounds.

Market Harboro' is in one way even more easy of access than Rugby; for an eight o'clock train from St. Pancras will convey the London sportsman down to many meets. And yet Harboro' has not half such a run upon it as it deserves; and especially is it little favoured by men who cannot neglect their toil or ties in town for a prolonged course of six days a week with foxhounds. With every possible advantage of situation, with a plethora of proffered accommodation, with a good name well earned—even with the halo thrown round it by Whyte Melville's best sporting novel—Market Harboro' is scantily peopled during the season by hunting-men. They who come are by no means of a nomadic class. They settle down for the winter, in solid earnestness; abjure all outer frivolities, whether of town or country; but lay themselves out for early hours, many long journeys by road, as few as possible by rail, and for a hunting life in its most ascetic form. Market Harboro', indeed, has for many years been more essentially Tailbyite than Pytchley; and has thrown its sympathy and interests especially into the well being of the former denomination. Thus, though it joins in with the Pytchley on a Wednesday and on Friday or Saturday, it is apt to consider itself "over the border," and to adopt the other pack more particularly as its own. On Monday it is Tailbyite to a man. So it is on Thursday; and so it is on any other day the pack may be ordered to leave kennel. On a Tuesday the Cottesmore offer themselves; and if Friday or Saturday are left vacant near home, the Quorn or the Cottesmore fill up the deficiency—a good hack home being no less a necessity than a desideratum. Harboro', in a less degree, suffers from the same complaint as Rugby. Hounds are kennelled far away; and a man hunting from Market Harboro' rides many more miles with his head towards home than to covert.

Northampton holds all the Pytchley country within reach; and, when the new line is completed, will be a more eligible resort than now—Blisworth Junction at present rather stopping the way. Hitherto it has not been much frequented; though, like Weedon, it stands on a high pinnacle as a soldier's quarter.

Weedon is on the present main line of the L. & N. W. Railway, and at various times has been in high repute and fashion. It has, like Northampton, the very sporting country of the Duke of Grafton at hand; and has, besides, the Bicester and the Warwickshire for variety. From Northampton most of the best meets of the Oakley are easily available. Lutterworth and Daventry are other little spots in the Pytchley. Both remain much what they were in the coaching days,— with plentiful welcome for man and horse; both lie well for hunting; but both are rather off the main line of railway.

The Pytchley advertise for four days in the week, under the mastership of Mr. H. Langham. Previous to the maintenance of a separate pack for the Woodlands, it used to be five. Four is as many as any one huntsman can work effectively; and the change is for the better. For five days a week is really the maximum allowance, permitting any of us to maintain full freshness and elasticity—even for our part as lookers-on. We often make six days—because we don't know which day to miss; and as sure as we miss one, that is told of as the best of the week. And *we* can sit in our saddles, rest and gossip, while a huntsman is hard at work. *We* can gallop to covert, and go home quick at night. The huntsman has "hounds' pace" to the meet, unceasing exertion all day (the check being his busiest time), "hounds' pace" again homeward, and on arrival the pack to be fed, perhaps sick puppies to tend, and certainly kennel correspondence to be carried on.

The order of days with the Pytchley proper is some-

The Pytchley.

thing as follows: The Kennels at Brixworth (some seven miles from Northampton) being taken as a central point. Monday is mapped out for the east, Wednesday for the west, and Friday and Saturday alternately for the north and south. And these four divisions, again, may be classed respectively as the Northampton, the Rugby, the Harboro' (north) and Weedon (south) districts.

The area of the Monday, or Northampton, district is, roughly speaking, outlined by the points of Kettering, Wellingboro', and Northampton. Though not so popular with the general public as the country belonging to the other three days of the Pytchley, it not only has its share of sport, but, taking an average of several seasons through, has probably been richer than the others. The Pytchley field generally (and who shall blame them? Certainly not those who know them) prefer the small gorse coverts and the grass, to the deep woods and the plough of the Northampton country. Not that *all* of the latter is plough, by any means. It contains one or two very fine tracts of grass. Round Harrowden, for example, there is excellent going, fences fully worthy of the grass, and generally a good scent. Another circle of nice country has for its centre Faxton—a village to which there is no better driving road than a grass track across the fields. Foxes from Old Poor's Gorse and Mawsley Wood constantly cross this, and seldom without leaving a scent.

On the other hand, much of this part of Northamptonshire is plough deep and heavy—such as would kill the rush of a true Pytchley field as thoroughly as, in another part of the county, the deep clay of Naseby crushed the charge of Prince Rupert's squadrons. Ah, it was bad generalship that accepted that as battle ground for cavalry, with so much rich riding land all round. It may be that, even then, there were oxers round every pasture between Naseby and Market Harboro'. A mailclad trooper, let his heart have been ever so loyal or his cavalier blood ever so hot, would have but little chance with *them* in his path. They frighten us now, when burdened with no heavier weapon than whip and spur, and wearing no weightier armour than Mr. White's stout headpiece. And 'tis my belief that these ox fences, more than all else, bar the way to Market Harboro's prosperity as a hunting-centre. Bold men, perhaps, battle with them for a year or two: fathers of families shudder as they look at them and decline further acquaintance at once. Discretion is the truest valour at Harboro'. You can't ride the country in its immediate neighbourhood *straight;* and the sooner you accept the obvious truth, the better for your bones and for your enjoyment of sport. A fair oxer is a very charming thing on an exceptionally good horse. On an indifferent one don't be induced to look at it. Moral courage is the card to play then. Such play soon comes easy. You may hunt for years from Harboro' without jumping a single oxer; and yet escape being called a coward.

To return to the Northampton district. In its midst is a chain of strong woods, wherein foxes are heartily and plentifully preserved. Sywell Wood, Hardwick Wood, Wilmore Park, and Gib Wood are almost continuous covert. Good foxes are always there, but not always to be induced to take a right direction, and you may often have to make up your mind to some hours in deep rides. This not being in accordance with the universal taste, the fields on Monday are often small and local, yet of a sport-loving class. Hounds, too, are to be seen at their best; as they can work at liberty and without pressure. Monday is also the day on which neighbours of the Oakley join in, often headed by their Master.

Near Northampton itself a light and sandy soil is the chief characteristic ; and scent is often weaker than on the strong land.

Some of the best Monday meets are Sywell Wood, Hannington, Great Harrowden, Hardwick, Pytchley (where once stood the Club House of the Hunt), Cransley, and Orlingbury. And, besides those already alluded to, the principal coverts are Biling Harbour, Overstone Park, Vivian's Covert, Blow Hill (at Great Harrowden), Cockaroost, Cransley Wood, and Holcot Covert.

"A Pytchley Wednesday" is a term that has long ago passed into a proverb, and been accepted as a type of a condition of things not to be seen elsewhere in full perfection. If you would learn to what colossal magnitude and manifold variety a hunting-field can attain, go out on a Pytchley Wednesday to a favourite fixture ! If you would observe how such a field can cordially subject itself to proper discipline, stand at the covert side as one of them ! If, again, you would put your nerve and self confidence to a thorough test, make yourself an atom in the Niagara-like rush to which the "Gone away" is a signal ! If you would mark in its most perfect form the first essential for a fox-hound in the Shires, watch the Pytchley bitches slipping to the front through the mad torrent! You may learn a good deal else—not the least valuable lesson being *to take care of yourself*. It is a trying, but not really a rough school. And, in truth, 'tis a very jolly one. Boy or man need ask for no happier schooldays than this can offer. But the earlier lessons should, I think, be taken young. Like tumbling or tight-rope dancing, the art of riding over a grass country in a crowd is more easily to be acquired while the nerve is fresh and the frame has not lost its first suppleness. You will scarcely hold your own in a twenty minutes' burst from Misterton to Stanford Hall, or in a scurry from Crick to Lilbourne, without some previous practice here or in a similar sphere. And if you come, middleaged and unprepared, the chances are you return disgusted, and decline to tempt the fates in the same direction again.

This Wednesday, Rugby, or Western district (call it which you will) is, if not absolutely the best of the whole Pytchley country, as good as any. Certainly it asserts itself as the most popular—the credit for which may probably be ascribed to the propinquity of Rugby—which town lies just beyond its western borders, and, with Watford, Cold Ashby, Welford, North Kilworth, and Lutterworth, may be taken approximately to mark the outline of Wednesday's arena. Small coverts, chiefly artificial, are entirely the characteristic of this district—unless we can bring in as an exception the Hemplow Hills, whose precipitous sides are covered with continuous plantation

The Pytchley.

and gorse. The soil over which you ride is not *all* under the sod; but as little of it has been given to the plough as is consistent with grazing farms and the necessity for winter forage; and, broadly speaking, it fully deserves the title of a *splendid grass country* —big but fair—competent to carry, and to scatter, the huge fields that embark upon it—seldom entrapping, but affording room for all. If there is a fault to be found with the Pytchley country it lies in the frequency of the villages, which come so near and quickly that it is often difficult for a fox to keep his head straight, still more to escape observation. Again, I am not prepared to say (though I am no more willing absolutely to gainsay) that it is consistently good scenting ground. A sharp scent and a firm one there often is. But apart from the causes, accidental and atmospheric, which may affect scent at the moment, I am inclined to think that huntsmen would scarcely speak of it as "a fine scenting country," and one they would choose as especially favourable for killing foxes.

To turn to particulars. Among the nearest meets to Rugby is Lilbourne Village—the Gorse close at hand, a river and railway hemming it in on one side, the field on another, and every knoll, hillside and road commanding the valley. And yet, by one means or another, by a cunning that does their race credit, foxes contrive to escape and give runs—often over the wide vale eastward to Crick, or northward to Stanford Hall. Swinford is almost equally near Rugby, and has Swinford Old Covert, with Stanford Hall (also a frequent meet) and its park coverts close by.

From Stanford Hall to Misterton, and from Stanford Hall to the Hemplows, or *vice versâ* in either case, will take you over a grass line fit for a king—if that king be but well minded and well mounted.

Crick Village is their most celebrated meet, and has one of their best coverts attached. From it they either run over the cream of the Warwickshire ground (possibly over what was so long the site of the old Grand Military Steeplechases), over the double-ditched fences to Lilbourne, perhaps by Claycoton to Stanford or (it *must* be) a good line *anywhere*. Misterton is their northernmost fixture, with a gorse belonging to the Hunt, an osier bed, many plantations, and Shawell Wood held by the occupier of Misterton Hall—and all held staunchly in the cause of foxhunting. But, indeed, it may be asserted fearlessly that no country is more heartily preserved than the Pytchley—and the Wednesday portion is as good as any. Landowner, tenant, shepherd and labourer, strive with one accord to further sport; and foxes, accordingly, are to be found wherever they are sought.

North Kilworth is another excellent Wednesday meet on the upper margin of the country. Hounds when brought thither (as also to Stanford Hall and Lilbourne) sleep out. Usually they work towards home in the afternoon; but often they have a very long jog back to Kennels on a Wednesday evening. Kilworth Sticks is a famous covert—with a run to be mapped out on every side. Northward it has the prettiest part of Mr. Tailby's country, westward there is a nice line to Misterton; southward there is every chance of a superb twenty minutes to

The Pytchley. 141

the Hemplows (merely to commence with); eastward there is capital ground about Welford and Sulby. There are good coverts, also, round Kilworth Hall—and another near South Kilworth Village. Welford and Cold Ashby, when advertised, are almost sure to lead to the Hemplow Hills, which for many years was nearly always the regular Wednesday afternoon draw, and where Mr. Topham always had not *one* fox, but a dozen, awaiting them. The bold steep front of the Hemplows looks over a most glorious flat grass country—the great pastures, strongly fenced, stretching to Stanford Hall and wide to the left of it. There was no part of the Pytchley domains of which Charles Payne, in his palmiest days, was fonder than this Crick and Stanford country: and he used to slip over it so quickly that half his field seldom knew when hounds were really running, when he was casting them, or when he was going for a point—to pick up his hunted fox or start a fresh one afoot. He initiated a dangerous school—one, indeed, in which he, and he only, ever attained success. *His* success was undeniable and brilliant—for there was a method and an instinct in all he did. But many a huntsman has tried in vain to follow in his footsteps; aiming at brilliancy, has merely achieved a character for wildness, and succeeded only in losing reputation—and perhaps place.

Other Wednesday meets are Thornby (with Firetail and the Thornby Spinnies close by) Winwick and Yelvertoft. Between Yelvertoft and the Hemplows lie the coverts of Yelvertoft Hillside (where some years ago foxes were so thick that Capt. Thomson had to surround it with nets and catch up several brace), and Lord Spencer's Covert. The existence of the splendid gorse of Watford is threatened by the new line of railway under construction by the L. & N. W. Ry.

Friday and Saturday with the Pytchley alternate with each other, in falling one week on the Weedon, the next on the Harboro' side. Thus, if Friday's fixture is named for the Harboro' neighbourhood, Weedon is credited with a meet on the Saturday—and *vice versâ*.

Weedon is on the main line of the L. and N.W. Railway; and, without offering so free a choice of trains as Rugby, is nearer to London, easily reached, and can give you as much hunting as you desire. Besides the Pytchley, it has the Duke of Grafton's pack at its gates, the Bicester running close up with their most favoured strip of country, the Warwickshire within comfortable reach, and the North Warwickshire to be met near Rugby once a fortnight.

The Weedon portion of the Pytchley country may be defined as included in the points of Northampton, Weedon, Badby, Braunston, Ravensthorpe, and Brixworth. Among the coverts of this district Badby Wood stands out as a grand stronghold for foxes. Much of the country round it carries a good scent; though across Burrow Hill (to look for exception) hounds often find it difficult to run hard. Braunston Gorse, again, is a splendid covert of a different type—being of artificial growth (and of course of limited size) and planted to overlook the tempting valley spreading to Shuckburgh, or, wider still, to the confines of the North Warwickshire. To ride with hounds to Shuckburgh requires some virtue in both man and horse. The country (all grass) is generally deep, the fences are big, and the pace often great. At Ashby St. Ledgers there is covert round the Hall, and the chance of a pretty trip into the Warwickshire or North Warwickshire territory. Nearer Northampton are the coverts of Harleston Heath, Nobottle Wood, Harpole Hills and Brampton Gorse, all owned by Lord Spencer, and consequently sure finds. Then there are Dodford Holt, Staverton Wood, Whilton Osier bed (with its most beguiling, and often mirth-giving, brook), Vanderblanks, and Buckby Folly. On the extreme south of the country, Stowe Wood, Everton Stubbs, Mantel's Heath, Preston Wood, &c., neutral with the Duke of Grafton's. These are more often drawn by the Duke than the Pytchley. Among the best meets on the Weedon side are Althorp, Weedon Barracks, Dodford, Brock Hall, Badby Wood, Long Buckby (famous for its crowds of shoemakers), Brampton and Holdenby. All these are also available from Northampton, and many are within reach from Rugby. By the way, it is not a very uncommon thing, during term time, to meet an undergraduate from Cambridge with the Pytchley on a Monday, and one from Oxford at Badby Wood later in the week. Round Badby, it should be noticed —and especially in the Watford direction—the country is principally grass, a feature that is common to a great deal of the Weedon district.

The Market Harboro' side (alternately Friday and Saturday, as above noted) is comprised within the landmarks of Harboro', Rothwell, Brixworth, Cottesbrooke, Naseby and Sulby. Most of this, too, is grass of the finest type: and the part containing the parishes of Clipston, Oxendon, Braybrooke, &c., is fenced in the most terrific style—timber being very frequently added to both sides of the stake-and-bound hedges. The late Jim Mason was wont to say, that no man could ride the fences from Waterloo Gorse to Dingley without three falls, however well he might be mounted. Waterloo Gorse stands in the centre of this formidable tract, and is consequently rather a dread than a delight—at least to men of ordinary constitution. There are many other excellent coverts scattered through the district—notably Blueberry and Berrydale near Cottesbrooke, Faxton Corner, Loatland Wood, Scotland Wood, Blue Covert (the planting of which is ascribed to the Blues, when last quartered at Northampton), Naseby Covert, Naseby Woolleys (where a fox is generally found in some corner of the garden). Talliho is another nice covert in a beautiful country near Kelmarsh, and Sulby Gorse is seldom without a fox. Marston Wood and the plantations about Marston Trussels are neutral with Mr. Tailby's. The meets for all these are Cottesbrooke Park, Lamport Hall, Fox Hall, Harrington, Kelmarsh Hall, Oxendon, Clipston Windmill, Naseby, Maidwell and Sibbertoft.

We need prolong this sketch of the Pytchley no further than to remark that theirs is, on the whole, a superlatively pleasant country over which to ride to hounds. It is less hilly and trying to horses than High Leicestershire; and, with the exception above

The Pytchley.

alluded to, is practicable, if big. The hounds have never been in better order than at present; and foxes are everywhere in abundance. The Pytchley farmers are all staunch supporters of foxhunting. A great many of them ride in the front rank: while one and all of them are hearty in the cause, and greet every foxhunter as a friend.

As regards horses to carry you over the Pytchley country, it is only necessary to repeat: Remember that a bad horse cannot get over it at all, and a second-rate one will only spoil your pleasure and ruin your nerve!

THE WOODLAND PYTCHLEY.*

First established as a separate, tributary, branch by Mr. Watson, the Woodland Pytchley is now in the hands of Lord Spencer—who, since resigning command of the entire country, continues, with an establishment at Brigstock, to hunt the woods twice a week. Both sides of the country benefit by this arrangement. The Pytchley territory in its entirety was too extensive for a single pack—and a single huntsman. Now the well-stocked coverts on the grass are rattled as frequently as they should be; and, on the other hand, the foxes of the great woods are no longer allowed the luxury of fat and idle living. We have all learned that no fox can travel so strong and straight as a woodland-bred one. But to do so he requires teaching and practice. He may have many a light journey, when merely fleeing from the noise of pursuit, of which one of his brethren is the immediate object. The more of such alarms he gets, the better for him and the better for all concerned—for, with the steady scent that most woodlands hold, it will require all the strength and all the wind he can muster to carry him out of distance. A larger per-

---

* ¡Vide "Stanford's Large Scale Map," sheet 10; also "Hobson's Foxhunting Atlas."

centage of run foxes are, perhaps, accounted for in woodlands than in the open; for, besides the advantage of a more consistent scent, hounds meet with few of the interruptions they have to contend against outside. Roads, along which the one old hound can alone puzzle out the line (and that only if he is not at once ridden over or surrounded)—fallow soil, dusty or clinging—sheep to huddle, in their provoking foolishness, across the very track—cattle to soil the herbage—manure to taint both earth and air—footfolk to drive poor reynard back in his footsteps or to send terror and excitement on the breeze—all these are wanting in forest hunting; and a virgin soil and an unhampered course remain in their stead. Hounds can then work for themselves—and work much better than when continually assisted. They can get back readily to the point at which they were first at fault.* And thus it is that woodlands are so good—nay, so necessary—a school for young hounds. It is there only that they learn self-reliance, and the art of hunting their game.

Again, although it is not given to *everyone* to like woodland hunting, there is a strong section of honest sportsmen to whom it recommends itself with intense force. The taste may be as inexplicable to

---

* On the other hand, as against all the advantages enumerated above, there are greater chances of changing foxes in the woods than in the open—where a huntsman can often detect the mistake. Also falling leaves, or, on certain days the drip from trees, are all against scent in woodlands. Hounds take longer to pick out a cold line in covert than in the open, and if a fox is once well ahead, you have not the same chance of getting up to him through the medium of a holloa.

outsiders as the fisherman's mania is to him who does not fish, or as the enthusiasm of the golfer to him who has never learned golf. But the passion does exist, and is quite as solid and lasting as that commanded by the more butterfly forms of the chase. Men who favour woodland hunting claim for it all the excellencies for hound-work above alluded to. They insist, too (with a pleasant self-satisfaction impossible to begrudge them), that whoever goes into the woods with hounds must go there for hunting only, and with none of the weak ulterior motives of company, coffee-housing, or dress.

But it must not be inferred that the whole of the country in question is one vast woodland—though it may be true that there is as much timber grown in it as in any similar area in England, and along the north west side stretches a tract of covert almost unbroken. There is an oasis of fine grass almost in the centre of the country, there is more along the eastern border, and a wide corner of open ground in the south.

The boundaries of the Woodland Pytchley are as follows. The Midland Railway from Wellingboro' to Market Harboro' is held to be the line of division from the main Pytchley now governed by Mr. Langham—except that Lord Spencer hunts the small coverts at Glendon and Rushton Hall, which are beyond the railway. The remainder of the outline is much as is shown on Stanford's Map* and is contained in the natural boundaries of the river Welland on the west and the Nene on the east. Its northern

---

* *Vide* "Stanford's Large Scale Map," sheet 10; also "Hobson's Foxhunting Atlas."

The Woodland Pytchley. 149

limits, in themselves rather indefinite as touching the Wakerly (or north-westerly) corner, are inaccurately put by the wielder of Mr. Stanford's paintbrush who, having no natural, or accidental, boundary to follow here has considerably curtailed the Pytchley territory. Glapthorne Pastures is the extreme point to which they can draw on the north-east. The Bulwick Woods are Pytchley; Laxton Wood is neutral with the Fitzwilliam, and Wakerley Wood contains a line beyond which the Pytchley right is not recognised.

The Kennels, as above-mentioned, are at Brigstock, a capital central point. But for the summer months Lord Spencer moves his hounds to Althorp Park. For cubhunting purposes the Pytchley Proper maintain their right to bring their pack into the woodlands; and, as a matter of arrangement, Lord Spencer has the privilege of teaching his young hounds near home.

Kettering, Thrapston, Oundle and Market Harboro' are the points from which the Woodland Pytchley are best met. But, beyond the early autumn and late spring, Harboro' generally turns its attention elsewhere; and, though the other three may invite visitors, as a point of fact few come and the field remains a small and almost purely local one. Kettering being only about two hours from London, and having a choice between the grass on one side and the rougher country on the other, might well be fixed upon as a good hunting quarter. Thrapston is a frequent landing point for Cambridge undergraduates, with a view either to the Woodland Pytchley or the Fitzwilliam,—representatives from which latter pack and the Oakley often come over the borders to join Lord Spencer.

The Duke of Buccleugh's grand woods form the backbone of the country, being always full of foxes, with the additional advantage of being well rided and tolerably easy to hunt. The chief of these are Weekly Hall Wood, Geddington Chase, Boughton, Old Head and Grafton Park. Between these woods and Brigstock Forest is a large tract of grass land known as Brigstock Parks—the fences of which are often too formidable to jump, but where gates are numerous and convenient, and hounds are to be seen but not interfered with. The same kind of ground stretches beyond Sudborough; and there *must* be a run if a fox takes over it. From Brigstock Forest there is another series of woods extending eastwards to Wadenhoe—comprising Lady, Lilford, Souther, Tichmarsh, Bullock, Oxen, Bearshanks, and the Wadenhoe woods, with again a good deal of wild grass interspersed and surrounding.

Turning to the north-west we have, besides, the neutral Laxton Wood, the Bulwick Woods, the great coverts of Deene—and, near by, are treeless wastes with only stumps still rooted. Westward of Deene Park are Penn Green, Excellent, Lodge Green, and Corby; and, farther southward, is Oakley Purlieus—all belonging to Lady Cardigan. Near Rockingham Castle are Mr. Watson's well stocked coverts—Porter's Coppice, Prince Wood, and Rockingham Cow Pastures; and south of these again the chain is continued with King's Wood, Swinehaw, Carlton Forest, the Pipwell Woods, and Stoke—till we get to Brampton Wood (the property of Lord Spencer). Between the river

The Woodland Pytchley. 151

Welland and these woods is another good strip of turf; and beyond these, at a short distance from Harboro', is Dingley looking across the stiffest of all valleys to Waterloo Gorse, over the boundary. In the southernmost portion of the country there are few coverts — below the Duke of Buccleugh's woods. And between Cranford Gorse and Finedon Poplars there is quite an open district of light plough and little fences, reaching to the Nene. Oundle Wood in the north east corner is a fine stronghold, and the river runs through a beautiful green valley, unblessed, however, by any tempting sheltering spots.

The days of hunting are arranged thus. Monday is a weekly advertisement, and generally for the northern half of the country—the road from Thrapston to Rockingham forming an approximate line of division. The second day of the week is alternately Thursday and Friday; and is more often in the southern half. But no attempt is made at an absolute rule — various considerations combining to render adherence to a strict programme impossible. The shooting season is not the least of these considerations —the upper part of the country being strictly under game-culture: so much so, that in the autumn there is sometimes difficulty in obtaining sufficient room for foxhunting.

The more prominent meets of the north are Rockingham Castle, Harringworth Lodge, Bulwick, Deene Park, Oundle Wood, Farming Wood (for Brigstock), Sudborough and Lowick. In the south are Finedon, Cranford, Boughton House, Oakley Hays, Hermitage Farm (for Brampton Wood), Weekley Hall Wood, Rushton Hall, and Dob Hall.

As a woodland country, pure and simple, it may be asserted that the "Woodland Pytchley" is not easily to be beaten. It has foxes everywhere, and in most parts carries a good scent — while the rides are navigable, though the woods are wet enough for sport in both spring and autumn. For the one who wields the horn there must be an endless fund of interest and amusement. Those who follow have work enough for wits and energy, if they would keep within hearing of hounds. *Seeing hounds* in woodlands is, to all practicable intent, a *façon de parler*. The ear must be the guiding organ more often than the eye—or—to leave the directing power with the hound—*he* may follow his nose, *you* must follow his tongue. And there is no crowd to carry you on in the mechanical way that in an open country may bring you forward (you know not how), till eventually you come up with hounds once more. In the woods you must act for yourself, and acquire a special interest. And it ends in your learning (however dull and careless a pupil) that foxhunting is an interest—not merely an exercise. It may be said that long and solitary rides home offer few point of interest except to the man of melancholy and reflection. But they are necessarily part of the self-discipline and rigour of habit called for in pursuit of sport in a woodland and thinly-populated country. They may even be improving. But at least they are open to the objection that the horse, though eminently a reflective animal, goes home better in company than alone. You, reader, and I, may have learned that silence is golden—but, I fancy, we would gladly take out the change in silver, to spend on a fourteen-mile ride to our dinner.

The Woodland Pytchley.

Again, amid a small company, and an independent one, there must be much more individuality of action than in a crowded current of humanity and horseflesh. And this alone must always add an interest. Where the field of action is open and easy enough for all, where most are successful, and where competition does not shut out, the day need seldom close on disappointment, thwarted ambition, or loss of opportunity. And thus moralising, we come to the practical point that you need not throw your money away too lavishly when mounting yourself for the country in question. You may, if you like, keep a good horse for Dingley, Rushton, &c., on the chance of a dive into the outer grass. But for home purposes and general occasion, something stout and shortlegged—with a blood head, and heels well protected (if you can hit upon such a combination)—will carry you well enough. An extra ten pounds on fair hack action will not be thrown away—if you would hunt far and late.

This summary of requirement is, of course, intended for the outsider who does not care to be in every field with the hounds, but he who does, and the huntsman, requires possibly as good or a better horse than in the largest jumping country. At any moment a fox may take to the open, and with little exception the fences are large and require a first-rate jumper. In other respects a horse is most severely tried for stoutness in the deep rides.

THE ATHERSTONE.*

A LARGE and varied country, with half its area in Leicestershire, half in Warwickshire; Coventry and Rugby mark its southern margin, Lutterworth is on its eastern boundary. It runs almost up to Leicester at its north-east corner; and Nuneaton is its centre. It touches the North Warwickshire in the south, the Pytchley, Mr. Tailby's and the Quorn along the east, the Quorn again and the Meynell on the north, and the South Staffordshire on the west.

Where it adjoins the Quorn on the north-east, a large strip (between Bardon and Grooby) should have been entered on the map in neutral colours, being the common property of the Quorn and the Atherstone. For the Atherstone have the right of drawing all the Bradgate Woods, and even half of Swithland Wood —though their title (independently of game considerations) does not include cub-hunting.

The Atherstone hunt four days in the week; and for this purpose divide their country about as follows—

Monday is credited to the Market Bosworth neighbourhood; and includes the district to the north of Hinckley.

---

* *Vide* "Stanford's Large Scale Map," sheets 9 and 15; also "Hobson's Foxhunting Atlas."

The Atherstone.

Wednesday is in the Appleby district, and points to the district between Tamworth and Ashby-de-la-Zouch.

Friday is for the Rugby country, and means the goodly tract south of Hinckley and westward as far as the Coventry and Nuneaton road.

Saturday is spent on the Birmingham side, *i.e.*, within the points of Tamworth, Coleshill, and Coventry.

The Kennels are at Witherley, about a mile from Atherstone (just within the borders of Leicestershire), are admirably situated for hunting the country, and possess the advantage of being close to a good railway station. Mr. Oakeley hunts the country in almost princely style.

The Friday, or Rugby, country is undoubtedly the pick of the Atherstone domain. On a Monday they go over some neat and pretty ground, to the south-west of Leicester; but on a Friday they must be all day in a land that is passing fair. Indeed, Rugby, as a hunting quarter, has the exceptional advantage of commanding the choicest portions of no less than four, or even five, Hunts. We have spoken of Rugby already, under the heads of the Pytchley and North Warwickshire: but there is no unnecessary repetition in averring that few places have such excellence of choice and variety as are to be found here—in hunting with Mr. Tailby's on Monday, the Pytchley on Wednesday, the North Warwickshire, or the Warwickshire, on Thursday, and the Atherstone on Friday; while for Tuesday or Saturday there may be the Quorn, the Atherstone or the Pytchley within riding distance—or the Duke of Grafton to be reached by rail. And all this wealth lies within two hour's journey of London! Truly Rugby would seem to stand out alone as a point of attraction for the sport-loving Londoner.

Or, for a man desirous of attaching himself to a single pack, there is Nuneaton offering him every facility of access and every opportunity of enjoying himself. It is only a few miles from the Atherstone Kennels; and less than two and a half hours from London. To be "sent to Coventry," again, in the literal sense, is to the hunting soldier the *summum bonum* of earthly happiness. There he will hunt from barracks four days in the week, and—if his means allow—will get leave from parade on both the other days, that he may rail to covert elsewhere, not far away. Lutterworth, Leicester and Market Bosworth, also, are by no means undesirable stations.

It is only on a Friday that the Atherstone command the giant field that constitutes the sole drawback to fashionable Leicestershire—a drawback necessarily begotten of virtue well appreciated. On a Friday you must be prepared to ride in a crowd, and to take your chance over a big country with a multitude all as anxious to be near hounds as yourself—or nearer. On other days with them you want a hunter; but he need have none of the qualities of a steeplechaser—nor need *you* have graduated between the flags. But on a Friday you must be quick to start, and bold to ride. Your horse must be able to glide over ridge-and-furrow, to keep his head straight, and jump his farthest when called upon, and to gallop twenty

The Atherstone.

minutes without a pull. For the Rugby country is nearly all grass, and the fences are fair but formidable. Scent lies well, and the fun is often fast and furious. We have begun out of order; so may continue out of order—and complete the Fridays before returning to the earlier days of the week. Brownsoever is the Atherstone meet nearest to Rugby; and, after its home plantations are drawn, the word is generally for Cestersover—which constitutes also the second draw from Coton. A very favourite fixture is Coton House, from whose snug little gorse, or from the Park spinnies, many a good gallop has led into the Pytchley country. There are also, on the borders and close to the Watling Street Road, two or three more small coverts tempting a trip on to the neighbouring soil. By the way, Mr. Stanford is open to a slight correction hereabouts, in that he has carried the Pytchley colouring over the river Swift, where it crosses the Watling Street Road—whereas the Atherstone country comes to the northern bank of the stream.

Bitteswell is another outside meet, which never fails to call in a large body of visitors from Mr. Tailby's and the Pytchley. As the hounds are generally brought here by rail, and as the Bitteswell Covert is very small and road-begirt, Ullesthorpe Station is often named instead of Bitteswell. For a second fox from either—should it happen to be inconvenient on the day to turn to Twelveacres, a terrible distance has to be travelled. For, excepting a little plantation or two (seldom occupied) not far from Ashby, there is no covert of any sort till Burbage Wood is reached, fully six miles away—the whole of the beautiful grass tract round Frowlesworth, Sharnford, Leir, &c., being completely wasted for want of a covert! (Since this was written I learn that a new covert has been formed in this fine ground.)

Burbage Wood is advertised for the great good stronghold of that name, and its linked neighbour Aston Firs. These woods take a good deal of drawing, and cannot be drawn too often. There is a capital country round them in almost every direction; and if you can stick to hounds there, and when they leave it, you will see sport frequent and excellent.

Twelveacres is, perhaps, the nicest covert in the whole of the Atherstone Hunt. It is a wooded fastness on the Watling Street Road; and famous runs have been credited to it, over the fine large grazing lands stretching to Lutterworth, or Misterton (in the Pytchley country); and it is an afternoon draw from Bitteswell, Newnham, or Coton. I know of no better chance for hounds—or for horsemen—than when the former start fairly thence on a fox with their heads pointed southwards or westwards. Both must be on their mettle then—for it is Leicestershire in its purest sense. Newnham Paddox is another pleasant fixture—a lawn meet, and good coverts all round the domain, including a gorse and many little woods. Coal Pit Lane, as it is called, borders the Newnham estates, has a spinney running up all its length, and leads to Wolvey Gorse. Three Pots is the meet nearest Nuneaton, and, after its spinnies, has Wolvey Gorse and the Newnham Coverts most handy. Or from a meet at Wolvey Village the programme may be varied by a

The Atherstone.

visit to Coombe. But the ordinary meet for the great woods in Coombe is Shilton Village—and no sounder coverts are to be found. Like all large woods they will bear, and require, hard and frequent work. Brandon Wood is the southernmost covert—for which Binley Common is usually on the cards. Newbold Revel and the wood of All Oaks, bring us back to the immediate neighbourhood of Rugby.

Continuing with their Mondays we find ourselves in the Leicester—or Market Bosworth—district. The latter town has more right to give a title; for Leicester is over the borders while Bosworth is almost the centre point of this division. On a Monday you will be taken over a lighter country than that of Friday—a very sporting country withal, carrying a fair scent and more than tolerably well supplied with foxes. There is a good deal of grass, and the ploughed land is not very deep or sticky. The fences are not difficult, but may be taken much as they come. The coverts—as is the case over a great part of the Atherstone country —are principally small. Hounds can thus usually get away on good terms with their fox, which is at least half way towards killing him.

The opening meet of the season is always Bosworth Park (the seat of the Dixie family), where there are the home plantations, with the coverts known as the Cow Pastures and the Decoy to draw. Then within three miles of Bosworth is Sutton Ambion—which may be termed the mainstay of the Monday country. This grand covert consists of a large horse-shoe shaped wood, with strong brambly undergrowth, which foxes frequent in number inexhaustible. Within its curve is a meadow containing Richard's Well—where tradition has it that the King drank after the Battle of Bosworth. But Shenton is the more usual meet for Sutton Ambion—hounds more often being taken northwards after Bosworth Park.

Next in an eastward direction is Cadeby Gate; and close to the fixture are the Spinnies of Cadeby, also Botany Bay and a number of little spots capable of holding a fox. Then, as we move towards Hinckley, comes Kirkby Mallory, with Kirkby Gorse and, again some small copses—further drawing leading on by Peckleton and Tooley Park. Normanton Turville (formerly the residence of the Rev. J. Arkwright, himself once Master of the Essex, and father of Mr. Loftus Arkwright the last Master of that pack) has small coverts round it and some more spinnies stretch up to Enderby, to the edge of the Quorn country. Earl Shilton is another meet with the same intent. Turning northward again, we come to Desford, with Lindridge Wood (thirty or forty acres of capital covert) and Nailstone Wiggs, a patch of rough growth like that of a common—two nearly sure finds, and doorways to a nice country round. Ratby Burrows is on the borders of Lord Stamford's property, and points to the territory that is neutral with the Quorn. At Barton-in-the-Beans and round Bagworth, Ibstock, &c., we get for the first time among the collieries of the Atherstone country. Here, however, they are scattered at considerable interval, and do not interfere much with the interest of foxhunting, which is carried on in wild, but fairly good ground, though inferior to that of the more southern Monday resorts. Shackerstone, too, has plantation growth dotted about in its vicinity—Congerstone Spinnies being those nearest to Gopsall Park (Lord Howe's seat). From Harris Bridge is drawn Sibson Wolds, a large gorse, surrounded by a belt of timber. Nearer the Watling Street Road, which is plainly marked across the centre of the country, we come to Linley Park with small coverts round the house. Red Gate is more often the advertised meet: and about here are plenty of foxes, and plenty of small fences and small grass enclosures. Caldecote, the property of Mr. Henry Townshend, is invaluable, though the coverts near it are but small. Years ago there existed Weddington Wood, (some 90 acres), which would furnish a whole day's amusement and employment. But this has long since been levelled and ploughed.

Wednesday is spent in the north-east, or what is known as the Appleby country. There is more clay in the soil, and more grass grown on it, than in the Monday district: and, as a consequence, the fences are stronger. On the whole, it is a good fair country for hounds; and, moreover, full care is taken of the foxes.

Gopsall (Lord Howe's seat) is generally the first Wednesday meet. There are numerous good coverts round the estate, among them some woods of considerable size—*e.g.* The Racecourse (so called from the long avenue running through it) and High Wood. Just north of Gopsall is Appleby (Mr. G. Moore's), with some plantations near the house, Birdshill Gorse, and Appleby Gorse. Round here there is good grass and fine scenting ground. Between

Appleby and Snarestone there is also an osier-bed—the old Snarestone Gorse having been done away with. From Appleby Gorse took place what is said to have been the best run of Col. Thomson's reign over the Atherstone. The gorse had been lately cut down, thistles constituted the only cover, and the earth was open. The Master ran his hounds through one side, while a terrier was put into the earth at the other. A fox was bolted, and they chased him an eleven mile point (fast all the way). He crossed the river Thame near Elford, then turned back about three miles beyond. Hounds caught a view of him as he swam the river again, overtook him as he reached a willow-bed in mid-stream, and there pulled him down.

Above Appleby we come to Willesley, near Ashby de la Zouch and the extreme north—the coverts, as in many other parts, being limited to small plantations. But more westward are the two big and useful woods known as Seale Wood and Grange Wood. Lullington comes next as a meet. And near here is a gorse, which (planted by a former Master of the Atherstone on neutral, or rather, unclaimed ground) is still undefined as belonging to either Atherstone or Meynell—a reference to Boodle's having met with no decided award. Seckington Tumulus is generally fixed for Thorpe, where are some good coverts and gorse. At Ammington, too, is a gorse and some spinnies—Shuttington Bridge being a favourite meet: and Grendon another, more to the south.

The Saturday, or Birmingham country, is the south-west portion—and lies below the Watling

Street Road, which passes through Atherstone and Tamworth. It is full of coalpits; and its other characteristics are big woods, small enclosures, rough hairy fences, and much arable. It is altogether difficult ground for hounds to run over; and is certainly the least-favoured part of the Atherstone country. The first large wood to notice is Birch Coppice, which is on the Watling Street Road about four miles from Atherstone. There are large strong coverts also about Baxterley—Kingsbury Wood being the chief in size and quality. The Black Swan is a frequent meet for the above; and Kingsbury Wood itself is often advertised. To the east of these is Merevale—from whose site a beautiful view of the Atherstone country is to be obtained. The coverts about here are many and large, headed by Bentley Park Wood—Bentley Tollbar being the ordinary meet. There are more woods again leading up to Oldbury Hall. Hartshill Hayes is the next large wood: and near here lives Mr. R. Alken, who, in spite of deafness, has not missed a day's cubhunting for years, during the summer has devoted his whole time to the care of coverts and cubs, and has done more than any one else to keep the country together.

Camphill has coverts round it—notably Haunch Wood: and from here we get into a very region of coalpits. Arbury (Mr. Newdigate's) is among a multitude of woods, strong and well-preserved—Cow Leighs, Park Wood, North Wood, and Coventry Wood, being the leading names. And these are joined on the south by Lord Aylesford's Woodlands; and Kench Grove to Corley constitutes another great range of wood. Working on through Corley to Birchley Hayes, Fillongley, Arley Wood, and Dale Wood, we get to Packington (Lord Aylesford's residence) and Maxstock—Filloughby, Packington, and Corley all being meets. Shustock is advertised for the extreme west, of which the river Thame is the boundary.

THE BILLESDON OR SOUTH QUORN.*

In dealing with the geography and characteristics of the Southern Portion of the old Quorn Country, it is not intended to refer in any way to the question so lately and unfortunately vexed. It stands on our Map* as Mr. Tailby's Country, and in describing it we may still make use of the name by which it was so long and honourably denominated. It is safe to affirm that in the palmiest days of Mr. Tailby's *régime*—when a loan of some of the Cottesmore woodlands gave a backbone to the open tract first worked separately by Mr. Richard Sutton—no pack in the Shires had such brilliant and continual sport. In two wet seasons especially—some fifteen years ago—Jack Goddard had a gallop every day his horn was at the saddle; and riding-men swore that Mr. Tailby was the only Master with whom to hunt. With Frank Goodall, too, runs came almost as merrily and frequently; and it was only when the sphere became limited by the woods being surrendered to the Cottesmore that the sun of success shone a little less hotly. Let it be understood that the following sketch is of Mr. Tailby's Country,

---

* "Stanford's Large Scale Map," sheets 15 and 16; also "Hobson's Foxhunting Atlas."

as it remained on the resumption by the Cottesmore of the territory they had left. After this his hunting-grounds were restricted to the south side of the turnpike road running from Leicester to Uppingham. The other boundaries were as coloured on Stanford's Map—the Wye Brook and the Welland marking the east and south east—the Leicester and Lutterworth turnpike the west, and Market Harboro', Lubenham, Husbands Bosworth, and Kimcote, points on the southern limit.

Leicester to Market Harboro', in fact, defines as well as any fuller term the extent of the territory of late years hunted by Mr. Tailby—Leicester being at one extremity, Harboro' at the other, and the road between, straight as a ruler, cutting the country almost exactly in half.

Either of these places commands the country; and of the two it is not unfair to say that you are likely to choose Market Harboro'. Leicester does not care about you, for it has sources of wealth far more extensive and deep rooted than the pockets of hunting men, while Harboro' is glad enough to welcome you to its comfortable hostelries and unlimited stabling. The one has grown into a great manufacturing centre; the other still remains as Whyte Melville depicted it—a neat little market town, owing all its position in the world to its attractiveness as a hunting quarter. Looked at even from this point of view, Harboro' has had its ups-and-downs. At one time it rivalled Melton. Oftentimes it has been a smaller Harboro'. But while fox-hunting exists in the Midlands, there will always be a strong staff of sportsmen gazetted to this most

The Billesdon or South Quorn.

central and tempting post. Within two hours-and-a-half of London (an eight o'clock train from St. Pancras bringing any of the nearer meets within a single day's work from Town), with three packs of hounds hunting up to its very gates, and the cream of the Shires spread round its walls, it must offer food for the most critical appetite—a field for the most ambitious temperament.

Besides Leicester and Market Harboro', and midway between them on the main line of railway, is Kibworth —consisting of a village, a station, and a group of hunting boxes. Kibworth lies quite in the centre of the Country; and is becoming every day more popular as a hunting base. Hotel accommodation it has yet to acquire; and its chief favour is found in the eyes of men who have a wife, and must needs have a house. In fact, Kibworth is more of a four than a six-days-a-week quarter. For the pack under notice has, with its limited sphere, been in the habit of taking the field only five days a fortnight; and on many of the other days a long journey is needed to reach, or to return from, another pack—be it the Quorn, the Cottesmore, or the Pytchley. If you would hunt every day, and still reside in the Billesdon province, you had better go further from the railway, and establish yourself at Billesdon itself—where your field of operations is wider and easier. It was at Billesdon that Mr. Sutton, and for some years afterwards Mr. Tailby, kept the hounds: and hence the B. H. button for the initials of the hunt. Billesdon, again, is not a spot possessing any greater resources of its own than most country villages. You must go there with a view to the pleasure of the chase—and for that purpose only.

The days of hunting have hitherto been arranged very simply as follows—The Midland Railway cutting the country in half, the southern portion has been chosen for Mondays, the northern for Thursdays, except that an extreme eastern corner has been left for an extra day on alternate Saturdays—when the Cottesmore are on the farther side of their own dominions.

Some of the Monday country is extremely good; and all of it may be termed fair. That of the Thursdays embraces a superb grass district that has no superior in the shires; while that of the Saturdays is on some sides very perfect—if very stiff.

Nearest to Market Harboro' on a Monday is Gumley, whose well sheltered and carefully tended coverts form a never-failing base of supplies. Foxton is sometimes named that footpeople may not know whether to assemble at Gumley, above Papillon Gorse, or round the spinnies at Lubenham. But Gumley is always the opening meet; and a standing dish throughout the season. For the afternoon there are the Laughton Hills to be drawn—overlooking the green valley to Theddingworth, and facing the neutral hills of Marston and Hothorpe. Were it not for railway and canal, this valley would bear a brilliant name. As it is, foxes seldom face it. And when they do, hounds must more often cross it alone. Marston in Mr. Stanford's map is coloured as being over the border—whereas its spinnies and the adjacent wooded heights are neutral with the Pytchley. You must take your

The Billesdon or South Quorn.   169

map in hand, and you must take your saddle there if you would really learn the features of the country. This sketch is only intended to help you to your bearings on arrival. Beyond Gumley are the meets of Mowsley (for the neat artificial coverts of John Ball, Jane Ball, and Walton Holt, with Bosworth Gorse as a link with the Laughton Hills). From Walton Holt westward is a beautiful line : and the Atherstone country may even be pierced at its best. The same course is possible from the other coverts ; and the Pytchley country is open and at hand ; but too often foxes prefer the home precincts. Another covert between Walton Holt and Ashby would be a true boon. Shearsby is put on the cards for any of the last-named coverts, or for Ashby New Covert. Bruntingthorpe, again, is for the latter or for Peatling Covert—both bordering on an open, and rather wasted, quarter of the Atherstone—and Kilby when named is meant for a trot to the Blaby Spinnies and the almost defunct Whetstone Gorse. Wistow has its Gorse, its Spinnies in the Park, and Peatling Gorse to fall back upon in the afternoon.

It will be gathered that the coverts of this Monday country are invariably small and artificial. When foxes run straight and choose an upland, and a westward line, there is good ground to be ridden over. There is of course more plough than in the north of the country, and seldom perhaps so good a scent. But there is a bit of pretty riding by Gilmorton and Peatling that is well worth experiencing.

In the Leicester neighbourhood we get to Stretton Parva, with, probably, Thurnby, for a morning draw,

Norton Gorse and Glen Gorse for the afternoon. Thurnby Spinney is but a little place. But with a good fox, or even a fair fox, it may mean a run of grand merit. Hounds *must* get away at his brush; and to save his brush he must travel fast over a long distance without a covert, and with grass underfoot. And the same conditions (given a huntsman quick to get his hounds from covert—and the hypothesis has seldom been wanting) apply fully to Norton Gorse. Grass paves the way in every direction; and to run to Kibworth by Burton Overy and Carlton is indeed a blissful progress. Glen Gorse has a good side and a bad. If a fox will but choose his line northwards or westwards, he has a hunter's paradise before him. But foxes are too often insensible to proffered happiness and the interests of their best friends. From the meets of Illston-on-the-Hill and Burton Overy, the probable draws are Norton Gorse and Shangton Holt. Shangton Holt—or, more familiarly, Shang Holt—was a great place in the days before the spinnies of Noseley had grown up. *Now* it is too apt to act as part of what the Tailbytes were wont to term the "home circuit"—meaning thereby Noseley, Rolleston, Keythorpe, Staunton Wood, and Glooston Wood. For, from the park plantations of Noseley a fox is almost sure to run through the Long Spinney or the Covert of Rolleston, or into the wooded glens and glades of Keythorpe (Ram's Head, Moor Hill, Vowes Gorse, and Keythorpe Wood included). From here he is certain to follow a gully to the woods of Staunton or Glooston, or both. All these coverts are from one to two miles apart. Go there as a stranger, you will see a fine run

The Billesdon or South Quorn. 171

every day. As one who has learned all their features you will seldom be amused. Herein, in fact, lies the bane of this little country. *It is too well known.* And a fine hound-run is often voted wearisome, because men anticipated its line, and could map out their whole path beforehand. But they don't all know their way over the Stonton Brook. Here their learning fails, and their shortcomings discover themselves. High authority has suggested that the Stonton Brook should be drained — guaranteeing that, in silver-mounted relics and stirrup leathers alone, full compensation for expense would be found.

Just westward of this home circuit is the meet of Carlton Hall, and the delightful covert of Sheepshorns —the latter ranking with Norton Gorse as a *certainty* for a gallop over the creamiest grass.

Stonton Wyvile is for Langton Caudle and the great strongholds of Staunton and Glooston Woods; and hounds are here or hereabouts quite once a week— and seldom without good result.

The Saturday country comprises a very limited space. The new railway, as jotted on the map, gives about its area. It depends for its sport almost entirely on the chain of woods facing the Cottesmore at Wardley. The Billesdon draw Allexton with the other pack; and they have also Stockerston Wood and Marabole Holt (otherwise Merivale)—and for these they usually meet at Allexton or Blaston. From these good fastnesses foxes should break over into Cottesmore ground more often than they have of late been willing to do. Slawston is more frequently a Thursday meet, and the Slawston vale, where practicable, is admirable.

You will meet the best and hardest of company in this Billesdon country. Mount yourself accordingly, and ride with confidence in yourself and your horse.

THE MEYNELL.*

To the north-west of Leicestershire lies the pleasant grass country of The Meynell, occupying all of Derbyshire that is huntable west of the River Derwent—together with a well-wooded portion of Staffordshire. The Meynell Country is touched on the south by the South Staffordshire (the River Trent dividing the two); it runs over the Trent to meet the Atherstone, and again returns within the river at the fork formed by the Trent and Derwent, where Lord Ferrers meets it on the south-east. The South Notts runs up the whole of its eastern side; on the north it merges into a hilly blank where only harriers are seen, and on the west is the North Staffordshire.

The Meynell Hounds are one of the oldest existing packs—their Kennel Book containing uninterrupted yearly entries from 1818, and there were nine-season hounds in that year's list. During the whole of this time, and up to Mr. Meynell's death about 1870, the hounds were kennelled at Hoar Cross, his place in Staffordshire, and, the Derbyshire side of his country being distant from home, was only hunted during the

---

* *Vide* " Stanford's Large Scale Railway Map," Sheet 9; also, " Hobson's Foxhunting Atlas."

first week of each month. For this purpose the pack was sent on the first Monday of the month to Kedlaston Inn (near Derby), whence it hunted three days, and returned to Kennels on Saturday. This was called the "Derby week;" and under this arrangement the best part of the country obviously did not receive its full share of attention. If a frost fell early in a month, the district would, as often happened, remain unhunted for seven or eight weeks. From the Hoar Cross Kennels, too, it was the custom to take hounds by rail to Ashbourne once a week for a day in the Upper country. At Mr. Meynell's decease the hounds were left by will to the Country; and Lord Waterpark and Mr. Clowes took them, on the conditions of a guaranteed subscription and of Kennels being provided in the centre of the country. Kennels were accordingly erected at Sudbury; and ever since it has been the rule to hunt two days a week in Derbyshire, and two in Staffordshire—the River Dove separating the counties, and dividing the Meynell territory into two portions very equal in size, but very different in feature. The days of hunting are Monday, Tuesday, Thursday, and Saturday; and the northern, or Derbyshire, half is hunted on Tuesday and Thursday—in order that all the hounds, which are divided into two packs, may each week have their turn in both open and woodland. For, whereas the country north of the Dove is grass from end to end, and such a thing as a large wood is unknown, south of the river it is in many parts hidden by woodlands for miles. On the Derbyshire side the soil is almost entirely devoted to dairy farming; and over a wide, undulating plain you see for many miles only good grass, small inclosures, and easy fences. It is the most tempting of all countries to "lark over;" jumping is offered every hundred yards: and the fences—top-trimmed, not stake-and-bound, and seldom furnished with a ditch of any moment—invite but never terrify. Consequently, hounds are hindered rather than horsemen; and sport is occasionally the sufferer. In fact, it is difficult for hounds to get room enough even with a moderate field and over capital scenting ground; and they seldom get away from their followers, except when now and again they slip on to the hills north of the country. There they have more than once been known to pull their fox down by themselves.

The Meynell country is not one much known, or visited, by outsiders. They know of it as a country of sport and pleasant riding; and a visit to it—even a day's trip, is a chance readily seized upon by men quartered elsewhere. But, apart from those who hunt in Derbyshire, or on its frontiers, because they live there, fewer hunting men bring their horses to the Meynell country than its many attractions would lead one to suppose. But, as may have been already gathered, it is not a country that could stand an influx of visitors. A crowd would at once spoil its own sport; and anything approaching to a Leicestershire field would choke itself, and its object. Added to this, there is little choice of quarter—Derby being the only resting-place offering, except the more distant points of Uttoxeter and Ashbourne. These towns all lie on the outskirts of the country; while at Sudbury, the site of the Kennels, the Inn would scarcely provide room and stabling for more than one or two sportsmen. Derby is undoubtedly a good situation. It commands three days of the Meynell, and has the South Notts and Lord Ferrers' to eke out the week. It is rather more than three hours from London (St. Pancras); and the Midland Railway offers further facilities, in the opportunity of taking train two or three times a week to join the Quorn near Loughborough, Syston Junction, or Leicester.

Thursday is especially the day of the week on which the Meynell are in the immediate neighbourhood of Derby—Tuesday being nearer Sudbury or Ashbourne, Monday in the Burton-on-Trent district, and Saturday on the Chartley side (and south of Uttoxeter).

Thus, as has been already stated, the two middle days of the week are in the Derbyshire, or grass, country—the characteristics of which vary but little throughout. Its coverts are entirely small and artificial: and are keenly preserved on all sides. Some larger coverts might be of advantage; for towards the end of a season it often happens that there is difficulty in finding a fox in some of these little places —though, when one is once found, two or three others are almost certain to be soon afoot, with the possible consequence that, after running hard all the afternoon, hounds have to be whipped off a fresh fox, when they should be near killing their own.

The horse for this country ought to be a quick jumper, yet easy to stop and turn. He should be shortbacked and strong—power and endurance being, perhaps, of more consequence here than mere speed.

For he will be popping in and out of the small pastures all day; and, though the fences are not such as to throw him down easily (except when now and again a stiff bit of timber may be encountered), they are high and scratchey; and a well-bred horse is apt to over-exert himself at most of his jumps—to avoid the sharp edges of thorns and stakes. And, travelling on grass all the time, a fox is not soon tired to death, nor likely to run his pursuers easily out of scent. The chase is therefore often a long one, calling for continued and severe exertion, and requiring a thorough stayer to carry a man in comfort and pleasure. As a sample of the Derbyshire country, and of the distance foxes occasionally travel over it, take the run from Hilton Gorse some five or six years ago. Hilton Gorse is to Derbyshire what Ranksboro' is to Leicestershire. To watch it drawn is a sight in itself—to get a good fox away is almost always a run. On the occasion alluded to they ran from this covert (which lies close by the River Dove) straight northwards to Snelston, near Ashbourne—a ten-mile point —and crossed only one ploughed field in the distance!

Above Ashbourne come the Derbyshire Hills, great rolling limestone formations, covered with grass—so steep that it is impossible to follow hounds, except by riding from one high point to another for an occasional view. But it is a fine country for harriers, whose game is not prone to carry the sphere of action so wide—the range on the north towards Wirksworth being particularly favourable.

Beginning with the Thursday, or Derby, side of the

grass, we have Radbourn as the meet nearest to the borough, also as the best known of all the Meynell fixtures, and as usually advertised for the first Thursday in each month. Radbourn Roughs, a stronghold of wood and osiers and reeds, is its covert. Sutton Mill, and Etwell, point to Sutton Gorse, Parson's Gorse, and Hilton's Gorse. The last-named is really a gorse, and a good one. Sutton Gorse, like many other of the coverts of the Meynell, has no longer any title as a gorse, but remains an excellent covert in the form of blackthorn. And these two stand out as two of the most celebrated holding-places of the Derbyshire country. Kedlaston (the seat of Lord Scarsdale, and three miles from Derby) has small coverts round the place, with Langley Gorse and Breward's Carr, of more substantial size and power, in the neighbourhood. At Egginton is Egginton Gorse, and some way to the east is Arleston Gorse. One of the farthest meets from Kennels is Stenson Lock, with Stenson Field Covert. But farther still is Elvaston Castle (Lord Harrington's) towards the junction of the Derwent and the Trent—a great lawn meet, from which hounds are taken to draw the cypress gardens. Even to this remote corner the grass stretches as sound and fair riding as ever. At Longford (Hon. E. Coke's) we get to about the centre of the Derbyshire country, and may see hounds there on a Tuesday almost as often as on a Thursday. Longford Carr is a capital covert, and there are other small ones also at hand.

The Tuesday country of the Meynell differs in no respect from that of the Thursday—small grass fields, artificial coverts of very limited size, light fences, and plenty of foxes, being conditions that apply to the whole of hunting Derbyshire. On a Tuesday, then, they are on the east of the county, towards Ashbourne and Uttoxeter, both of which places are on the border line between the fox hunting flat and the harrier hills. And it is close to this boundary line that we meet with the only exception to the above description of the Derbyshire ground—for between Ashbourne and Cubley we find a rough, undrained, often sedgy country, with scrambly, untrimmed fences, frequently intersected with broken watercourses; while just below Norbury is a strip of flat watermeadows—pleasant enough when foxes will run over them, but they generally prefer to turn upwards towards Snelston.

It may be noted here that water is not a large ingredient in the fencing of Derbyshire. Indeed, beyond four or five small tributaries of the Dove, few opportunities of testing the powers of a water jumper are to be met with : though, as is the case in most countries where brooks are seldom encountered, there is often a disproportionate amount of difficulty and disaster whenever the real occasion offers. These few streams drain the country by running southward, at right angles, into the Dove—the Somershall brook taking the westernmost valley, the Saperton Brook (running from Cubley to Foston) the next. After these we meet with the Longford, or Sutton Brook (emptying itself by Egginton) with another from Radborn and Dalbury joining the main stream at about the same spot. These, with the stream draining the Kedlaston district into the Derwent by

Derby, are the only brooks giving a chance of a wetting.

To continue with the meets and coverts of Tuesday, we have Brailsford and Mercaston—half way on the main road between Ashbourne and Derby—as more often belonging to that day than Thursday. Brailsford has some eight acres of strong gorse, full of foxes. Mercaston is for Breward's Carr and Ravensdale Park, which are coverts of wild natural wood with an undergrowth of fern; and nearer Ashbourne we come to the Ednaston coverts, at one time particularly good. In the north-west corner of the country, and close to Ashbourne itself is Bradley—the burial-place of Old Meynell, of Billesdon Coplow fame:

> Talk of horses and hounds and system of Kennel,
> Give me Leicestershire nags and the hounds of Old Meynell.

Hard by is the Limekilns, close up to the Hills, for which foxes are very prone to set their heads when disturbed. It has happened more than once that, quite late in the afternoon, hounds have been carried even over the high summit of Atlow Winn—to the great distress of horses and men. Dropping south of this Ashbourne-and-Derby road, we find a noted hunting-ground in Shirley Park, a wild stretch of wood and heather. Shirley Park contains no house, but Osmaston Manor was built close by, by the late Mr. Wright, who maintained Shirley Park as a great nursery for foxes. And hounds are advertised to meet at either place. Westward of this is Snelston (Mr. J. Harrison's), with its surrounding copses and plantations, where the needed animal is always to be found;

and directly south is Cubley—or, as it often appears on the cards, Cubley Toll-gate, and its small but certain gorse.

At no great distance from this is Bentley Carr, a gorse and plantation jungle—at present rather out of repair; and eastward still we get back into the centre of the Derbyshire country, and to Longford (already mentioned). Two or three miles below Longford is Barton Park, where Mr. F. Bradshaw (a staunch friend to the Hunt) has a capital little gorse. At Saperton is a strong covert in the shape of a large square plantation; and, nearer still to the River Dove, is Foston Hall with its coverts. Three miles west of Foston lies Lord Vernon's place at Sudbury—whose fine old Hall was at one time the residence of the Dowager Queen Adelaide. The wide deer parks are, by Lord Vernon's courtesy, at disposal for exercise of the Meynell hounds and horses; and the pack is daily walked out among the deer (by no means a small or useless privilege). For the Kennels are only separated from the Park by the high road; and lie about one mile from the village, and two from the station of Sudbury. Almost within sound of horn from the Kennels, on the north, is Sudbury Coppice, of oak and underwood, and conveniently quartered by its cross rides. In the Park itself there are also some small spinnies. Still more to the westward, Lord Waterpark has made an excellent blackthorn covert in the meadows adjoining the Dove—his seat at *Doveridge* being a frequent fixture. He has other coverts, too, above the House, which extend to within a short distance of Eaton Wood, which is again a meet. Eaton Wood itself is a large stretch of timber on the hillside overlooking the Dove, and is a sure find. Here, by the way, is a heronry; and it is curious, when spring-hunting is still going on, to look upward at the outstretched limbs of the herons, as they try in vain to accommodate their length of leg to their narrow nests. Wardly Coppice, a wood of some ten acres, is close to Eaton Wood; and with it we have nearly exhausted the Derbyshire portion of the Meynell country.

South of the River Dove is, as we have already observed, the Staffordshire half of the Meynell country, and it is hunted on Mondays and Saturdays. Hitherto the Burton neighbourhood has been chosen for Mondays, the Uttoxeter and Chartley side for Saturdays. In future, however (in order to suit the convenience of a large number of subscribers in and around Burton), it is intended to reverse the two days. For present purposes we will retain the old denomination, and call the Burton side their Monday country.

Briefly, then, the main features of the territory below the Dove are the two great woodlands known as Bagot's Park and the Forest Banks (or Needwood Forest)—the two running into each other and covering many miles of ground. Bagot Park, the property of Lord Bagot, but containing no residence, is on the south bank of the Dove, is celebrated for its grand timber, and contains, besides other large coverts, no less than fifteen hundred acres of wood in one piece. Here, too, is a large heronry. Forest Banks stretch round southwards over the whole centre of the country below the river—almost the entire distance between

Burton-on-Trent and Bagot Park being comprised in Needwood Forest. This Forest is, of course, nowadays all enclosed; but many large woods remain, the intervals being filled with light plough and rough grass—with foxes abundant everywhere. Monday, as hitherto employed, may be taken roughly as relating to that part of the country which lies east of the main road from Sudbury to Lichfield—the Meynell kingdom of course being understood to stop short at the river Trent, where the road in question reaches it. Among the leading meets for this section of the woodlands are the New Inn (about six miles from Sudbury, and three or four from Burton-on-Trent), Rolleston (Sir Tonman Moseley's), and Anslow Village. And the woods for them are those of Rolleston, a large wood called the Hen Hurst, Needwood House Coverts, Brakenhurst Wood, the Hoar Cross Coverts, and the various strongholds pertaining to Birkley Lodge, Yoxall Lodge, and Hollybush Hall. South of these again, are Wichnor Park (Mr. Levitt's) and Dunstall Hall (Sir J. Hardy's). And all but the two last-named form part of the old Needwood Forest.

East of the Trent, beyond Burton, the Meynell have a strip of country adjoining the Atherstone—rough but light plough, hilly and broken by coal digging, but by no means bad scenting or useless for hound-work. It should be observed—somewhat in falsification of a previous remark—that the county of Derbyshire claims this corner, which is comprised within the boundary points of Calke Abbey and Melbourne on the East—Hartshorn, Bretby Hall, and Lullington on the south. At the two former places the Meynell touches Lord Ferrers' country—Staunton Harrold (the Master's residence) being quite contiguous. Gorsty Lees (a large wood) Draketon, Bretby Park, and Foremark, are all meets and good coverts; while Walton-on-Trent is the fixture for Catton and Lullington.

On a Saturday the Meynell are in their Sudbury or South West country — consisting chiefly of Bagot Park and part of the Forest Banks, the Blithebury Coverts, Lord Bagot's Coverts round Blithfield and the Kingston Woods, stretching west almost as far as Lord Shrewsbury's place at Ingestre—each of these names representing a meet. West still of Bagot Park and Uttoxeter is Chartley Park, a wild grassy upland plain, with large woods and a good gorse called Fradswell Heath—or *The* Heath. Then there is Loxley Park and its coverts near Uttoxeter, Carry Coppice, Gratwick Wood, and Hand Learson Wood, and the whole comprise a fine rough woodland country. Chartley Park, with Chillingham, is one of the only places where the wild breed of old English cattle still remains. Bramshill, in the corner west of Uttoxeter and above Phillips' Gorse is again a very good grass country extending by Checkley towards Tean into the woody part of the North Stafford country, and all this southern district is excellent for hounds, if not delightful for horsemen.

THE BICESTER AND WARDEN HILL HUNT.*

OF all the good grass countries of England, none is so easily accessible from London as the Bicester, and none is better provided with convenient quarters. Two hours' journey will land you at the towns of Bicester, Buckingham, Brackley, or Banbury, all of which are excellent bases from which to hunt with the pack in question, and offer a variety of choice besides. Of these, Bicester is undoubtedly the most central, being as near the middle of the country as a country so straggling and tortuous can be said to have a middle. It is only some three miles from the main Kennels, at Stratton Audley; commands all four days of the home pack, and has its Wednesdays with the Heythrop or Duke of Grafton, and its Fridays with the Duke or South Oxfordshire, to fill up the week—besides the opportunity, if desired, of a weekly gallop with the Baron's staghounds. Many Oxonians keep their horses at Bicester, or even hire there—Oxford itself being just outside the country, and commanding its best meets only by rail. Buckingham has the packs

---

* *Vide* "Stanford's Large Scale Map," Sheet 16; also, "Hobson's Foxhunting Atlas."

of Mr. Selby Lowndes and the Duke of Grafton, to occupy spare days: Brackley and Banbury have the Duke, the Warwickshire and the Heythrop to fall back upon, when the pack they subscribe to is not in the field.

The Bicester hunting days are professedly three in the week. Practically they are four—Monday being always added to the card by Lord Valentia, the present master. The other days are Tuesday, Thursday, and Saturday; and the distribution is as follows:

Monday is, perhaps four times out of nine, devoted to the Oxford Woodlands, four times more to the Tingewick Woods, and on the odd occasion to the lower Northamptonshire country, about Farthinghoe or Thenford—of all which sections we shall have more to say anon. For the moment it will answer the purpose to remark that Monday may be spent in very happy fashion,—or it may be otherwise. Tuesday is the day for the Bicester Flat—as the country near that town is called. Thursday is for the Claydon Woods and the Aylesbury Vale; and Saturday for the upper country, where it runs into Northamptonshire above Banbury.

Taking your map in hand, you cannot but remark upon the wonderful eccentricity of outline displayed in the boundaries of the Bicester country. Starting from near Oxford on the south, it wriggles a sinuous course among the neighbouring Hunts, as if all had combined to squeeze it out of existence. Its chief bulk is its southern portion, where the Heythrop support it on the west, the South Oxfordshire are at

The Bicester and Warden Hill Hunt.

its base, the Whaddon Chase (better known as Mr. Selby Lowndes') touch its eastern flank, and the Duke of Grafton's pinch it into a neck on the north east. Above this it has an attenuated existence between the Warwickshire and the Duke, till it reaches the Pytchley at Badby. The river Cherwell on the east, where it runs from Banbury to Oxford, is one of the few natural boundaries that give any excuse for the configuration of the country. Above Banbury, on the same side, the high road pointing to Coventry is accepted as the march, till we get north of Fenny Compton. For its other boundaries it is, in the absence of any noticeable landmarks, sufficient to say that Mr. Stanford's colouring has been laid on correctly, according to the outline accepted by the Hunt. The natives complain that at certain periods in recent history they have suffered some loss of territory, both in the far north and in the extreme south. For, until late years the Bicester used to hunt right up to Shuckburgh and Ladbrooke, where the Warwickshire now reign supreme; while on the south they held more of the Oxford woodlands, and even dipped below the river Thame as far as Ricot. At that time the country required no less than three sets of Kennels, to allow of its whole length (some forty miles) being properly worked. Thus, the main Kennels were at Bainton, there were rougher lodgings for hounds at Rycote in the far south, and Chipping Warden in the north. At the present day the main Kennels are at Stratton Audley, the southern ones have been abolished as unnecessary; and Thorpe Mandeville has been chosen to take the place of Chipping Warden. For

P

every other Saturday hounds are now sent overnight to Thorpe Mandeville; and, after hunting all day on Northamptonshire soil, have to make their way homewards across country—often a journey of terrible length.

The Bicester country is, as a rule, excellent for hunting and delightful for riding. In most parts it carries a good scent; and nowhere is it too formidable to cross. A good horseman on a fair animal will find himself at home everywhere; and as a school for man or horse there is no better. For the fences are everywhere negotiable; and, while quite sufficient to induce a horse to rise vigorously, may be taken at almost any point, in the full confidence that you see the worst and are venturing nothing impracticable. In the Vale of Aylesbury a certain number of, not too difficult, doubles are to be met with: and it is as well that you and your horse should be prepared to encounter them —and be able, also, to face the frequent brooks. Otherwise the Bicester country may be set down as a very artless one; and you should be able to get over it comfortably, even if you cannot flatter yourself that temperament and teaching have given you a claim to the highest honours of horsemanship. Your stud should, as elsewhere, be made up of as good material, as your purse, or prospects, seem fairly to allow. But, though the country boasts of a most liberal proportion of grass, it can scarcely be said to require—except in the most chosen, and most trying, northern corner—a class of cattle so rare and so expensive as the oxers of the Pytchley and the Quorn demand. A *stout* horse is essentially necessary; for the distances are long;

The Bicester and Warden Hill Hunt.

and the woods and the Vale often ride distressingly deep.

Another great point in favour of the Bicester country is the plenitude of foxes throughout its length. Blank days are altogether unheard of; and foxes are readily found as required. Possessing every requisite for sport in its pleasantest form, and every advantage of easy accessibility (with the best of accommodation to hand at any of the quarters named), it should be especially tempting in the eyes of hunting-men, who, making London their chief base, are yet willing to go far enough afield to escape the sphere of suburban packs.

It is often possible to reach the Bicester from London after an early breakfast, and to return for dinner. For this purpose you would probably fix upon Leighton, or Bletchley, on the L. & N. W. Railway, for your horses to stand. Both these places are a few miles outside the eastern limits of the Bicester; but command many of their best meets. And either can be attained within an hour and a half, from Euston-square. And Bicester itself admits of a morning journey—*every* hunting day if you will leave Town by 7.15 a.m.—on some few occasions if you do not start till 9.

Before taking the days of hunting in order, a better general idea of the country will be gathered by noting its leading features as follows: Its head and neck, as comprised in the many-angled strip above Banbury, and nearly to Daventry, is Northamptonshire quite in its orthodox sense—mostly grass, with fences often very formidable, and here and there a bottom that is scarcely to be jumped. The centre of the country is formed by the Bicester Flat: separated on the east from the beautiful Aylesbury Vale by the Claydon Woods. The Vale runs down the whole of the south-east of the country: and hitherto the Baron has run the stag over it on the same day as the Bicester have been pursuing the fox. It is rumoured, however, that some arrangement may be arrived at by which Thursday may find the one animal or the other at peace. Light plough runs down the western edge; and the deep Oxford woodlands fringe the south.

With these two sets of woods, besides those of Tingewick, on the north-east, the Bicester justly lay claim to as good woodlands as are to be found within the bounds of any hunt. Well foxed, and with the best of their country near some of the largest, they form a grand foundation upon which to build high-class sport. The Claydon Woods occupy every Thursday during the winter, till March—after which, in deference to the wishes of the neighbouring farmers, the field are bidden to where their passage is likely to do less damage than over the rich pastures of the Vale. The Oxford Woods, which for the most part come under the denomination of The Quarters, are to a great extent neutral with the South Oxfordshire. On one side (that of Brill) they have, as we shall see presently, a capital country. The Tingewick Woods stand about one day a fortnight; and have fair grass on every side. All these, being grown on stiffest clay, become very deep in winter; and harden to such an extent in summer that it is difficult to ride in them with hounds until after the autumn rains. Thus, strange as it may seem, they are not available for cub-hunting; and the Claydon Woods are seldom entered before October.

Monday, then, being almost always occupied either in the Oxford Woodlands or the Tingewick Woods, we may get on to those coverts, and take them more in detail. The Oxford Woodlands, or The Quarters, cover an immense area on the east of Oxford. The whole were at one time the privilege and perquisite of the Bicester Hunt; but at various times their boundaries have suffered—till now it is difficult to define distinctly where the right of Bicester ends, that of the South Oxfordshire begins, and where a mutual interest exists. Briefly, the present boundary lines run thus. Of the Quarters proper, Hell Copse and York Woods belong to the Bicester, though dovetailed into the South Oxfordshire Woods of Holton, Waterperry, Shabbington and Oakley. Horton Wood is the right of the Bicester until Christmas, when it goes into the hands of the South Oxfordshire. Staunton Great Wood, Staunton Little Wood and Holly Copse, running into each other, are all neutral between the two packs.

A rough deep country is this district of The Quarters. Few gentlemen's residences adorn the neighbourhood. The land round and between the woods is of a poor, undrained, description, though carrying a fair scent, especially on the borders of Ott Moor, where the sluggish Ray is ever flooding the country. Very bad indeed is the riding hereabout; but should hounds go eastward, towards Brill and the Vale, they soon get into the finest of the country. Islip Town-End is the meet for this part—Prattle Wood, on the borders of the neutral territory being generally drawn, before proceeding into The Quarters. From Menmarsh Guide Post they go at once into The Quarters; Horton Common or Village is for Horton Wood and The Quarters; Boarstall Tower and Oakley point to Hornage Copse and Boarstall, with The Quarters to follow. Whitecross Green is for the wood of that name; and at the top of this portion of the Monday country is Arncott, with Arncott Great and Little Wood, Piddington Wood and Boarstall Wood to draw.

The Tingewick Woods, on the north-east, supply ground for most of the Mondays not spent in the Oxford Woods—though hounds are also very frequently in them on a Tuesday—Stratton Audley and other Tuesday meets being no distance away. These are very strong coverts, with deep rides and much rushy undergrowth; and take a great deal of drawing. They are, fortunately, full of foxes—and of foxes that will go straight and far. The group is composed of Tingewick Great Wood, West Wood, Round Wood, Gawcott Wood, and Stocking Wood—with a beautiful grass country on the south and east, to the Claydons, while north and west is light plough.

Turning now to Tuesday, which is always given to the Bicester Flat—we have Langford Lane, or Gravenhill Wood, for the meet nearest the town of Bicester. The wood is a large covert on the top of a hill, very difficult to get away from with hounds; and whenever a run comes off there is sure to be a large body of pursuers left behind. From here they may run south-

The Bicester and Warden Hill Hunt.

ward over the low meadow country swamped by the Ray; or, again, they may take a line north or west over light plough—perhaps reaching Middleton Park, a great stronghold. This strip of plough up the western border is nearly all the arable that the Bicester Country contains; and it is so narrow that a fox very soon travels off it. It should be added, too, that the "Steam Cultivator" has no place in this district, and the soil is consequently only thinly turned.

Middleton Park is another favourite meet for Oxford. The Park (the seat of Lord Jersey) is very extensive, is thick with foxes and tempts them to cling to its limits, till too hot to hold them. Stoke Lyne (more generally put on the cards as Stoke) is in the midst of the light plough, and has some very holding, and well-preserved, coverts belonging to Sir Thomas Peyton—whose place, Swift's House, stands among them. Next, to the north, and on the same description of soil, is Tusmore, Lord Effingham's house and Park—the property adjoining that of Stoke, and equally well-stored with foxes. Shelswell (Mr. Harrison's) has several very good coverts, is situated on the borders of the grass, and is invaluable to the Hunt. No place in the Bicester country lies better for hunting than Shelswell (or Stratton Pasture, as this part is often termed)—its outside coverts running up towards the Tingewick Woods, with the Claydons imminent beyond. The Kennels at Stratton Audley (three miles from Bicester) stand in capital country. About a mile and a half away is a large, and famous, gorse covert—known as Poodle Gorse—surrounded by strongly fenced grass: and a fox from here is very likely to cross Pounden Hill into the Claydons. At Caversfield are coverts, and there is another very good gorse at Cotmore—the meet being Skimmingdish Gate or, perhaps, Bicester Windmill. Below Bicester, Weston-on-the-Green is in very deep, wet, ground. It has three good woods, however, viz., Weston Wood, Park Copse, and Warnhoof—foxes are plentiful, and leave quickly, without hanging. And this brings us to Bletchington Park, Lord Valentia's residence, and Kirtlington (Sir H. Dashwood's)—the outside meets of this part of the country—the Cherwell running just below and dividing the Bicester from the Heythrop. Bletchington has Busby's Spinney and Harris' Gorse; the Park Coverts and even the gardens of Kirtlington always hold foxes.

Of the four Thursdays in a month, the Bicester employ quite three in the Claydon Woods—for which Edgcott Village, Charndon Common, Steeple Claydon Claydon Park, Finemoor Hill, and Grendon are in turn the meets. For the remaining Thursday the changes are rung between the three fixtures of Ham Green, Waddesdon Cross Roads, and Chilton. The above woods are chiefly of stunted oak, with a strong undergrowth of briar and rushes—Grendon Wood in particular being one of the most difficult woods conceivable for hounds to draw. Foxes but seldom make their earth, or breed, in the damp clay of these great woodlands; but prefer to lay up their progeny outside—resorting to the woods when the corn is off the fields, or when winter drives them in for shelter. At any rate, there are always plenty to be found when hounds

The Bicester and Warden Hill Hunt. 195

are in covert; and no sooner is one on foot than others crop up at once. Thus it is essentially necessary that hounds should be very even in their work, and carry a good head—or to a certainty they will quickly change foxes. The rides are desperately deep and holding; and the man who goes through them with hounds will frequently send his horse home at two o'clock more than half tired—though he may never have jumped a fence, or even been out of covert. But once outside, you embark on a country that fully justifies the Bicester men in their rapturous eulogies on the merits of the Claydon Woods. There is a splendid grass country on every side—whether you gallop to Goddington Gorse or the Tingewick Woods—or, on the other side, over Muswell Hill, or to Blackgrove Gorse —or, again, a different direction, to The Quarters—or, another line still (nor by any means the worst) to Gravenhill, near Bicester.

The woods mostly belong to Sir Harry Verney, of Claydon Park, a true fox preserver (a preserver, indeed, of any kind of wild animal. It was in one of his coverts that hounds killed a badger last autumn). The Duke of Leeds owns one of the largest woods, Finemoor Hill; and Grendon Wood belongs to the Pigotts of Doddershall, an old Bucks family. All the country round the Claydons is good scenting, and fair and pleasant to ride over—though very deep indeed in mid winter; the woodland foxes of course are stout; and they travel long distances before they die.

Of the three Thursday meets outside the woods, Ham Green is close to the edge; and the Duke of Buckingham's coverts at Wootton (Gipsy Bottom,

New Wood, The Grove) are the usual draw.* Very sporting coverts they are; and frequently act as the halfway house for a good travelling fox on his way between the Oxford Woodlands and the Claydons. Chilton, near Thame, overlooking the Aylesbury Vale, is always the Bicester meet for their opening Thursday; and is a very popular rendezvous—tempting the presence of many of the South Oxfordshire Hunt, a great number of Oxonians, and a strong force of the Baron's men. The first draw is generally told off for Nottley Abbey (where Squire Reynolds always finds a fox or two)—on the borders of the Old Berkeley and the South Oxfordshire. From here the Bicester last year ran a very long point, over the flints and through roughest woods, to West Wycombe. Another very favourite covert—though scarcely so good a certainty—is Chearsley Firs, which stands by the side of a brook just big enough to tempt, and always provocative of lavish grief. From here to the Claydons or the Wootton Coverts is a very pretty gallop — the latter line probably taking hounds by way of Ashenden, where Baron Ferdinand de Rothschild a few years ago bought a charming property from the Duke of Marlborough, is now building a house, and has some well-preserved little coverts—the chief of them called the Decoy. Waddesdon Cross Roads (four miles from Aylesbury) is in the best of the grass. The fences here are, perhaps, more intricate than in the rest of the

---

* Tithenhall Wood, Ham Wood, and Oring Hill, close to the fixture and between Wootton and the Claydon Woods, should be added.

The Bicester and Warden Hill Hunt.

Bicester country—doubles being very frequent, though none of them are strongly built. Coverts for this meet are none too plentiful; though Blackgrove Gorse, on Sir Astley Cooper's property, is a sure find; and a recently-made covert on Mr. Lee's Hartwell estate is very promising. The Bicester here join the Whaddon Chase (Mr. Selby Lowndes'); and so have frequently to fall back for a second draw on the Wootton Coverts, the Claydons or Chearsley. As has been already pointed out, the fact of the staghounds choosing Thursday for their day of meeting—instead of Monday, as in the time of the late Baron Meyer de Rothschild—leads to a good deal of inconvenience to farmers and field; and it is eminently desirable that a better arrangement should be established.

Saturday with the Bicester is in the northern length of their country, past and beyond Banbury. The meets of Aynho Park, Souldern Gate, Croughton, The Barley Mow, Finmere, Tusmore Park, and Baynard's Green, with Astrop, and Thenford (the two last being also occasional Monday meets), are all considered within reach of kennels, and hounds accordingly go to them by road on the morning of hunting. But for Helidon, Byfield, Fenny Compton Wharf, Prior's Marston, Lower Boddington, Trafford Bridge, and Thorp Mandeville, the pack has to be sent overnight to Kennels at the last-named place—this happening every alternate week. The former places of meeting are very numerously attended, being within easy reach of Banbury, Brackley, and Bicester, and there are plenty of foxes in the area embraced within these three points — though it is rather a poor scenting country, of light plough, and with fences so small that the field are ever on the backs of hounds. Aynho Park (Mr. Cartwright's) is a most useful place for cub-hunting; as is also Tusmore Park (Lord Effingham's), and Evenley Park, which is generally the first draw from the Barley Mow (close to Brackley, and on the borders of the Duke of Grafton's Hunt). The *entente cordiale*, by the way, between the Bicester and the Duke of Grafton's Hunt is so complete that, for the border meets of either the neighbouring territory is always "stopped" by the other. Fritwell gorse is always called upon from Souldern Gate and Baynard's Green, and is a most reliable covert. The Finmere and Mixbury plantations are much favoured by foxes; and often lead to a gallop to Tingewick, or tempt a run thence. Astrop and Thenford are, as above mentioned, occasionally kept over for a Monday—should the Saturday district appear to afford it. The former is the property of Sir William Brown, and contains both coverts and foxes—for Rosamond's Bower is a sure find, while Willifers gives another excellent chance for brook-jumpers, the stream being close to the covert, and just of enticing width. At Thenford the Laurels and Gorse are certainties, as are the neighbouring coverts belonging to the Farthingho estates, and Cockley Brake. The Northamptonshire country in the extreme north is short of coverts; at Helidon there are only spinnies; at Byfield there is a covert called Griffin Gorse, celebrated for good foxes, though not a certain find; at Fenny Compton four spinnies; at Priors Marston a small, and not very certain gorse; at Boddington a good covert, Boddington Hill is to be depended on; near Trafford Bridge are some good coverts, Warden Hill is a stronghold, with Red Hill Wood, Grange Wood, besides some coverts at an outlying property of Lord Valentia's. Eydon has a good gorse and the laurels round the house are a sure find; at Thorpe Mandeville is Geff's Gorse. This is all a fine upland country, chiefly grass and all very strongly enclosed. It carries a very good scent, is wild, with few people about in the fields, and wants a better horse to cross it than any other part of the Bicester country.

From what has been said it will be gathered that the Bicester are everywhere exceptionally well off for foxes, and—save in two small corners, where the want is already being rectified, for coverts also. It should be added—as a point conducing in no slight degree to the comfort of hunting in a country—that all the roads have smooth turf sides, along which you may canter to covert at best pace: and, every road being enclosed, there is no delay occasioned by having to open a lot of gates—as is the case in many parts of the Midlands.

THE HEYTHROP.*

THE Heythrop is another varied and pleasant Country in the Oxford Circuit. It seldom happens but that hounds can run hard over one part of it or another—whether across the wolds and stonewalls, when rain enough has fallen to make scent cling to the light plough—or, in dryer weather, along the grassy vales which cross its face in many directions. And when there *is* a scent on the wolds, the Heythrop bitches can often leave their field behind them. The coverts are small, hounds generally get away close to their fox, and have frequently raced right away from horses. For they can fly the stonewalls in their stride, carrying as broad a head as across the field—nor dwelling a second to bring the gallopers on to their backs. Pretty riding, too, is this stonewall country—never a snare in the fence, and the ground always light and sound going. You might not care to ride over stone walls *every* day—but you are not called upon to do this with the Heythrop—for it is seldom more than twice in the week that they cross the wolds. A loose stone-

---

* *Vide* Stanford's Large Scale Map, Sheet 15; also "Hobson's Foxhunting Atlas."

wall is in itself a pleasurable, and encouraging leap. Horses can make no mistake, and seldom fail to jump it safely and well. Even should they be a little careless, the wall rarely takes advantage of them—but allows its upper story to crumble quietly before the onslaught. There being no ditch on either side, you can give your horse full leisure with a view to his jumping off his own spot and landing as he chooses. In fact, you may ride a fair horse over a five-foot wall, with considerably less tremor than, with most of us, is involved in a venture against four of stiff timber—especially if, in the latter case, a tolerably wide ditch (away from you) be given in. One of the few objections to stonewall jumping will be found in the stiffness of back and neck, consequent on the first day or two of essay. An old hunter accustomed to them will get so near to a wall that he rises almost perpendicularly, and—*mutatis mutandis* as to head and tail—descends almost vertically on the other side. To accommodate yourself to this form of calisthenics, your body is at one moment lying along his neck, and at the next it must be thrown back on to the crupper—your spinal cord being called upon to perform the hinge-action required. Let this performance be executed fifty-four times in a single day (as an old Oxonian assures us occurred to him when at college)—and small wonder if a certain degree of torturing stiffness is your lot on the next. Granting you no longer possess Oxonian youth—and the faculty of going some distance out of your way for the sake of a jump—you must yet in a stonewall country often find yourself an extraordinary number of times in the air, with none of Oxonian suppleness of backbone to help you through your allotted task.

The Heythrop vales are nice sound grass, somewhat deep in wet weather, and in themselves rather narrow and limited. But foxes are always fond of running a valley rather than crossing it; and so the turf lowlands are generally made the most of: and they carry a capital scent. Their fences are fair stake-and-bounds to be taken at a fly, and as a rule are well within the compass of a hunter. Besides these two descriptions of ground, the Heythrop have one large broken woodland, known as Whichwood Forest, and various pieces of rough inferior country, here and there — more particularly down their eastern boundary.

The Heythrop country lies north-west of the town of Oxford—having the Old Berkshire and the Vale of White Horse on the south, the Cotswold and North Cotswold on the west, the Warwickshire on the north, and the Bicester on the east. The river Charwell marks the eastern boundary—the others as coloured on Stanford's map (with no other distinctive natural features to denote the limits of the country), except that the southernmost corner, from Witney and Eynsham downwards, should have borne a neutral tint, as it is held in common by the Heythrop and the Old Berkshire.

Oxford itself stands a little wide from the best meets of the Hunt, as it does from those of the Bicester. In fact, there is very little good country in the immediate neighbourhood of Oxford—though you may get lots of excellent hunting by riding some distance to covert. The Oxonian in good credit thinks a good deal less of having a second hack on the road (his hunter having gone on overnight) than we should who hunt elsewhere. There is a choice of four packs at Oxford, and it is not more than an hour and three-quarters from London. Still, few men fix upon Oxford as a hunting quarter, without having been drawn into allegiance with Alma Mater, professedly for more serious ties. Chipping Norton (about three hours and a-quarter from Paddington) is not far from the centre of the Heythrop country; and accommodation, sufficient if not extensive, is there to be had, with the option of days with the two Cotswold packs and the Warwickshire, and occasionally with the Vale of White Horse and the Old Berkshire. Thus Chipping Norton (where, moreover, the Kennels are situated) may be written a capital hunting-base—in many respects equal to its neighbour Banbury (which we have already noticed under the head of the Bicester). As to horses, it is essentially necessary they should be speedy. Large horses you do not want; but they should be wiry, strong, stout, and quick.

The Heythrop hunt four days a week—besides a frequent bye-day, which the country, being everywhere thickly stocked with foxes, well affords. These four days are Monday, Wednesday, Friday, and Saturday; and are regulated as follows—Monday is generally within close range of Chipping Norton, and up to the Warwickshire border; Wednesday is fixed in alternate weeks for Oxfordshire or Gloucestershire, with once every other month in Tar Wood—in the corner neutral with the Old Berkshire; Friday is on the Cotswold side, and takes in almost all the stonewall country—with, of course, its intersecting vales; and Saturday comes near Oxford, into a region where woods are frequent and deep clay prevalent.

The Monday meets are only four in number—viz., Heythrop (the residence of the present Master, Mr. Albert Brassey), Chapel House, Pomfret Castle, and Boulter's Barn. This limited portion of their territory is an undulating description of country, plough and grass mixed—with a considerable proportion of vale. There is good ground round Heythorp, where there are quite ten or a dozen nice coverts, after working which, hounds are taken on to Great Tew. Here there are many small plantations, leading round to each other. Foxes, consequently, are apt to keep within the home confines. Chapel House has good gorse coverts; after which hounds would probably go on to draw the large withy-bed at Salford, and eventually all the gorse and brier coverts at Addlestrop (itself sometimes a Wednesday meet). Pomfret Castle has Badger's Gorse close by, with Swerford Heath two fields away; and Great Tew to fall back upon in the afternoon. From Boulter's Barn they draw Sarsgrove —a fine wood of Lord Ducie's; and then get on to another equally good covert at Churchill Heath.

Of their Wednesday country the portion in Oxfordshire is by no means their best. It is a big rough, chiefly upland, country—some of it plough, some grass—the fences fair, but the ground by no means favourable for scent. The meets are Deddington—for Aynho Spinnies; North Aston for Deane Hill Gorse, and Steeple Aston Gardens—whence they may draw on to Barton, or back to the wood of Worton Heath, near Ledwell. And the meet of Ledwell Village may be taken as intended for the same coverts in reverse order. Barton Gates has the coverts of Barton, with Rousham Spinnies and Tackley Heath and Wood, to follow.

The Wednesday fixtures held in Gloucestershire mostly point, on the other hand, to stiff grass vale. They are Bruern Abbey, where there are large coverts; Gawcombe, with two fine woods facing a beautiful valley which stretches right up to the Kennels at Chipping Norton; or they proffer another equally good line, if a fox crosses back over the brow and dips down for Slaughter or Bourton-on-the-Water. Indeed, the Slaughter Vale is, perhaps, the most favourite strip of the whole of the Heythrop country. From Addlestrop, with Oddington Ashes, you are also likely to find yourself in the Gawcombe Vale. Bradwell Grove is regularly advertised for the first Wednesday in each month. There is a large covert near the house, with Jolley's Gorse afterwards: and here you get on to the stone wall country, and may not see a hedge all day. From Burford you have Windrush Gorse, to be followed by Jolley's Gorse and Westwell Gorse. These last two meets are quite for a wold country—where the coverts are small, the walls all rideable, and the pace often tremendous. Tar Wood, in the corner below the railway at South Leigh is held in alternate months by the Heythrop and the Old Berkshire: and is always hunted by the former on a Wednesday. It is a deep wood, with heavy going on both sides.

Most of the Fridays are also spent on the wolds—the meets ranging up the west of the Heythrop kingdom, and the country partaking much of the character of the Cotswolds adjoining. Cheltenham is generally well represented on this side. From Farmington Grove and New Barn—the two extreme meets on the south-west—hounds will draw the Wood, and the Sherborne. From Barrington Park they have Windrush Gorse, with Westwell Poor's Lots and the Wood of Tangley for the afternoon. When, however Barrington *Inn* is advertised, it more often means that Westwell Gorse will be first drawn, and Sherborne kept for a second fox. Bourton-on-the-Water is for Lord Redesdale's Gorse. Tangley has quite a day's work in itself—being possessed of numerous plantations in hollows leading from one to the other : but sometimes Rissington Spinnies are reached later in the day, with the prospect of a run over a fine grass vale. Eyford is also among the walls, though there is a frequent chance of gettting to Slaughter Copse and Vale as the day progresses. Longboro', for variety, is all vale in the morning, with Sezincote and the wolds in the afternoon. Bourton-on-the-Hill, in the far north-east, has a large wood on its hill : after which Batsford Park is generally reached, and a stiff country entered.

Saturday is devoted to a wide tract on the southeast, Whichwood Forest and Blenheim Park being the two leading features. Whichwood Forest, though now disforested in the technical sense of the term, still covers an immense area below Charlbury; and contains as much as a thousand acres of wood in one piece—besides numerous smaller woods almost touching each other, and a huge acreage of tree stumps and uncultivated ground. It *ought to be a* grand place for cub-hunting; but hounds are not allowed in it till later in the autumn—and the same remark applies to Blenheim. Thus, all the cub-hunting of the Heythrop has to be done in the smaller coverts. Cornbury Park is the meet for Whichwood Forest proper; Shipton Barrow for a gorse near, and for the coverts at the upper edge of the Forest. Wilcot is for the Wilcot Spinnies and Chase Woods, after which the rest of the day may be spent in Stockley Wood. Eynsham is in the deepest, most stiffly fenced, and most holding, part of the country, and has Cogg's Wood previous to a move on to Blenheim. The latter is a mass of large woods, from which foxes seldom travel far—though last season a good run thence was put on record. Dean Cross Roads, not far from Charlbury, is a good meet, with a fine vale for some three miles round—Dean Grove being the draw. After this, hounds have to fall back upon Dytchley Woods. Sturges Castle is for Tackley Heath, Rousham Spinnies, and Barton—all amid plough and heavy going. Kiddington Gate points to the same sort of country—indeed, all up the side of the Charwell, may be set down as the worst ground in the Hunt. From Kiddington the order is generally for Glympton Heath (a large rough gorse), with Kiddington Wood and Glympton Wood to fill up the day.

THE OLD BERKSHIRE.*

SOUTH-WEST of the town of Oxford is the very sporting Country of the Old Berkshire. Some forty years ago the Vale of White Horse and the Old Berkshire were one Hunt—under the latter denomination. But the extent of ground being considered too wide for a single pack, the western portion—from Cirencester and Malmesbury, to the River Cole, and (north of the Thames) nearly to Bampton—was told off as a separate province, and carried with it the title of the Vale of White Horse (though the site of that ancient configuration and rite really is still in the Old Berkshire as it now remains).

The outlines of the present Old Berkshire Country follow very approximately the marks suggested by hill and water. High downs separate it on the south from the Craven; the River Cole forms its western boundary; and—with the exception of a turn over the river—into the Heythrop kingdom as far as Witney on the north, and again as far as Nuneham Park into the South Oxfordshire on the east—the Thames defines it on the remaining sides. Any little

---

* Vide " Stanford's Large Scale Railway Map," Sheet 15; and "Hobson's Foxhunting Atlas."

The Old Berkshire.

eccentricities of boundary may be taken as accurately set down on Mr. Stanford's Map—except that the extreme south-west corner should extend another mile and a half, to include Hinton, &c.

The pith of the Old Berkshire consists in its Vale. Practically it has two vales—the one of the Thames, the other of its tributary the Rosey; and it is the valley of the Rosey that is known, and widely known, as the Berkshire Vale. Limited in extent it may be; but it is enough to form the foundation and whole of one excellent day in the week, while aiding and contributing frequently to other two. Whether in this Vale, or elsewhere, the Old Berkshire is with slight exception an excellent country for houndwork. Foxes are found everywhere in abundance: and almost everywhere the scenting properties of the soil are six-to-four against them. Treadwell—many years ago—scored higher with the Quorn than any of his numerous predecessors; but fallacious and odious as is, usually, the comparison of kills numbered, it is pardonable to put on record that with the Old Berkshire last season he brought fifty-seven brace of foxes to hand—while hunting only three days a week! Apart from the old huntsman's merits, it must be obvious that the country is stocked with foxes in an exceptional degree. On every side they are carefully nurtured and cared for: and, not only are they always to be found when wanted, but, once afoot, they must go for their lives—with a good scent—and hounds unhampered by a swollen field. For, except on a few days, fixed for instance, for Challow and neighbourhood—when the Great Western brings passengers from east and west, from

Oxford or from the Duke of Beaufort's, and from the Vale of White Horse, there is seldom anything approaching to a large field : and hounds have such a chance as they do not often get elsewhere. With almost a plethora of foxes it is not astonishing that many of them lie out in the open throughout the winter. Thus it never does to be coffeehousing or loitering behind when the old Berkshire hounds are on the move, even between covert and covert. For at any moment information may be brought of an outlying fox; the pack are laid on at his brush, and may be fields away in a minute. Of late years foxes in these parts have shown a wonderful partiality for ivy-covered trees ; and many good gallops have begun by Reynard being whipped out of his perch, to descend like a meteor on to *terra firma*. And a fox is no less extraordinary than a cat in his power of leaping from a great height without harm to himself.

Of Hunting Quarters for the Old Berkshire, Oxford is of course the handiest with regard to London (being distant but one hour and three-quarters by Great Western) ; and has, as noticed under the head of the Heythrop and the Bicester, the advantage of touching also those two packs, as well as the South Oxfordshire. At the same time Oxford stands a little wide of the best meets of at least the three first-named ; and, though you may hunt most days of the week from the city in question with one pack or another, you must make up your mind to many miles of roadwork in the attainment. Faringdon and Abingdon, though in point of time much further from London (Paddington Station)—the delay contingent on branch lines nearly

The Old Berkshire.   211

doubling the journey)—are, once arrived at, much more commanding as points in the Old Berkshire Country. Of the two, Faringdon is to be preferred, as not only dominating all the best of the Berkshire Vale, but as placing you also within reach of most of the fixtures of the Vale of White Horse.

The Old Berkshire take the field three days in the week — viz., Monday, Wednesday, and Friday. Monday is in the best of their Vale ; Wednesday is on the eastern or Abingdon side ; while Friday is in the semi-circle embracing Faringdon on the west and north—an occasional Monday or Friday being taken to account for the Bampton Corner, north of the Thames, and in every second month Monday is devoted to Tar Wood, neutral with the Heythrop.

The Monday country, though limited, embraces the pick of the beautiful grass lowland through which runs the Great Western on its way between Didcot and Swindon. It cannot be said but that the railway is exactly where it is least wanted—but this is a drawback so frequent all over the hunting-fields of Great Britain that it calls for no special comment. Wantage on the east, and Knighton Crossing on the west are, roughly speaking, the limits of the Monday district ; which, again, runs up to the Ridgeway of the Lambourn Downs on the south, and embraces as far as Hatford on the north. Sloping down from the heights on which the outline of the White Horse is annually scoured, the face of the country gradually merges into a deep grass vale, through which—to the north of the railway—runs the Rosey, sluggish and formidable. The fences of the Vale are mostly to be jumped without difficulty—five out of six of them at a fly, the remainder at a double effort, where a hedge-grown bank has a ditch on either side. Here and there, possibly, you may come across a fence of a strength of build and a width of double ditch that precludes an absolute jump—and in these you must be content to seek a hole through which you may pop from bank to bank on either side. The Bishopston neighbourhood, for instance, will supply examples of this nature. In the Vale you had best be mounted on a bold, strong-jumping horse, of square build and on short legs. Ugly looking places have often to be faced; and a horse must have pluck and power to carry you with true comfort. All over the Old Berkshire country you want a *hunter*: in the Vale you must have a bold and active one.

The Downs, as we have said, run along the southern border of the Monday country, the Blowing Stone is the meet just below them, on the edge of the Vale, and immediately under the figure of the White Horse—said to have been originally cut on the hillside to commemorate a battle gained by King Alfred over the Danes about a thousand years ago; though by many people it is supposed to have had a still earlier origin. Legendary lore has not much to do with our present subject; but it is so insolubly wound up with the locality under notice that it will not be out of place to mention that at Compton they shew you Wayland Smith's cave—wherein, tradition has it, the invisible smith lived and worked. He would only take sixpence for shoeing your horse; and he would only shoe him on his own terms, which were—that you tied your horse up, put down your sixpence, went away and remained out of sight till he had finished. This legend is amusingly worked into Sir Walter Scott's "Kenilworth"—the scene of which is laid partly in this neighbourhood. At Kingston Lisle is another curiosity—the Blowing Stone, which gives its name to the fixture. It is a stone of about three cubic feet; and is pierced with holes, which when blown through are said to produce a sound loud enough to be heard at Faringdon. The coverts in view when the Blowing Stone is advertised, are those of Kingston Lisle—both meet and coverts being popular. The Kingston Spinnies, by the Canal, are almost sure to produce a run—generally over the Vale, though it is always on the cards for a fox to face the hills. The Downs will carry a hot scent if wet enough; but if dry and hard, hounds cannot act with great vigour over them.

Woolstone also overhangs the Vale, and is named for the small but very useful wood of Uffington—while Uffington Station means Uffington Gorse, which is always regarded as a *great place*. Childrey Canal Bridge and Challow are two of the most popular meets of the Hunt—the best of the grass lying all round, with no drawback to its charms save such as is contained in the presence of the railway and canal, here running side by side. Sparsholt is the usual covert from Childrey. From Challow Station and Goosey Green a move is generally made to Woodhill Gorse, a nice covert of four acres, facing south-west, the property of the junior member for Berks, almost a sure find, and from which a gallop over the grass is bound to follow. From Baulking Green hounds work down the valley of the Rosey—the Whissendine of the Old Berkshire—a brook feasible enough in many places, but generally with treacherous banks and bad bottom—a plunge into it more frequently involving a lengthy stay. Hounds run well over all this part of the Vale—in the Challow district more especially; and the country being all grass and the fences rideable, there is little room for improvement. Shillingford is a meet near Faringdon, with a gorse at Coxwell that always holds: and from Hatford they go up to Pusey and Buckland. On the north bank of the Thames they have a piece of Oxfordshire, which they hunt sometimes on a Monday, sometimes on a Friday. By the river side is Shifford with another meet, Yelford, just above. From here they work up to Cokethorpe Park, Boys Wood and Barley Park—which almost touch each other. A very natural line for a fox to take from here would be by way of Lew Gorse towards Bradwell Grove or Whichwood Forest, in the Heythrop Country. Curbridge would be fixed for Lew Gorse—once a capital covert—now recently restored, and should again be very valuable as a connecting link with the big coverts of the Heythrop. From Black Bourton they begin by drawing Hadden Copse and several other small coverts—from which they might get at once over the stone walls of the Heythrop. In the other direction, down the Thames Valley, are beautiful grass watermeadows, which, however, are often very deep—while the fences are tremendous, the ditches being in many cases wide open drains leading down to the river.

The Old Berkshire. 215

Friday has three meets in the south-west extremity of the Berkshire Vale. Longcott is for Beckett (Lord Barrington's place) with the Laurels and coverts round the house; after which they have Knighton, by the railway copse, Compton Wood and Hardwell Wood. From Shrivenham they get to Beckett, Staines Wick and Bourton Spinney. There is beautiful ground from here down to Swindon; but there are no coverts to tempt foxes to take this direction. Bishopstone lies in a very big country, containing the coverts of Hinton Spinney and Dore's Covert, after which they work back to Bourton and Beckett, or up the Vale. As you leave the vale you will find yourself in an open country of mixed grass and plough. Badbury Hill (by Faringdon) leads to Coles Hill, where are Lord Radnor's coverts of Watchfield Carr and Swan's Nest, with the Buscot Woods in the north-west corner of the country—the latter fastnesses being big woods with rides that are still very heavy in spite of efforts towards gravelling them. Coming round Faringdon you find the Fox-and-Hounds, Littleworth, as the next meet—for a small wood known as Haremoor, and Faringdon Grove—the two almost touching; while sometimes hounds get to Hatford Gorse, with every likelihood of running into the the Vale. Buckland (Sir W. Throckmorton's) is a nursery of foxes. It has its gardens, the Warren and the Ashbeds, which are invariably occupied. Here also is Barcot, a small but thick covert, belonging to Lady Theo. Guest, where foxes are afforded every protection.

The Wednesdays of the Old Berkshire being spent on the east of the Kennels at New House on the

Abingdon side of the territory, we get into a country whose chief characteristics are plough and large woods. The open consists almost entirely of arable, crossed by many small grips; and with the fields divided by open ditches. Of the woods (Tubney Tree being the meet), Appleton Common (Bessels-Leigh the meet), and Bagley (Foxcombe Hill, near Oxford) are the chief—with Wittenham on the extreme east. Wytham Wood is the great overhanging covert looking down on the Thames near Oxford—for which Cumner is the meet—the woodland being the property of Lord Abingdon. From the fixture of Marcham Park they draw the Marcham coverts; and from Steventon Green they have Milton Hill Gorse and Hendred Cow Lease—the latter being a wood with grass on its south side and plough again elsewhere. Sutton Courtney is for Culham and Milton Hill. South Moreton and East Hagborn are fixtures in the extreme south-east, from which they draw East Hagborn Spinney and Cholsey Lease, in a cramped close country, where grass and plough alternate. Nuneham Park and Woods are kept for cub-hunting purposes by the Old Berkshire, and are then handed over for the winter months for the use of the South Oxfordshire.

THE SOUTH OXFORDSHIRE.*

A TWO-DAYS-A-WEEK Country, carrying fox-hunting up to the very gates of Oxford, the South Oxfordshire completes the quadrilateral, of which that city is the central point, and the Bicester, the Heythrop and the Old Berkshire form the remaining components. Like the others it has its rough and its smooth, its plains and its hills, its vales and its woods; and like the others it puts the chase in an excellent form within reach of young Oxford—who never, if they can help it, miss Lord Macclesfield's Mondays in his Vale.

The South Oxfordshire Country is bounded on the north by the Bicester, the east by the Old Berkeley, the south by Mr. Garth's and the South Berkshire, and on the west by the Old Berkshire. The Thames is a rough guide to its western limit as far as Oxford, after which the Cherwell and the Ray take up the march. Turner's Wood, Shabbington Wood, and Waterperry Wood are within the boundary along the north, though the latter is left out on both the maps alluded to. For the rest it need merely be said that its limits are correctly pencilled on the maps; and

---

* *Vide* "Stanford's Large Scale Map," Sheet 15; and "Hobson's Foxhunting Atlas."

that on the extreme south-east it again reaches the Thames at Henley.

At first glance the sphere of the South Oxfordshire would appear too extended for only two days a week. But as a fact the brow of the Chiltern Hills cuts off the whole of the south-eastern portion as virtually useless—the Chiltern Forest covering a wide area of chalk, with mile upon mile of inhospitable beech wood. Thus the Hunt seldom finds itself there except by accident; and even in the latter case the majority turn their heads homewards. Foxes occasionally travel on to these scentless heights from the Vale; but seldom, if ever, take a downward course from the Hills. So, well-preserved as is all the rest of the country, it would be difficult to find room for the chase more than twice a week. Lord Macclesfield has now hunted the hounds since 1857, after two year's previous experience of them in 1845. They became his own property in 1860, since which the judgment of one of the best authorities in England on the points of a foxhound has not been wanting in the task of continual improvement. Though in his sixty-ninth year, Lord Macclesfield still rides up to his hounds as vigorously as ever, while he hunts them with all the accumulated experience of so many years of practice.

As to hunting quarters for South Oxfordshire, there are only Thame and Oxford to point to, unless we take in Aylesbury as commanding its Mondays, and offering, besides, its Vale under the auspices of the Baron, the Bicester, the Old Berkeley, and Mr. Selby Lowndes. Henley is the only other noteworthy town touching

The South Oxfordshire.

the country; and one would as soon think of Cowes as a hunting centre as Henley-on-Thames.

The horse for the South Oxfordshire should be an animal that has been bred to stay and taught to jump. He should have learned that water is not a matter of fear and that a double ditch requires something approaching to a second sight, or at least a pause for a second spring. If there be a double instinct required for the fences of the Vale of Aylesbury there is a double argument for its brooks. A horse that has been outpaced, or has been well ducked, hates the very sight of water. On the other hand, familiarity breeds contempt very readily as applied to brook jumping. Take the converse—A Leicestershire horse, however bold and dashing at most descriptions of fences, is seldom good at water; for the simple reason that he rarely encounters it, and then is asked to perform among a number of other hesitating ignoramuses all exaggerating the danger and discouraging each other. An Aylesbury horse, on the contrary, has learned by precept and practice, that water jumping, being part of his daily office, must be acquired—and, consequently, he acquires it.

For practical purposes the Country may be considered as divided into three very distinct sections—to wit, the Vale, the Oxford Woods, and the Hills. And in this way we will proceed to take them.

The South Oxfordshire Vale runs from the north-east corner of the Country across its whole breadth—say, in a direct line to Nuneham Park. As far as the town of Thame it may be spoken of as part of the Vale of Aylesbury, and is readily recognisable as such from the frequency of water and double fences. Below Thame, by Tetsworth and Stadhampton, we get into a light flying country, still beautiful grass,—but not so deep and trying as that of Aylesbury—easy to ride over, and, on the whole, good scenting ground, notwithstanding the fact that the farmers keep their stock out all winter as thick as the land will bear. The South Oxfordshire farmers, by the way, are ever most friendly to foxhunting; and are themselves generally capital sportsmen. It is a boast in the country that "Ware Wheat!" is a cry never heard. By way of further definition it may be added that the meets and coverts of the Vale extend to the foot of the range of the Chiltern Hills on the one side, and as far as the railway between Waterstock and Littlemore on the other. Three Pigeons is perhaps the best known meet of the South Oxfordshire. From it they draw Gale's Gorse, Fern hill, and the Old Paddock; and from Fern hill a good fox will often cross the river for a spin over a beautiful part of the Bicester territory, to Chearsley or Chilton. Haseley is named when it is meant to draw Haseley Wood, Latchford, and Cornwell Gorse. The last-named is the property of the Master, and very frequently gives a gallop over the grass, prefaced by the Haseley Brook. Meeting at Thame hounds draw Thame Park, the Tythrop coverts and Emmington; and from these they are likely to run directly into the Vale of Aylesbury. From Tetsworth they work Adwell and Wheatfield; while from Shirburn Castle (where the Master lives and keeps his hounds) they have the Shrubberies, Clare Copse, Brookside, and Pyrton. Brightwell Park

The South Oxfordshire. 221

is a well-known meet—for Ashleys, Brockes Furze, Cadwell, and Holcombe. Stadhampton is for Chislehampton, after which we get west of the Thame Brook, where we have Baldon for the Home Coverts, Sandford Brake, Garsington Hays, and Allen's Gorse. The woods of Nuneham Park are lent by the Old Berkshire after the latter have finished cub-hunting. Bullingdon Barracks and Waterstock are for Open Magdalen, Brasenose Wood and Coombe Wood—all this western corner between the big river and its tributary the Thame being of a light plough description. Throughout the South Oxfordshire Vale proper the coverts are small. This, added to small fields and good foxes, puts everything in favour of sport; and most of their best runs of late years have been in this part of their country. Even last winter, in spite of the lengthened frost which they had in common with their neighbours, was marked as a good season in the Vale.

Friday is always held in the deep clay woodlands that, passing the town of Oxford, run a corner into the Bicester country, and are here and there neutral with that pack. (For more exact definition vide Bicester aforetold). Wet grim woods are these, dark within and cold without; but they make hounds, and they give a certain amount of sport, though their depths are unfathomable and their rides bid defiance to a stranger.

"The Quarters" is a designation quite as frequently applied to these great coverts, and perhaps more correctly, than that of the Oxford Woods—inasmuch as some of the cluster lie in Buckinghamshire. It may be repeated that the two Stanton Woods are neutral with the Bicester; while Horton Wood is hunted by that pack up to Christmas, after which it is taken over by the South Oxfordshire. Waterperry, Shabbington, and Oakley Woods belong to the latter. The principal meets for the Quarters are Holton Stonepits, Forest Hill, Stanton St. John, Stow Wood, Park Farm, and Menmash Guide Post. Several of the Friday coverts are close to Oxford, to wit, Headington Wick, Stow Wood, Noke, Woodeaton Stow, and the Elsfield coverts; and a fox running over the Marston Meadows will sometimes go quite into the suburbs of the town. Shotover, Brazenose Wood, and Open Magdalen are also quite close to Oxford (the two last being, as above-mentioned, generally drawn on a Monday) and a fox may be found within a few hundred yards of the Brigade Depôt—the soldiers of which are, of course, staunch friends of foxhunting.

Of the Chiltern Hills all that need be said is that Nettlebed and Chinnor Hill are about the only regular fixtures—and hounds are seldom advertised to meet beyond the brow.

THE SOUTH NOTTINGHAMSHIRE.*

JUST north of the more fashionable countries of the Shires comes that of South Notts. On the roll of its history appear many names whose celebrity, confirmed in more notable spheres, was first established here. Mr. John Chaworth (grandfather of the present J. Chaworth-Musters) hunted it in 1805. Mr. Osbaldeston held it about 1810. Lord Middleton (grandfather of the present) had it for some years, and in 1823 presented the country with a pack purchased from Mr. Chaworth for 1000 guineas, and gave them most of the horses besides—Mr. Lancelot Rolleston (father of present master) taking the reins of government. Mr. Dansey hunted it for a few seasons commencing in 1830, and, though no rider, showed excellent sport. The kennels were then at Lowdham. It was afterwards retaken by Mr. Chaworth—or, rather, Chaworth-Musters, as he had then become—who hunted it till 1844; after which the country remained vacant till taken in hand by his grandson, Mr. John Chaworth-Musters of our day. After undergoing a few minor changes, the Hunt is now in the joint hands of Mr.

---

* *Vide* "Stanford's Large Scale Railway Map," Sheet 9; and "Hobson's Foxhunting Atlas."

Lancelot Rolleston (son of the above) and Mr.
P. H. Cooper, who have built the present substantial
kennels.

But apart from its association with names of renown,
the South Notts has merits of its own. Certainly, it
is not a flying grass country; it boasts of no resort of
fashion; and attracts few strangers; while in many
parts it has to contend against a teeming manufacturing population; and some of its best ground is
only now in process of being opened up. But it has
a strong body of county residents to lean upon; and
it meets with staunch and substantial support from the
whole society corporate within the fold of the city of
Nottingham. It has good foxes and plenty of them;
capital grounds for making hounds, and innumerable
excellent walks for rearing its puppies—the last virtue
constituting not only a point of excellence in itself,
but a proof that the farmers really love fox-hunting.
It is chiefly plough, and the greater part of its area
is hilly; but it generally carries a fair scent, and
hounds work well over it.

The position of the South Notts may be described
as having the Quorn along its southern edge, the
Meynell on the west, the Belvoir on the east, and the
Rufford on the north. Its boundaries follow the Trent
along the south-west from Belper nearly to Nottingham, and the streams of the Smite and the Deven all
up the east. Its other limits are defined by custom
rather than by nature, and are correctly set down on
the chart; though Mr. Stanford's rendering of the
neutral corner of Sherwood Forest (in the north) must
not be taken as too strictly accurate—Thieves' Wood,

The South Nottinghamshire. 225

though claimed by the South Notts, being kept exclusively for the Rufford, and Haywood Oaks being also a place of meeting for that pack. Nottingham and Derby may be said to furnish a base to the country, which for practical purposes, again, may be divided thus— First, there is the strip of Derbyshire, running up the length of the country between the river Derwent and the coalpit valley of the Erewash, and resembling in character much of the best ground of the Meynell; secondly, between the valleys of the Erewash and the Leen are the Woods on a soil of loam upon limestone; in a third parallel section is the tract of light sandy ground where once grew the Forest of Sherwood (the name being still retained); fourthly, there is the clay of the open Oxton country; and fifthly, there is the low-lying ground on the south bank of the Trent, known as the Vale. Three days and a bye-day being the weekly work for the hounds, Monday is allotted to the Woods, Wednesday to the Oxton country and the Forest, Friday to the Vale, and Saturday (the extra day) to Derbyshire or to any district that may seem to require a visit. All north of the Trent is more or less hilly; only the southern Vale being flat and unbroken. For a visit to the South Notts, Nottingham is the most central quarter; though Derby, too, commands one side of the country, and has the Meynell besides. Each is about three hours from London (St. Pancras or King's Cross for either); and the travelling sportsman might well take his horses on to either place, after having tasted the sweets of the chase from Leicester *en passant*. With the completion of the railways in progress (promised at a very early date) Nottingham will find itself within distance, by morning train, of all that Melton commands, and will on any day be able to join in with the Quorn, the Belvoir, and the Cottesmore on their best ground.

That foxhunting is popular in Nottinghamshire is apparent enough at the covertside—where, perhaps, as large fields assemble as in any Hunt which does not resent the application of the term "Provincial." This popularity extends in a rather embarrassing degree to the countless hordes of workmen whose hands produce the wealth of Nottinghamshire. The sound of the horn, or the barest chance of hearing its music, has a magic effect on these good people; and coal and iron and cotton hose may look after themselves whenever hounds are in the district—one and all of these "merrie men" leaping forth as gaily to the note as ever did bold Robin's followers in these same jolly green woods. Thus to draw coverts in the neighbourhood of where tall chimneys grow thickest, it is often necessary to make a descent from far away, and take these sportsmen unawares.

Kennels have been lately built at Gedling, where there is a station on the Great Northern Railway, and which is as nearly as possible the centre of the country. Mr. John Chaworth-Musters used to keep them till about Christmas at Annesley, and afterwards at Wiverton. It is a curious little coincidence that the present masters of the three Nottinghamshire packs, the South Notts, the Rufford and the Grove were all initiated in their calling through the medium of carrying the horn at Oxford with the Christ Church Harriers.

You may see a good deal of sport in the South

The South Nottinghamshire.

Notts country on a second-class horse; but, as elsewhere, you will never see *the best of it well on a bad one.* The hills are severe; the woods are deep; the Oxton district is heavy, and so is the Vale. The latter is strongly fenced; but, curiously, more falls are got on the sand of the Forest than anywhere else. For, as on other light wold, hounds travel at a great pace over it when the soil is moist. It has the reputation of bearing only easy fences—which are disregarded accordingly. But these fences grow stronger yearly; and, treated thus lightly, are apt to retaliate by turning over the rash sportsman, who, forgetful of the pace, has been taking liberties with them, and with his horse.

Taking the days of hunting in detail, we have Monday in the Woodlands—a series of large woods commencing beyond Annesley in the north, and covering an area so large that it is very difficult indeed to drive a fox right away from them. They are separated from each other only by strips of grassland; and a fox, by moving from one to the other, finds scope enough to keep hounds at a distance, till his circle is narrowed and he is too tired to go. They are much broken by hill and dale; but within their rides are deep and wet. The Annesley Woods, belonging to Mr. Musters, run into those of Lord Cowper and Mr. Rolleston—the whole being in consequence more often denominated collectively the Annesley Woodlands. They are great strong coverts, full of foxes—the largest wood being that of High Park, which is a hundred and fifty acres in one piece. Then there are Park Springs, Morning Springs, William Wood, and

Annesley Forest Plantations; the last being an extraordinary fastness, covering, in all, as much as two hundred acres with gorse and young trees—and requiring toil and perseverance in drawing. The meets for these woodlands are Linby Cross, Linby Windmill, Annesley Park, and Lodge Farm—Annesley. The best chance of a run from the Annesley Woodlands is for a fox to take across to Watnall (some three miles of open), or to round that place and keep on to Wollaton—either line being fairly good, and presenting a course of light plough and nice fences. Moving southwards, we find the area of the woods narrowing about Nuthall and Strelley—both in extent and capacity.

Lord Middleton's woods at Wollaton are fine coverts, and the prospects of sport promise well—great efforts towards a supply of foxes having been set on foot. Their proximity to Nottingham, however, renders it impossible to hold a meet in the immediate neighbourhood—and it is customary to work southwards from the Annesley Woods in an afternoon.

Wednesday taking the Sherwood Forest and Oxton side, brings us into two distinct varieties of country —the former being a thorough wold, generally hard on the surface, and never deep, even in the wettest weather—the latter all clay land, of which a certain amount is allowed to carry grass. On the whole, the Wednesday country is considered the most reliable district for sport. It holds a good scent (varying according to soil and degree of rain, in addition to the ordinary wide mutabilities of "the phenomenon");

The South Nottinghamshire.

its coverts are of reasonable size ; and its fences are good and fair—while across the Forest you may gallop as freely as on old turf. As regards fences, it should be noted that throughout the South Notts territory they are all of a plain and simple nature, and to be taken at a fly. Oxton itself is the great centre point of this district, and is the property of Mr. Henry Sherbrooke—one of the best and oldest supporters of the Hunt. His coverts are Epperstone Park (a strong and very holding wood), Oxton Bottoms (a long bed of swamp and reeds), and Graves Lane, a wood which is held as neutral with the Rufford. Meeting at Gonalston and Lowdham, hounds get on to Mr. Francklin's property, to draw Thistley Coppice, Bleasby Gorse (one of the best coverts of the South Notts), Hallaughton Gorse and Wood—the Wood being neutral with the Rufford. Thurgarton Priory, by the death of whose proprietor, Mr. Milward, the Hunt has lately lost one of its most valued members, is a meet for the same coverts. Woodborough is the fixture nearest to the Kennels: and from it they have Mr. Heymann's good Gorse, Ploughman Wood, Bulcote Wood, and Gedling Wood, and Mr. Howett has planted a new gorse on his stud-farm in this neighbourhood. Heymann's Gorse is a most favourite draw. It has round it a considerable extent of grass, with strong fences. It always holds a fox, and generally gives a run. On the site of the old Forest, Sherwood Lodge is advertised for Mr. Seeley's coverts—Cockliffe Hill Gorse (another good place) Ramsdale Gorse, and the plantations round the House. Bestwood is the property of the Duke of St. Albans, and has large coverts round the Park, for which foxes appear to evince no great fondness—and the same may be said of Papplewick. Newstead Abbey, (formerly the residence of Lord Byron) however, has generally a fox or two in Mr. Webb's coverts.

On Fridays the South Notts are in the Vale, *i.e*, south of the Trent; where there is much heavy plough; interspersed, however, with patches of good grass. It is not a good scenting district; and, though bordering on some of the best of the Belvoir country, foxes have not of late years travelled in that direction as often as might be wished. The abundance of material for riot is another objection, as interfering considerably with the work of hounds. Nearest to Nottingham is the meet of Ratcliffe-on-Trent, from which they have Edwalton Hill (consisting of wood, thorns, and gorse), Bridgeford Gorse (both of these belonging to Mr. Musters), Tollerton, with its two little woods; Cotgrave Gorse, Mr. E. Smith's Gorse (the same good sportsman also owned Harlequin Gorse, from which Mr. Musters had his great run about 1872) Marshall's Hill, and Blackbery Hill (the latter the property of Lord Manvers). Colston Basset, the seat of Mr. Knowles, has its Gorse, together with a newer one called Blanche's Gorse—from either of which a nice gallop into the Duke's country may be hoped for. A line by Key Wood (Mr. Knowles's property in Belvoir territory) and thence into the Hickling parish would in this case be the *desideratum*. From Colston Basset hounds would draw on to Cropwell Hoe Hill, also Mr. Musters's—whose place at Wiverton is the next meet. His coverts here are Smite Hill Gorse (neutral with the Belvoir), Langar Lane End (strong thorn and gorse), the Moats, and the new plantation near the House; also Cropwell Hoe Hill, and Cropwell Lings nearer to Bingham. East of the Nottingham-and-Grantham Road is the estate of Lord Carnarvon, which extends to Shelford, but contains no coverts of any importance—foxes bearing scarcely their fair proportion to hares and other game. From here the south bank of the Trent —in some places a considerable height above the river —forms a narrow and almost continuous strip of covert nearly to Newark, and is a very difficult piece to draw, hounds having scarcely foothold. Meanwhile, the field riding above have the advantage of a beautiful and extensive view over the landscape north of the river. After Shelford comes East Bridgeford, where Mr. H. Martin keeps up the memory of his friend, the old "Jack Musters," by steadfast care of the foxes. On the Flintham estate (Mr. Hildyard's) there is generally a litter or two—his coverts being the Barleyholme, Coronation Covert, and a portion of the Trent bank. At Hawkesworth, close to the Coronation Covert, are a couple of small and useful spinnies. South-east of these is Sibthorpe Gorse, on the property of the Duke of Portland—ten strong acres of gorse and thorns, and close to Shelton, where lives the Rev. Banks Wright, in sight of whose blue leathers we have often been only too glad to live through a gallop. Mr. Fillingham's estate at Syerston has small coverts and an artificial earth which is often occupied. Stoke owns occasionally; and between here and Newark remains little but a few osier beds, and the presence of a keen fox preserver in the person of Mr. Ripon Brockton.

With good foxes and a good scent the Vale should be the best part of the South Notts country; but foxes have not run with vigour of late seasons hereabouts. Chances of sport will improve much when the neighbouring coverts of the Quorn and Belvoir are once more occupied with old seasoned foxes.

Turning, in conclusion, to the strip of Derbyshire that runs up the west of the South Notts country, and which is always visited on a Saturday, we again find ourselves on a different description of ground. Small grass inclosures and pleasant flying fences give to this part quite a Meynell type. It is only during the last few years that all this territory has been reopened for foxhunting; but, the ice having once been broken, it would appear as if all antagonism were happily melting away. For their work here hounds are brought by train from Gedling to West Hallam or Breadsall—from either of which stations all the coverts can be reached, and which are, consequently, usually named as the meets. From West Hallam they draw Lady Wood, the property of Col. Newdigate (in whom the Hunt has a good supporter), Shipley (a covert of some extent), Hopwell (where Mr. E. Pares is throwing all his energy into resuscitating his share of this Derbyshire district), and the Dale Plantations. Locko has hitherto been withheld from the Hunt by the present owner. From Breadsall they work Horsley Carr (a splendid fastness—being a large valley of rough natural covert), Cloves Wood, and Hays Wood (all three belonging to Mr. R. Sitwell —one of the mainstays of the South Notts in this part); and they have also Coxbench Wood and Chaddesden Wood.

Right in the north of the Derbyshire province the Hunt have a small covert of Mr. Jessop's, and Bloomer Wood (a fine wild covert of the Duke of Portland's). From these a fox will occasionally run across to the Annesley Woods), or he may even strike upwards to the Derbyshire Hills. Mr. Musters has also planted a gorse near here. Other coverts hereabouts are Brook Hill Gorse (Mr. Coke's), Langton, and Newton Wood (Lord Hartington's good covert)— the meet for these being Middlebrook Bridge, on Selston Common, whence the choice offers of drawing the above or turning to the Annesley Woods.

THE EAST KENT.*

KENT is scarcely the county a hunting-man would of his own free will select as the most delectable sphere for his pursuit—unless, indeed, he be wedded to change, and, having experienced the smooth side of foxhunting in one quarter, should suddenly find himself bitten with a desire to try the rough elsewhere. Kent is eminently available from London; and it has three packs of hounds to choose from. But the " Garden of England " is laid out in a manner scarcely compatible with foxhunting in its most successful form. It would be as fair to expect that a high-class cricket match could come off on a lawn—though bat and ball have been wielded there by most of us at one time of our lives. But if the nomade foxhunter is not likely, voluntarily, to pitch his camp in Kent, he only after all represents a small section of the hunting field—except in some few of the most fashionable resorts — where men gather yearly from every quarter and corner of the kingdom. Her Majesty, if you serve her, is graciously pleased that you should hunt, and gives you every encouragement towards doing so—except as regards assisting

---

* *Vide* " Stanford's Large Scale Map," Sheet 23 ; also, " Hobson's Foxhunting Atlas."

you to the means, or appointing your station so that you may command the best countries. On either of these heads the soldier is treated with scanty liberality; but, for all that, he will join the chase to the utmost of his ability *wherever* he may be—and, truth to tell, if his C. O. be at all a decent member of society, *parade* is but seldom allowed to stand in the way. Thus, he is much more likely to be stationed at Canterbury than at Leicester, at Dover than Northampton, or at Shorncliffe than either—and a hunting he must go, be the country good, bad, or indifferent. Or, again, you may have been born to own, or to occupy, a goodly acreage of crops. Your property, it is true, may not pay for your hunting *every* year; but it will find you a new stud—and give you something handsome to invest, besides—at least once in seven seasons. At any rate, it is too good to leave; and certainly it does not take up all your while. During the winter months time would hang sorely, were there not some other object to turn to. What better than foxhunting? The country gentleman, of course, inherits a love of the hound and the horn, with his patrimony and family traditions. And so the three classes combine to set the chase on its legs, and to keep it there as steadily as the ground will allow; —making the best they can of the result. While the other two are scattered over the extent of the country the soldier will have his headquarters at one of these chief centres, and at the points which happen to be the most accessible from London. It is, therefore, from *his* point of view that we may mainly take the geography of the East Kent.

If anything could have raised the Hunt to a position of eminence, the enthusiastic exertions and profuse liberality of the late Master must have done so. When Lord Guildford took the Country in hand, some few years ago, it scarcely contained a fox, and all ardour in the cause appeared to have died out. He not only succeeded in rousing the slumbering interest of his neighbours, but he found them a new pack of hounds; built magnificent Kennels in his park at Waldershare; took the whole expense of establishment and country on his own shoulders; and by degrees brought round the covert-owners, almost without exception, to his way of thinking. Everything connected with the Hunt was done in first-rate form; the hounds gradually became a pack, good in the field and fashionable on the flags; and at the present moment the whole of the Country—one small portion alone excepted—is thoroughly stocked with foxes. On his retirement at the end of the last season he lent hounds and Kennels (with the privilege of using the Park for exercise) to the country, and headed their subscription-list with five hundred pounds—Mr. Mackenzie taking over the reins of government.

The East-Kent Country comprises the extreme south-east corner of England—a line from Whitstable to Canterbury, and Canterbury to Ashford, cutting it off from its neighbour, the Tickham. It goes south as far as the Military Canal at Hythe, where it encounters the Romney Marshes, which are only practicable for harriers. Ashford is situated in a flat grass vale, worthy of any hounds—but this, the most favourable ground in all Kent, is practically and obstinately

The East Kent. 237

useless—for want of foxes. There are coverts in it, of which foxes would avail themselves as gladly as would the pursuing force: but the Ashford Vale is no place for them. The rest of the East-Kent Country is mostly a cold plough upland, thickly studded throughout with great woods; and to drive a fox through them, hounds must be thorough workers, keen of nose, and stout of frame and heart. Here and there in the valleys are patches of hop-garden (deep and holding in winter); but hops do not flourish in the soil of East Kent as freely as further west. The valleys, consequently, are more often merely marked by a single breadth of meadow bounded by fairly strong wattle hedges, constituting the only fences to be met with for miles. Great unfenced fields of arable cover all the upper ground, especially where, between Canterbury, Sandwich, and Deal, much of the land assumes quite a wold character. Further south, however, on the high ground above Hythe and Shorncliffe, cultivation is of a much closer description, and a fair sprinkling of grass comes in about Acrise and Reindean. As a rule, East Kent is not good scenting ground. Hounds have the best chance of killing their foxes in cub-hunting—before the leaves have fallen to any extent—or when, now and again, one of the early spring months brings a steady, good-scenting period. You need not have a very expensive horse to enter the woods with the East Kent, or to see many of their runs. But if hounds slip away close on their fox, and at best pace dip in and out of one of the above little valleys as they run from wood to wood, only a very respectable hunter will carry you up without chancing a fall. But, even allowing for these contingencies, you need not ruin yourself in first outlay. To jump a strong fence out of deep ground, or a stiff stile out of a wood, will be a test to occur occasionally, and establish a standard which may be reached without very wild extravagance. After mentioning that Canterbury is about an hour and a half from London (Victoria station), and Dover about two hours, we may pass on to the leading points of the country as usually hunted.

The East Kent advertise for three days a week, and generally add a bye day. Monday, Wednesday and Friday are their regular days of hunting, leaving Saturday open for the extra. Beyond setting apart Wednesday for the south of the country, *i.e.*, for the Ashford Vale, or the upper ground just above it, they keep to no absolute rules in allotting their meets. Monday is more often within easy reach of the Kennels, while the longer journeys are generally taken on Fridays. The Kennels themselves are a very frequent Monday meet, with a view to the home coverts of Waldershare, which are numerous, and— it is needless to add—abundantly stocked with foxes. Easling Wood is the great stronghold of the series. The Half-Way-House, on the Canterbury-and-Dover road, is for a thousand acres of woodland under the name of Woolwich Wood. The Black Mill is named for the Nolden and Sleden Woods, each of some hundreds of acres. Lydden means Lord's Wood and Alkham Valley—the latter being a rough natural covert in the hilly district between Folkestone and Dover. Swingfield Park is another large wood at no great distance from Alkham. At Swanton there are smaller coverts, from which it is not unlikely to get on to Reindean and the better country. Sir. W. James's place at Betshanger stands the Hunt in good stead; and there are good coverts of less extent about St. Alban's.

Of equal importance in the Wednesday country as Waldershare in that of Monday is Beachborough, the property of Mr. Brockman—nephew of the former Master. The House stands just under the hill, and covert is plentiful on the slope and below. Ashley Wood is the chief fastness, and there are foxes everywhere on the estate. On the high ground above—and giving a line very commonly taken from Beachborough—is Acrise (Mr. Mackinnon's seat), with a nice wood, in the midst of the best of the East-Kent upland, where there is a good scent and something to ride over. The Pillars, near by, are a prominent landmark, and consist of a high clump of trees, by a small covert. Hawkinge Hill immediately overlooks Folkestone, and has small, but holding coverts in its neighbourhood. Under the hillside, again, is New Inn Green—being, with Beachborough, one of the only meets on the low ground from which sport is to be had. Its coverts are Thorn Wood and others. Mersham, Sellinge Lee, West Brabourn, and Aldington are all meets in an excellent grass country; but it is seldom thought worth while to bring hounds to chase the wild goose in their midst. There are fine coverts, too,—if only foxes might be encouraged to take to them. Certainly it is no fault of the farmers of the neighbourhood, who — as throughout the East-Kent country—are staunch, to a man.

Among the more distant meets and coverts, generally taken on a Friday, are Evington (Sir F. Honeywood's) in whose woods is a capital show of foxes. Far away on the west of the country is the Denge, a huge woodland, for which they meet at Petham or Godmersham—the latter owned by Mr. Kay, an excellent fox-preserver. Elham as a meet has Elham Park, another big wood, from which good foxes are often started. Next come the Covets (or Coverts?) enormous woods, with a fair sprinkling of foxes of late years; and Walderchain Wood—for which Woodlands Breachdown is the usual fixture. White Hill is also a big wood with another of like description, Gorsley Wood, facing it. Trinley Park is another meet and extensive covert. North of the Canterbury-and-Dover road Adisham and Wingham lead to smaller coverts and a lighter soil—except where, by the river Stour, you may get on to the watermeadows. Hounds are hardly ever taken nearer the sea, on the north, than the South-Eastern Railway (to Ramsgate) — except when, about once a year, meeting at the Barracks at Canterbury, they go to draw Blean and its vicinity.

THE TICKHAM.*

THE Tickham occupy Mid Kent — the only packs touching them being respectively the East and West Kent. The sea, or rather the outflow of the Medway, bounds them on the north, while on the deep lowlands on their southern edge no one has for years—if ever —been adventurous enough to keep a pack of foxhounds. In point of fact, Mr. Stanford, without perpetrating any absolute error, carries the Tickham Country considerably lower in this direction than hounds are ever taken to draw—though no doubt they are at liberty to dip as far among the currant gardens of the Weald as they may choose. Mr. Hobson's Atlas gives a very just idea of the limits within which the Tickham look for their foxes. For it has long been recognised that the deep vale by Staplehurst, Headcorn, &c.—through which runs the South-Eastern Railway to Ashford, and through which winds the stream of the Beult, is unsuitable for the chase. Much of it is grass; but that grass is more than fetlock-deep in winter. The rest is in a great measure devoted to fruit gardens and like high-

---

* *Vide* "Stanford's Large Scale Map," Sheet 23; also, "Hobson's Foxhunting Atlas."

cultivation. That it has *not* hounds of its own, is much to the disadvantage of those over the border, who drive many a good fox across, never to return— for, not only is there no pack to drive him fairly back, but once across the march, he is treated as a vile beast and shot down accordingly. Truth to tell, poor Reynard's sanctity, though seldom openly assailed, yet holds no universally strong place in the creed of the Mid Kent landowners. I presume there are not two of them who would directly order a fox to be destroyed, and perhaps not one who would boast of having done so—much wickedness as there is upon the earth, whether that earth be grass or plough, Leicestershire or Kent. But only comparatively few among their keepers have had it pointed out to them that the pithy dogma "No fox, no Box" could ever possibly bear any application for them. The latter, consequently, think they are fully and honourably carrying out instructions when they allow the old foxes to eat up a certain number of their rabbits under their very noses. But in a shooting country no heart that ever beat under velveteen could bear with complacency the sight of an earth, round whose mouth lie many feathery proofs of a vixen's careful catering for her young. There is more gold for "Gaiters" to be got out of a single shooting party than the most liberal of M.F.H.'s can afford him in a season. So the vixen and her litter find a home elsewhere; and under the influence of these Malthusian principles, small wonder that woodlands, which should swarm with foxes, are often drawn in silence.

There is an argument, seldom openly advanced, but

too often acted upon (not in Kent only, but wherever the owner of gamecoverts either goes off to some more popular country for his hunting, or else does not hunt at all)—" Foxhunting is out of place here. The country is altogether unfavourable ! And so I don't feel called upon to preserve foxes." Put in other words, this is the most selfish and ungenerous reasoning possible. It simply means "I can go to a better hunting country—or could if I chose. As for *you*, my neighbours, who are obliged to stay here—it does not concern me whether you have sport, or not; and accordingly I decline to make any effort to assist you !"

Great woods of hazel and Spanish chestnut are the leading feature of the Tickham Country. Oak and ash and other timber are scattered freely over the acres and miles of thicket; but the bulk of the covert is a low and densely thick growth—cut down about every twelve or fifteen years for conversion into hoppoles, hurdles and wattle. The rides through these jungles are merely accidental cart tracks, made in carrying off the last-cut portion of the wood. Riding up them, you, as often as not, find that all path has entirely disappeared, and you are brought up short by the growth of years—through which a horse cannot possibly struggle, and even a hound can only force himself slowly. In the autumn the under-covert is so thickened by the help of the briars that a pack can in some places scarcely crawl. Carrying a head during cub-hunting must be out of the question; and at no time can they rattle a fox with a front so wide and a pace so strong as, for instance, in the hollow woods of the Fitzwilliam or the Pytchley. A fox can, therefore, take his own time about leaving; generally goes away with a long start; can betake himself to a similar refuge almost as soon as he chooses; and is, consequently, about as easy to catch as Cetywayo. Nor with such difficulties in the way of your own progress, is it at all an easy matter to keep within hearing of hounds. You may often have to gallop a mile round to gain a point of a few hundred yards; and to retain your cue of the line of chase under such conditions must require an absolute instinct. Woodland Hunting is a pursuit, and a taste, of itself. Some of us are very fond of it: some prefer to gallop over the open. The former division may well pay a visit to the Tickham—where (if they would live with hounds) they will often have to gallop quicker in the woods than outside. Between the woods they will meet a rather cold-scenting plough everywhere except on the ridge of hills between Debtling and Charing (and which, as the backbone of Kent, runs from one end of the county to the other). On the top of these is a good deal of grass, with light fair fences: and here hounds can often travel a great pace. But elsewhere the country, where not taken up for growing hops or hop poles, is given up to corn; and thousands of acres are unfenced, except here and there by hurdles. The hop gardens are mostly deeply trenched by hand, and everywhere heavy and sticky in winter; while the corn land is thickly strewed with the sharpest flints—from which hounds and horses alike suffer. Indeed, a right good hound is wanted in Mid Kent. If he has not lots of music (yet be free from riot) he is useless in the big

The Tickham.

woods—where, too, he requires all the dash that can be bred in a foxhound, if he is to cope with his game. Again, for the open, he must be ready to put his nose down and willing to keep it there; while his feet must be perfect to combat the flints, and his frame untiring to carry him through the day. In woods of such size, so difficult to ride through, and none too lavishly off for foxes, a single mute hound may rob the whole day of its chances of sport. And, again, the flints of the open ground are so severe, that a hound will seldom really face them for more than three or four seasons, and at all times at least a sixth of the pack are in hospital with cuts. The present Tickham Pack owes its foundation chiefly to hounds purchased when Mr. Musters broke up his Kennel in South Notts. Since then the present Master, Mr. W. E. Rigden, whose father had the country for some forty years, has made every effort to establish a high and uniform standard—by infusions of blood from the Fitzwilliam and other leading Kennels—with the result that he now possesses an excellent pack. And that hounds should be of good class in a rough and difficult country as much as in a more fashionable one is self-evident—for the greater the difficulties to contend with the more need for good qualities on *their* part—added to which, the foxes of a wild country are invariably stronger than those matured in a more artificial sphere. Mr. Rigden has lately built beautiful Kennels at Wren's Hill, near Newnham; which in themselves are worth a visit.

The horse to ride with the Tickham should be

strong enough to carry you up-and-down hill, and to go through deep ground from beginning to end of the day. The whole country is very undulating, consisting, as it does, of a series of salients running down towards the sea at right angles from the main ridge already alluded to. As with the East Kent, you may often ride all day without having to take a single leap; but when, now and again, a fence is met with, its proportions are, practically speaking, magnified by the necessity of jumping out of deep ground. And, as such fences as exist are built and bound into an unyielding wattle—or in the case of the frequent hogbacked stile which forms the only exit from a wood—your horse must have jumping power when the necessity comes. His hocks, too, must be clean and strong, or they will certainly fly; and his feet must have a growth and breadth of horn that will bid defiance to the flints. Finally, when mounting yourself for Mid Kent, you had far better buy something already blemished (and consequently cheaper); for a season among the flints is certain to leave its mark in cuts and enlargements. There is yet hope for improvement in the surface of the county of Kent —to be found in the fact that while to grow corn in the present state of the market cannot possibly pay, more and more of the uplands are being laid down for grass. Let the revolution really establish itself, hounds will go quicker, horses will gallop on sound turf, and fences must spring up to give a fillip to the pleasures of riding.

The Tickham is professedly a five-days-a-fortnight country—and as the season advances, it often reverts to its avowed allowance—hunting Monday, Thursday and Saturday in one week, Tuesday and Friday the next. But for the greater part of the season Friday is developed into a Thursday *and* a Saturday; and three days a week is the rule.

For the Monday (Tuesday in alternate weeks) they retain the centre of their territory; of which their chief meets and coverts are as follows—

Otterden is fixed for Mr. Wheeler's good coverts—natural woods, but not of the great size so frequent in the county, though stored with foxes beyond the average. The Black Post, Hollingbourn is also for some small woods; and from here you get on the grass of the hills, of which most is seen on the initial day of the week. Rodmersham, and Torry Hill (Mr. Leigh Pemberton's) are for Kingsdown Wood. Tunstall (Mr. G. Webb's) and Woodstock Park lead to Mr. Twopenny's coverts, where there are always litters of cubs, and Cromer's Wood is one of the most certain finds in the Hunt. Linsted Village has little coverts near it; Doddington is another common fixture; but Leeds Castle (seat of the late Mr. Wickham Martin, who was a member for the county and a good supporter of foxhunting) is usually advertised for Kings Wood and various plantations in the neighbourhood. And below this, as above-mentioned, hounds are seldom taken—on account of wet ground and fruit gardens. From the Squirrels, Stockbury they draw Long Tun (a good place for foxes) and get again on the top of the hills and to the better country. Sharsted Court may be on the cards for either Monday or Thursday. It is the residence of Mr. Faunce De

Laune, Hon. Sec. to the Hunt; and Sharsted Wood is always a find.

Thursday is always on the Canterbury side. From Stone Stile, Chilham they take Mr. Hardy's coverts. Lees Court is the seat of Lord Sondes, who owns a great part of that side of the country. At Belmont are many small woods of Lord Harris's, who has the interest of the Hunt at heart. He also owns Longbeech, a wood of 1500 acres, which is a certain find, and, large as it is, not very difficult to get away from. Syndale, the property of Mr. Hall, son of the last Master of the Tickham, is surrounded by fox coverts, and is a near and favourite meet for foot people from Faversham. The Kennels are a frequent meet for the woods in the neighbourhood. Eastwell is for another "King's Wood" at Challock which was once a good fox covert. Occasionally hounds go down to Cale Hill Park on a Thursday, where in the small woods close by they are likely to find and get into a nice piece of country. The great woods of Blean—stretching seven miles, from Whitstable to Canterbury—and part of which are hunted by the East Kent, used to be great places for cub-hunting, besides availing for at least once a fortnight during the season. There is now so complicated a division of interest in their possession—and that interest leans so largely towards the gun, that they have lost half their value for fox-hunting.

Saturday being for the Chatham and Maidstone side of the country—the meet of The Hook-and-Hatchet, Chatham, is with a view to the great woodlands near that town. Rough, ugly, coverts are these, stretching right down to the Medway; but they hold

The Tickham.

lots of foxes, and stout ones. From Bredhurst are big woods still, separated one from another only by a few fields. At Debtling we get again to smaller coverts and the edge of the grass. From Rainham (on the main line of the L. C. & D. Ry.) they draw Rainham Park, which generally holds a good fox. From Bobbing Court (where lives Mr. Richard Knight, a good friend to the Hunt) they have Wardwell and Calves Hole, where some litters of foxes are bred every spring. Now and again a trip is made into the Marshes by the sea: and Tong Mill, opposite the Isle of Sheppey is usually named. Blacketts is the chief draw; but the search is more often for an outlying fox. From this region they had an extraordinary long run two years ago, following a gallant fox right across the breadth of their country to Staplehurst (a point of between fifteen and sixteen miles), where—scent having been cold all the way—he fairly beat them.

The hounds nearly always sleep out the night before the Saturday meets, lying at the Bell at Bredhurst, where rough Kennels have been provided.

THE VINE.*

HANTS is a county, over every acre of which the fox is hunted, as he has been uninterruptedly for at least the whole of the present century. The Vine, on the best authority, claim a continued existence of quite eighty-five years, during which time there have been many variations in the limits of the country hunted under that denomination.

Almost the whole of Hampshire lies upon chalk—the depth at which the chalk is found below the surface constituting the only variety in the face of the country. Between Basingstoke and Winchester and across the breadth of the county it almost reaches the top of the ground, and, with a sprinkling of light soil above it, forms a wide stretch of wold. Formerly all this district was a rough down—the process of subduing it to agriculture bringing about also the change of definition. Beyond this wold tract, on either side, we find a surface bed of deep clay, and of these two varieties the surface of Hants may be said exclusively to consist. The Vine Country contains both samples, and in itself bears no other divisions

---

* *Vide* "Stanford's Large Scale Map," Sheet 21 ; also "Hobson's Foxhunting Atlas."

beyond the extent of these two respectively. If it does not quite "go without saying" that neither description of ground is likely to carry at all times a strong scent, such is a fact—the statement of which will scarcely occasion surprise. There are good packs of hounds in Hampshire; and there is good hunting. But there are few rapid bursts to be looked for; very little galloping necessary; and watching hounds with their noses down will be the study and recreation provided for you. It is no bad school, though, nor an unworthy resort for maturer age. Hants nursed Tom Smith till he rose to command the Hambledon, the Craven, and eventually the Pytchley; and it soothed the declining years of Assheton Smith when he retired from Leicestershire. It taught the one, and it found food good enough for the other—after all his varied experience. And of all the small fields which come out hunting in Hampshire, it may safely be said that a far larger proportion make a study of the sport than amid the more crowded assemblages of fashionable districts. Every man has plenty of room, and plenty of time to look about him; and most avail themselves of the chance, to learn the sport more thoroughly than where the chief concern must necessarily be to outstrip as many of your neighbours as you can. (At least this is the way I must be allowed to put it—from the plough point of view.)

The Vine Hounds belong to the country: and are a capital pack—offering another instance among the many we have nowadays of the determination to attain a high standard of hounds, whatever may be the country they are called upon to hunt. It is in this direction that the Hound Shows of late years have worked so much benefit. A standard of excellence is there laid down by the best, acknowledged, judges, and presented for the study of Masters and huntsmen. The latter have at the same time the opportunity of comparing for themselves the picked representatives of the best kennels, and establishing a model for their own guidance more easily and satisfactorily than they could hope to by any other means. For, if as an alternative—instead of additional—course, you visit a number of separate Kennels, you find in every one—take which you will—that in each class there are one or two hounds standing pre-eminently above the others; while, again, if you pursue your studies below these elect, your search for knowledge cannot but be more or less swayed, and your judgment influenced, by the opinion of those who have had the making of the pack under observation—and who may, or may not be, the soundest of authorities. Moreover, granting the argument that the showyard and its results afford no criterion of a hound's nose, and behaviour in the field, yet his points for actual work bear so much more proportionate weight in the minds of the judges than his mere beauty of appearance that at least he must be bodily suitable for the field. And, though in a less degree with the hound than the horse, it may be asserted that a well-shaped animal is more likely to be a good performer than one of faulty make.

Then, again, besides the opportunity given by Hound Shows of filling the eye with the truest model, every facility is now granted by Masters of Hounds for access to the blood producing it; and thus every kennel in the kingdom yearly sends forth its matrons for the most desirable cross. For their own credit huntsmen will seldom use a hound in kennel that is faulty in the field (even should there be no restraining influence exercised by the Master); and if not considered good enough to be used at home, there will certainly not continue to be any great call upon him from outside. This alone constitutes a considerable safeguard against the propagation of hereditary vice in the search after symmetry and fashion.

The Vine Country as at present hunted, lies within much narrower limits than those laid down by the maps—inasmuch as Pamber Forest, and all to the north of it, has been lent to the South Berks. With this exception, both Mr. Stanford and Mr. Hobson give, on the whole, an accurate outline of the boundaries—which only here and there follow any direction suggested by natural features. The Vine Country, it will be seen, has the Craven and the South Berks touching it on the north, Mr. Garth's on the east, the H.H. on the south and south-east, and the Tedworth on the west. Basingstoke is the only quarter a visitor would take up. It is easily accessible, too, from London on the morning of hunting—a nine o'clock train from Waterloo landing one there by a quarter past ten. The soldiers often take a trip thither from Aldershot; but unless the L. and S.W.R. stretch a point in favour of hunting, and their own interests, and stop this train for them at Farnboro, a much earlier start is needed. The Kennels of the Vine are close to Overton station. They aim at no palatial grandeur; but are in a good position to command the country. It is found that some two-and-forty couple are by no means too many for the work of hunting three days a week; for the sharp flints of the wolds in some parts almost hide the ground, and play terrible havoc with the feet of hounds. Horses do not suffer in the same degree, as they move on the top of the chalky soil, and so only expose their hoofs to the ragged edges of the flints. The configuration of the country, as divided into the wold or upper ground, and the woodlands, is plainly visible on the map—the former stretching from the south of the country up its whole width to Ewhurst, north of which, and including the Wolverton, Kingsclere and the Vine neighbourhoods, is termed the Woodlands. As a definite distinction the latter is nowadays quite a misnomer. As a matter of fact, *all* the coverts of the Vine are big woods, chains of which are as freely laid across their wold country as in what they call their Woodlands—which section of their territory no doubt earned its name when it included Pamber Forest (once a thousand acres) and other vast tracts of wood now hunted by the South Berks. The only absolute difference now existing consists, as has been mentioned above, in the character of the soil and the style of its culture. On the light ground of the wolds the fields of corn or roots are divided only by broad growths of hazel—they can be scarcely called hedges, as, save by the roadsides, they are planted with no view to fencing-in or fencing-out. They merely serve to mark an outline, and to be cut down now and again to make wattles, &c. They are pierced with frequent holes, through which the rider may move at his leisure, or at

The Vine.

the least he may make certain of a doorway at the corner of each field, big enough for the passage of a waggon. In the "woodland" part of the country, on the other hand, the ground is much deeper, while the enclosures are small, and are separated one from the other by broad banks with a ditch on one side. A strong steady horse is therefore the animal required here; and, as *anything* will carry you over the wolds, it follows that the same horse will *answer* your purpose throughout the Vine country. Taking into consideration, then, that pace is not altogether a necessary quality in your mount, it is safe to say that a cobby, shortlegged, class of horse will be found the best conveyance with the Vine; and that you need never put yourself in the unhappy position of hazarding at every jump two hundred guineas more than you can afford.

Of Tuesday's leading meets and coverts we have Clerken Green or Oakley Hall, for the woods on the south-east, viz., St. John's Wood, Dean Heath, Bull's Bushes, South Wood, &c.—all well preserved. Dean Gate is for Ash Park, Bramdown, Berrydown, and Burley, a number of contiguous woods generally holding foxes. Popham Beacons means Cobley, Southington Scrubs or the Steventon coverts; or hounds may be taken to Black Wood (neutral with the H.H.). At Freefolk Wood, or from Laverstoke House, they draw the former, or Laverstoke Wood, Round Wood, &c.

On a Thursday they have Hannington for Hannington Scrubs, and the Dean's Woods. From Ashe Warren they go to Nutley (a noted source of good runs), Kingsdown, or the Great Dean Wood another fine stronghold. We here get into a chain of large coverts, the chief links of which are Hey Wood, Warrene Bottom, Sheeplanes, Long Wick, ending again in The Dean's Woods—foxes much preferring to hang to the line of covert as long as they can. They meet also at Malshanger, or Manydown Park. From the former they would reach the lastnamed woods; and from Manydown go to Worting Wood (another covert of repute) for first draw.

On Saturday they have Sherborne St. John, or The Vine (where lived Mr. Wm. Chute, the founder of the Hunt) for Morgaston and The Vine coverts, Sherborne Wood, &c., West Heath or Ewhurst Park, are set down for Wyford, Fishwires, Scears, Halton's Coverts and the Ewhurst Woods (foxes being frequent everywhere). Kingsclere or Wolverton Park are intended for Wolverton Wood, Sandford Wood, and the surrounding coverts, or a move may be made westward to Fro Park (which is neutral with the Craven), The Pine Apple—Brimpton, Blacknest, Ashford Hill Cross Roads or New Inn—Baughurst, are all meets for Kingsclere Holts, Redlands and the Baughurst Coverts.

THE SOUTH BERKSHIRE.*

THE South Berks Country rides the Thames about Reading. Indeed, it might almost be called the *Reading Country*—that town being its one base. Under Mr. Hargrave's Mastership everything connected with the Hunt is done on a scale that can only be termed *superb*. He has a beautiful pack of hounds numbering sixty couple); the Kennels—at the "World's End," about two and a half miles out of Reading, on the Bath road—are very perfect; and the men are mounted and turned out exceptionally well. In Roake of the South Berks, by the way, West of the Vine, and Treadwell of the Old Berks, we find that three contiguous packs are now hunted, with eminent success, by men who have wielded the horn for the huge fields of the Pytchley, the Cottesmore and the Quorn respectively; and who do their work none the worse in a quieter field of action, that they have experienced the dash of high-scenting grass, and the rush of an overwhelming multitude. In South Berkshire it is *hunting* always, the scent to be sought, the line to be picked out—except when on the Downs

---

* *Vide* "Stanford's Large Scale Map," Sheet 21; also "Hobson's Foxhunting Atlas."

of their northernmost limits plentiful rain has moistened the surface, and a straight fox starts close in front of hounds. Then there is galloping free and fierce—never a fence to hinder, never a lion to turn you from your path. But the rest of the upland is chilly wold; and the deep lowlands carry none too vigorous a scent.

The South Berks lies thus, with reference to its neighbours—On the north it has the Old Berkshire (west of the Thames), and across the river the South Oxfordshire, with some of the beech woods of the Chiltern Hills in the loop of the stream. The eastern boundary is defined by the little river Loddon, which separates it from Mr. Garth's country. On the south it has the Vine, and borrows from it all its tract of woodland and fir plantation that is contained between the streams of the Kennet and the Loddon, down to and including the Forest of Pamber. On the west is the wide territory of the Craven. Henley to Newbury gives the widest points of the South Berks; but Reading is sufficient mark for the traveller, wishing to make trial of the country. It is within an hour's journey from London (Paddington); and the 9 a.m. train will ensure his being in time for most of the meets.

The South Berks advertise for four days a week—occasionally treating themselves to a byeday in addition. Their country is naturally divided into two parts, differing widely in their nature—the one being the light soil of the downs and wold, the other deep clay and woodland. For distinction's sake we may speak of them respectively as *The Hills* and *The*

The South Berkshire.

Woodlands, by which terms they are more commonly known in their own locality. Thus the Hills are hunted twice a week, Tuesday and Friday, the Woodlands on Monday and Thursday. Should there be a byeday, it will take place on Saturday, wherever room can be found. In the stiff deep country of the Woodlands you must have a strong horse and a steady one. He must be able to move through the dirt; he must have length to cover the wide deep ditches, and sense—or education—to walk and climb over the thick-grown banks that divide the small inclosures between the woods. "Long, low, and wide," the old description, is still the best here. The same horse will carry you well enough over the wold and common of the Bradfield and Bucklebury district; but, if you have variety in your stable, keep your best galloper for the downs in the north-west corner of the country. He need have no notion of jumping, but he must be able to gallop down hill without faltering, up hill without distress, and, at a pinch, for half an hour without a pull.

Taking the Hills first, it must be noted that the Tuesdays and Fridays alternate with each other every week between the down and the wold—in the tract of ground which is north of the Kennet and west of the Thames. The Downs are at their best when much and recent rain has fallen; and then you may have a gallop for which a thoroughbred is none too fast. Where, however, the down has been broken up into wold, and the flints lie thick on the weak ploughland, there can never be any pace; and hounds must labour on incessantly to earn blood. The coverts are the same, on a smaller scale, as in the low country—viz., woods of hazel and other underwood, beneath oak and various timber. They are difficult for hounds to get through, until the early winter has thinned the dense luxuriance of vegetation: and they seldom attain a consistency that allows a pack to drive its fox rapidly before it.

Of the leading fixtures for the Downs are Aldworth and Streatley, for the stronghold of Unhill—a large and well-stocked wood in a most hilly country, and whence many a stretching scurry has taken place. Another frequent meet with a view to Unhill is The Grotto, Basildon, where lives Mr. Arthur Smith, one of the pillars of the Hunt. Besides Unhill, hounds may draw on to the Streatley Woods, Bennett's Wood, Nutgrove, Portobello, Long Copse, and so on, southwards, to Coleridge. More to the westward are the two favourite meets of Compton and Hampstead Norris. The former is on the Downs, and points to Compton Wood, while from the latter they draw Hampstead Beech Wood (Mr. Lowseley's) and Down Wood—thence getting to the flints and arable, and perhaps working down to the Eling coverts and on to Fence, on the boundary. Frilsham House (the seat of Mr. T. Floyd, another good friend to the Hunt) is the next meet, from which they go to Hawkridge for that gentleman's coverts. These are of considerable extent, and within their area is a fine gorse. From them the hounds move on to Coomb Wood (by the way, is there a Hunt in England that does not contain a Coomb Wood, variously spelt?) or the Yattendon Coverts. Bradfield and Ashampstead Common are

The South Berkshire.

just beyond. Both are frequent meets, and both have strong and extensive covert. The Bladebone at Bucklebury, and the Three Crowns at the same place, are other meets for this wild western district, where hundreds of acres are left to rough gorse and common, round which foxes will ring and twist till at their last shrift. Henwick and Cold Ash are similar wastes; Carbyns Wood, Hartshill, Blacklands, and The Hockett are the principal coverts; and Thatcham Gate is occasionally set down as a place of rendezvous—from which also the Westrop Coverts are reached. Jack's Booth is advertised for the Englefield Coverts; and the White Hart, Theale, for the Tilehurst Coverts, Tidmarsh Bottom, and the Purley Coverts. The De la Bere Coverts may be taken next, or may have a meet for themseles. By the side of the Kennet, or of the bigger river, the country of course becomes deeper.

But the deepest, and, perhaps, the most sportgiving, part of the Hunt is the Monday and Thursday country, the Woodlands, in which we include their own territory proper, south of Reading, and all that they borrow from the Vine. Here they have woods of great size, many foxes, and generally a fair scent. Often they have good runs; and would have many more—were their career not so constantly interrupted by the frequent-recurring covert. The riding portion of the South Berks field give this district quite the first place in their affections. They say they here find something—nay, a good deal—to jump, and that hounds are often going fast enough for the excuse. They would prefer that these leaps should be flying ones rather than banks, and that these banks should be sound instead of rotten. But they aver themselves "thankful for small mercies"; and are content that, if from this style of obstacle they fall often, at least they fall soft. The banks are wide and thickly planted; so that a horse should wade, and push, as far as he can, before preparing himself for a spring over the ditch, which may be deep enough to bury him and broad enough to take in two at a time. Between the woods the enclosures are small; and you are hardly in one of them before it is time to be out again—and then you have to choose as quickly as possible where your hindlegs will stick least, and where they will land on soundest ground. There is nothing airy even in first flight, over the South Berkshire Vale; though the pleasure is often rich and satisfying, as pudding to a schoolboy.

In the Old Vine Country the principal meets of the South Berks nowadays are—Silchester Dials for Pamber Forest, which, though much reduced, is still an immense jungle tract of hazel and oak sapling, sedgey and thick withal. Foxes there are here; but they are seldom young—an anomaly we must leave to others to explain. Farthest on the outside of the borrowed territory is Pamber End Gate, or Beaurepaire Park, to draw Beaurepaire Gully, or Newlands and Cranes, Grocus and Pepper Wood, all well preserved and faithful. From Bramley Village they have a good covert in Bramley Frith; and afterwards work back to Silchester. Aldermaston Village more often comes on a Thursday; gives them Pace's Gully, Wasing Wood and Burnhams; or takes them eventually into the fir plantations which cover the country across to Mortimer West End. It is queer riding among these miles of fir trees; but you must get through them quickly—leaving it to your horse to do most of the steering—for, as in the rougher portions of Mr. Garth's country, hounds generally own to a lively scent. If the meet be the Round Oak, Padworth, the early part of the day is spent among the fir trees; and then they probably find themselves in Padworth Gully or Upton Park. The three fixtures of The Kennels, The Swan at Burghfield Village, and The Bell at Grazeley all lead to Penge Wood, the Burghfield coverts, and Beech Hill —the last-named being also often a meet. Sulhamstead House is for Major Thoyts' coverts there, with Brazenhead, Boar Moor and Omer's Gully to follow, and so on to Starveall. At Twyford Gate they get Mr. Wheble's coverts, and Mr. Hargreaves' at Maiden Erlegh. Wokefield Park (Major Allfrey's) has excellent coverts, from which they generally get quickly away, and may run down to Strathfield Saye. Shinfield is quite on the border adjoining Mr. Garth's. By the side of the Loddon are many small coverts, among the little meadows; foxes are plentiful and the scent good. Chequers Green, Strathfield Saye, is more often an after-Christmas meet, for the Duke of Wellington's property. And though permission is withheld till late in the winter, foxes are then usually to be found.

The South Berks cross the river (the Thames) about once a month, for their province in the shire of Oxford. No particular day is set apart for the beech woods adjoining Lord Macclesfield's territory. But they seldom go there on a Friday, and Thursday is, perhaps, most frequently chosen. Nuffield Common is their outside meet. It lies just below the hills; and is for the great Mongewell coverts, where a fox is generally to be found. From here they come on to Ipsden, and get among the beech woods. Checkendon is for Hammond's Wood; and The Fox at Cane-End is for the strong beech woods at Wyfold. From Goring Heath they draw homewards for Mapledurham and the Whitchurch coverts.

MR. GARTH'S.*

MR. GARTH hunts a great expanse of varied country on the right bank of the Thames—from about Reading as far down the stream as the environs of London will allow (practically Weybridge or thereabouts), and southwards to include Aldershot and its precincts. Henley, Maidenhead, Windsor, Staines, and Chertsey are all posts on the northern border—none of their names with a foxhunting ring about them. Woking may be on the way to Happy Hunting Grounds; but it is certainly not *in* them. At Aldershot, the soldier say, there is "a deal of hunting;" but their share is as much in the passive as the active form. They are rattled about at home daily, and forced into the open at least once a week. The training is no doubt for their good. At any rate they learn to be quick enough away whenever opportunity offers; and never hang in covert when it is open on the London side. But if any human being has realised exactly the amount of enjoyment experienced by interesting Mrs. Reynard before hounds on a warm April morning, it is the stout and elder captain of an infantry regiment as, on a lovely July

---

* "Stanford's Large Scale Map," sheets 21, 22, and 16; also "Hobson's Foxhunting Atlas."

day, he skirmishes at the double through the dark dustclouds of the Long Valley. Breath has failed him long ago. Were it left him, he could make no use for it; for his tongue is swollen and dry, and black as pariah dog's, while his lips retain as much life as an old shoe. But the staff-hounds are raging fiercely on his track—their hoarse voices ringing savagely into ears. Though his heart sinks and his limbs almost refuse to act, he must run on; for, though it is pain and misery to go forward, a worse fate awaits him if he stops to be caught.

But it is from Aldershot that Mr. Garth's field is chiefly recruited; and the soldiers go out with him gratefully on his good ground and his worse—thankful that they can see a grand pack of hounds at work, even though the arena be not always such as will do them justice. Reading, however, would probably be found the best immediate base for a visitor. It commands the best of Mr. Garth's, and the best of the South Berkshire. It is less than an hour's journey from London; and the nine o'clock train from Paddington Station brings very many of the good meets of either pack within distance on the morning of hunting.

Mr. Garth has rough places to hunt over—heather wild as Exmoor, and fir woods fit to harbour red-deer. Indeed, the wild stag might be allowed to roam between Aldershot and Windsor, and be trusted to do no more harm than on the Hills of Devon and Somerset. What an opening for a grand sport! Mile upon mile of forest ground are now of scant use for hounds—or even for the gun. Most of it is Government ground—and a Conservative Government is several degrees less cautious than one of Liberal tenets. Crops are few and far between in this great moorland area. Mr. Bisset could re-establish staghunting, when it had virtually died out in the west; could not some one with influence and energy set it going amid the wilds of Bagshot Heath and Windsor Forest?

All of Mr. Garth's country, however, is not rough. The Reading side is in parts nice enough. Between the Kennels and Wokingham is a stiff bank-and-ditch country; there is some pleasant riding by the side of the Blackwater; while in the neighbourhood of Tilney Hall and Blackwood, touching the Vine, there is good ground and well fenced—though this, too, is under the plough. Taking it throughout, Mr. Garth's can hardly be termed a good scenting country, though like all others it varies much with season and circumstance. The Heath is often difficult to run over, even when a fair scent prevails; for a fox invariably shirks a bee line across the heather, and runs the beaten tracks, which crossing and cutting into each other, irresistibly tempt him to double and twist. Thus hounds are constantly over-shooting the line, and time must often be lost in getting back to recover it.

Mr. Garth's hounds are a pack of high class and character, and of a size almost unique among foxhounds of the present day—some of the dogs standing fully 25 inches. And this is attained without loss of quality, or addition of lumber. The bitches by no means strike the eye as being of extravagant size; and the pack generally gives the idea of smartness and dash. The Kennels are at the Master's place at Haines

Hill, near Twyford station, and about seven miles from Reading. Everything, both in kennel and field, is extremely well done; and Mr. Garth has shown untiring energy and determination in battling against the difficulties natural to the country.

Your horse for this country should be active and strong, if not necessarily of three-figure class. He must be nimble and surefooted as a goat—or as a middle horse in an R.H.A. team—if he is to cross in safety the hidden ruts and holes of the heather; while, for the other country, he must be able to move with tolerable ease through dirt, and to lift himself on to a high bank or fling himself over a wide ditch.

Mr. Garth advertises for four days a week—Monday, Wednesday, Friday, and Saturday. Monday is for the home district, Wednesday for what may be termed the middle country. For Friday hounds go overnight to Hartford Bridge, near Winchfield Station, to hunt in Hampshire, and beyond the Blackwater; while on Saturday they go upon the Heath. The Monday country has plenty of coverts, which, as a rule, are of no great extent—though there is a large wood on Bowsey Hills, for which they meet at Hare Hatch, close to the Kennels. Hall Place is the next fixture, and is for Ashley Hill (Sir G. East's). Between the Thames and these hills are wide open fields, with very few fences to be seen, till Billingbear Park is reached. This brings them close to Haines Hill and Mr. Garth's property—the main covert being Charity Wood—(a very favourite place). Shottesbroke Park is for Great Wood and Mr. Wiggett's Gorse—which is also in great repute.

Mr. Garth's.

Wednesday, too, is mostly in a cultivated district. Bearwood Lodge is fixed for the Bearwood coverts and Fox Hill Gorse. Barkham Combes, joining Bearwood, is another good place for foxes—and the names of Messrs. Walter and Simonds ought to be recorded as hearty friends to the Hunt. From the meet of The Greyhound at Finchhampstead, hounds go to The Fleet and Farley Hill; and sometimes the Bound Oak, Farley Hill, is named, for Sir C. Russell's coverts at Swallowfield Place. Luckley Park is for the Luckley Coverts and Finchhampstead Ridges.

Friday runs sometimes on rough, sometimes on smoother lines. Greywell Hill and Andwell Mill are very favourite meets for the same stretch of covert —the two being at opposite ends of a woodland some two or three miles in length. For an afternoon draw a move is more frequently made to Hods and Bells (a great covert). Dogmersfield Park (Sir H. Mildmay's) has various good resting-places for foxes, the best being Coxmoor. From Clere Park they draw Old Park Gorse, and back by Bourley Bottom, under the Long Valley. These coverts are Government property; and under this proprietorship cubs are yearly bred in security. Beacon Hill on the cards is for the same draws, with Ewshot Wood on the southern border of Mr. Garth's dominion. But Tilney Hall on the west is for a better country, enclosed with bank and ditch; and has a good covert in Blackwood, the property of Mr. Harris. Sherfield Green has some coverts in its neighbourhood, from which hounds are likely to work back in the course of the day by Greywell.

Saturday, as above mentioned, is on the Heath; and the meets are not numerous. Wentworth, belonging to the Countess Morella, is a rare place for foxes. Silverlands, close to Chertsey, is for the coverts of Fox Hills and subsequently for Ottershaw. Red Lodge, Swinley, is on Government heath, and this kind of ground is drawn over for many miles. Easthampstead Park (Lord Downshire's) is just between the Heath and the Billingbear country; and is named equally for Monday, Wednesday, or Saturday. It is a chosen and secure haunt for foxes; and a run may be had from it in any direction. The Easthampstead and Chertsey districts show best sport in spring—when, getting close away at a wild fox, he may be driven for miles.

THE H.H.*

It is not easy to describe any one Country in Hampshire, without repeating much that may have been already written about another. Undulating wold, with flints brought to the surface by the disturbing plough; close cropped down overlying the virgin chalk; occasional clay-covered vales—these are the characteristics of Hants throughout; and the sphere of each Hunt differs only in the degree in which it partakes of each variety. The staunchest friend to Hampshire cannot say that it is a quick-scenting country. Foxhunting is studied there, and made the most of; but it is foxhunting in its colder, more laboriously scientific form, rather than in its warm and soul-stirring sense. At least so the natives lead us to believe—and who is likely to give an opinion so fair and favourable as they? The H.H., or—in full, and quite as commonly—the Hampshire Hounds, hunt almost entirely on this sea of wold—their country taking up a great part of the high ground marked on the maps as the Hampshire Hills. It is only along

---

* *Vide* "Stanford's Large Scale Map," Sheet 21; and "Hobson's Foxhunting Atlas."

their south-eastern border that they get off the unfenced uplands, and enter upon a stiffer country, where there is a good deal to jump, and here and there a certain amount of grass to cross. Woods of the true Hampshire type, dense of undercovert, and through which hounds can only force their fox with difficulty, are their coverts, varying a little in size and frequency, — and perhaps in trustiness—but everywhere naturally capable of holding the animal in any number to which he may be encouraged. And, on the whole, the H.H. country has its full share of foxes; and is at least quite as well off in this respect as most of its neighbours.

Mr. Deacon has been master for the last eighteen years, and his own huntsman for fifteen; and during the whole time has scarcely missed a day. His hounds are almost entirely of Lord Portsmouth's blood, and many of them of his lordship's breeding, the young draft from the Eggesford Kennels being every year sent to Mr. Deacon. The H.H. Kennels are at Ropley (where also the master resides)—Ropley being a station on the L. & S. W. Ry., midway between Aldershot and Winchester, and about fifty-five miles from London (Waterloo station). For a four-days-a-week country a very strong pack is kept up, giving full allowance for the numerous casualties caused by the flints. The Master is thus also enabled to carry out his principle of bringing on every year a large entry of young hounds—youth being, in his opinion, an ingredient that should enter largely into the composition of a working pack, if it is to retain the dash that alone will allow of hounds *driving* over cold scenting grounds. His old hounds, consequently, are drafted as soon as they develope the slightest sign of pottering, or any of the numerous failings to which age is prone. The result is that the H.H. make all that is possible out of such scent as may be given to the day, and the ground will carry. If they do not often get the opportunity of *racing*, it is no fault of theirs. The bitch pack, especially, look like "flying"; and cleaner necks and shoulders are not to be found on hounds. But whereas on the wolds there is seldom a scent which would bear unabashed the epithet of *burning*, in their better country the coverts are so thickly scattered that a burst can seldom last many minutes. Should hounds be fortunate enough to get away from the first stronghold at the brush of their fox, they are bound to find themselves almost immediately in the depths of another, whose very density will tempt the stoutest fox to hang. Even should he be so gayhearted as to prefer an instant onward course, the chances are all in favour of his exit being anticipated and thwarted—by someone wise enough, and wicked enough, to reach the other side of the covert before him. At least so say those who should know, and who have gained their knowledge under suffering.

The towns of Winchester, Basingstoke, and Farnham constitute outside points conveying a very good idea of the extent of the H.H. country; and any of these may be chosen by the visitor wishing for insight into the "craft" as practised on the Hampshire Hills. Basingstoke is not only the most handy to the Londoner—the 9 a.m. train from Waterloo landing him at Basingstoke at 10.13—but it is situated almost at the spot where the Vine, Mr. Garth's and the H.H. all touch. Thus the H.H. have these two packs on their northern boundary, Mr. Richard Combe's and Lord Leconfield's on the east, the Hambledon on the south, and the Hursley and the Tedworth on the west. Larger fields attend the H.H. than are found with any of the other packs named—two hundred, or even two hundred and fifty, horsemen being a frequent muster. For, once a week (on a Tuesday) the Hambledon men troop in; and on a Saturday the army turns out from Aldershot.

That you are better off on a good horse with the H.H. than on a bad one, is a matter easily proved. To turn out of a lane, over a bank and a quickset at a moment's notice, requires a hunter; and for a hog-backed stile out of a wood you had better be on the same—if immunity from disappointment or fall is an object. And, again, as the chalk and loam are very holding in wet weather, a strong galloper is positively necessary when hounds run, and you would be with them. So, if you are a resident, and would see the sport, by all means mount yourself on a stout good horse. Whether, as a traveller in search of change and capable of buying the best, you care to launch into extravagance for the sake of a trial visit into Hampshire, must be for yourself to determine.

The hunting-days of the H.H. are Monday, Tuesday, Thursday, and Saturday. The three latter all take them into a very similar class of country, as afore noted: but Monday very often brings them among banks and ditches, with smaller enclosures—

many of which are grass. And this part is usually termed the Chawton district—its limits being comprised within a line drawn from about Bentley Station, by Alton, to Faringdon in the Selbourn neighbourhood. Mr. Stanford's map, by the way, by no means gives accurately the boundary of H.H. on this side; as it extends eastward here as far as Farnham— besides which, it should be added, the Woolmer Forest is a tract which no less than *four* packs claim a right to draw, viz., the H.H., Mr. Richard Combe's, the Hambledon, and Lord Leconfield's. In point of fact, the limits of the H.H. country in this direction have been so frequently altered, by loan of territory and otherwise, during the last half-century, that modern custom—rather than ancient right—has to do with its present geography. The Monday country, then, takes the south-eastern corner; and extends northward about as far as Preston Oakhills. Of its meets Medstead Green, Windmill Hill—Bradley, Preston Oakhills (where there is a very large covert), New Inn—Lasham, and Lasham Village are all on the lighter and more open ground. Chawton House is considered the best meet in the Hunt, and lies among the stiffest of the banks and ditches—some of which are too formidable for the powers of any horse. Between Chawton and Hartley there is more turf than is to be found elsewhere in the dominion; and it is quite the best scenting ground. Binstead Church, Hartley, and the Temple (near Selbourn) are other fixtures in the bank-and-ditch country; and Rotherfield Park, near Alton, is also a Monday meet.

Taking it all through, however, there is perhaps

more sport to be obtained on a Tuesday than on any of the other three days. It is held on the Winchester side, and along the south of the country. The Hambledon men come out on that day, and it is quite the most popular with the hunt itself. The most easterly meets are the Anchor Inn—Ropley, and West-Tisted. From the latter there is a capital line by Merryfield up to Rotherfield, good going, though on plough, and with much nice fencing by the way. Working westward, we have the meets of Bramdean Common, Brookwood Park, Cross-Roads-Beauworth, and Tichborne Park—and plenty of good woods are met with throughout the district.

Thursday has the worst side of the country allotted, viz., from Basingstoke, Ellisfield and Ropley westwards, and to the north of Alresford. Large woodlands over-run a great part of it; and the open is all wold, with little or nothing for riders to do—though hounds must work busily all the time, and patience is the leading virtue for both the pack and the field. It is quite an open question as to whether small fences, or none at all, are most detrimental to the interests of hounds patiently puzzling over an indifferent scent. A *whole* field likes to gallop when it can: but only a portion will jump without occasion. These latter, however, are ever finding excuse for indulging their propensities, wherever easy fences are offered them; and so are less easily restrained. These, perhaps, are the greater sinners. But on this point we must leave each huntsman to form his own opinion. Let him, however, bear in mind that, until he gains the Happy Hunting-Grounds, he will never have the blissful privilege of handling hounds without a field of horsemen to over-ride them : and meanwhile he must bear his trials as best he can. To continue with the Thursday meets, we have Brown-Candover, Stratton Park, Abbotstone Down, Bighton Wood, on the Winchester side; and Nutley Church, Farleigh Park, and Ellisfield Church, nearer Basingstoke—the woods forming almost a chain throughout.

Saturday is more especially the Aldershot day, and is held in the north-western corner, between that place and Basingstoke. The principal meets are Upton Gray, with the coverts of Sturts and Pudding; Herriard Park; South Warnborough, with Easters and Vinney to draw; Froyle Park; Golden Pot, Sutton Common; Marsh House, Bentley; and Five-Lanes, Holybourn; Hoddington House, &c.

THE TEDWORTH.*

NINE-TENTHS of the Tedworth country is situated on the high table land, round whose base run the Kennet, the Avon, and the Test—the border line of the counties of Wilts and Hants nearly bisecting it from north to south. Downs and light wold—all unfenced —divide this table land between them. For the rest, there is a narrow strip of low land in the north-west corner, termed the Pewsey Vale; and there are heavy woodlands on the far east. Marlborough is about the extreme northern point of the Tedworth; Andover is close to its eastern boundary; Stockbridge and Salisbury mark its southernmost limit; and Devizes is just over its north-west frontier. With reference to its neighbours (and being in itself of considerable size, it touches many), it has the Craven on the north, the Vine and H.H. on the east, the Hursley and Earl of Radnor's on the south, the South and West Wilts on the west, and the Duke of Beaufort's on the north-west. The Salisbury and Devizes road traces its western, and that of Salisbury and Stockbridge its southern boundary. Beyond these lines of demarca-

---

* *Vide* " Stanford's Large Scale Map," Sheet 21; also " Hobson's Foxhunting Atlas."

The Tedworth.

tion you must be guided only to a certain extent by the colouring of Mr. Stanford's map. He should have carried the north-eastern frontier of the Tedworth considerably wider, so as to include Savernake Forest and a tract of country of which Froxfield, Shalbourn, and the edge of the hills by Ham and East Woodhay, give about the true outline. Andover, being most easily reached from town (in an hour and three-quarters from Waterloo), is the point you would probably choose if minded to run down to the Tedworth, as it is attainable on the morning of hunting.

And now, having noted its position, we may proceed briefly to note upon the Tedworth country. It is not one that will bear lengthy description, for it has no great variety in itself beyond that conveyed in the summary already given. Its coverts are, generally speaking, smaller and farther apart than those of its neighbour, the Vine. Its face, where disturbed by the plough, is of the same cold, flinty and chalky, nature, over which hounds can only really run on exceptional occasions; but its Downs often carry a dashing scent. You may safely say of the Tedworth as a scenting country, that *you either run fast over it or cannot run at all*. Close at your fox on a favourable day, you may race him from find to finish more surely than over the best pastures in the Shires. For he can never run his foil by doubling down a hedgerow, nor at the last moment save his brush by lying down in a ditch. In a quick spin over the Downs it often happens that Reynard is to be seen all the way, as he rises brow after brow of the undulating sheep-walk, till at length he drops back to hounds to be rolled over in making his first turn. But this is not every day. The wold, now and again, will carry you on as briskly as the short crisp turf of the Downs; and you may leave turnips and stubble and fallow behind you gaily, with no time to turn out of your way for the one row of hurdles that offers its services for a leap. But often the wold is cold, and hard, and heartless: and even the Downs frequently will not help you, if you give them time to think about it. *Then* the Tedworth Country is in its inhospitable mood. Would you obtain at a glance a fair idea of the Tedworth Hills, betake yourself on a clear day to the top of Beacon Hill, a few miles from the Kennels; and let your eye wander over the sweeping undulations that roll smoothly away as far as vision will follow, like nothing else than the broad unbroken rollers below the Cape of Good Hope, in what is there termed a calm. Mile upon mile of unruffled surface, without a break to cross the scene or impede the view. The Downs dotted with sheep, like the white floating forms of seagulls; the green turnip fields and occasional coverts, as darker shadows cloud cast amid the sun-like glare of the cornfields—all go to make the simile more fitting.

A drawback—of more magnitude than would be supposed—is contained in the presence of the hares on the Downs. They may not interfere much on a strong scenting day. But they baffle and bother terribly when hounds are called upon to stoop to their work—for they flutter and skip across the line, not singly, but almost by the score. Flints are an enemy to hounds all over Hants and Wilts; and wring the

The Tedworth. 281

pockets of Masters quite five per cent. beyond ordinary estimate, in reference to number of couple in Kennel. And now for a point of heresy—The truest and most cat-like feet are *not* those that wear best over this razor-strewn wold. A flatter—and consequently less orthodox—foot stands more work than one fashioned on the accepted model. A greater surface, and more elasticity, is required ; and the inferior shape will last longer than the pattern mould. Cuts will inevitably come. And on the small rounded sole they inevitably come nearer, and sharper, to the supporting ligaments —while at the same time the rigid conformation from shoulder to foot, insisted upon by our leading judges, precludes a light footfall to save the shock and ease the cut. Without venturing to impugn their judgment, I would urge that a point must in practice be stretched for this special field.

The Kennels at Tedworth Park are the property of, and lent by, Sir John Kelk, without whose assistance the Hunt would last year have probably fallen to the ground. They were originally built by Mr. Assheton Smith; and the hounds presented to the Country in 1858 by his widow. In any notice of the Tedworth it would be impossible to avoid allusion to that prince of hard riders, who, after a notable career in Leicestershire, returned to Hants to raise the local Hunt to an eminence that was never aimed at before, and to spend a sporting old age where he could still gallop to his own hounds. The reflection of age having come over him may, or may not, have influenced Assheton Smith, who, as a sexagenarian, was a bolder and stronger man than most of us at forty—but there is an unquestionable advantage offered to advanced years, in the absence of fences in the Tedworth country. Very few backbones can then stand with indifference the jar of landing over big jumps. Yet the spirit may be strong as ever; and the heart leap as gaily to the sound of hounds in cry, as in early boyhood. Where can a better, safer, outlet be found than on the Downs and unfenced acres of the Tedworth—where the pack will often burst their fox as quickly as in the Vale of Belvoir, and where a horse may be extended without a pull from the start. Assheton Smith was an *octogenarian*, when, on the occasion of one of his last meets at Tedworth Park, he had two such gallops in the day; and the old man rode as close to his hounds, and as keenly, as in middle age. There was a *rare* scent. His first fox broke from a covert hard by, with miles of open country before him; and his great hounds—loping along like wolves—never lowered nor raised their heads, till after twenty-seven furious minutes, over down and wold, they galloped straight into their fox. In the afternoon they pulled down a second without a check—making up a day's sport difficult to beat. These hounds were of almost unparalleled size. Several of them were allowed into the breakfast room; and could all put their heads on the table as they stood. My informant (an eyewitness) gives their average as at 26 inches or over—a height that puts Mr. Fenwick Bisset's great staghounds to shame. Their descendants in the present pack retain no such giant dimensions. But they are a true built working sort; and with the country well held in the interest of foxhunting,

The Tedworth.

Sir Reginald Graham, the new master, has no bad prospect before him. Fricker, the huntsman, has—in one capacity or another—been nearly half a century in the Tedworth Kennels—which, it may be mentioned, are about half a dozen miles from the station of Grateley on the London and South-Western line. Tedworth itself, stands so exactly on the border line, between Hants and Wilts that (as every will-making lawyer has heard) Assheton Smith, in dictating his last testament, bequeathed House and surrounding estate as being all situate in Hants. The House went as willed; but the heir-at-law stepped in, on the plea that much of the *estate* was in *Wilts*, substantiated his claim and gained possession.

The Tedworth Hounds take the field four days in the week, viz., Monday, Tuesday, Thursday and Saturday —for which number they have ample scope in their extensive range of country. Monday is more especially for the Downs, and the west of the country: and the meets are—Woodford Bridge, from which they draw up the brook side towards Amesbury, where Sir E. Antrobus has good coverts: High Post, for the gorses on the Downs, with Amesbury to fill up the day: while Porton Firs and Amesbury are named for the same draws. Netheravon and Newfoundland are altogether for the open country up the stream, and for the patches of gorse on the Downs. From Elbarrow, on Netherdon Down, they go to the gorses of the Downs along the border by the South Wilts Country. From Everleigh there are nice coverts near, and plenty of foxes, at Sir John Astley's. Indeed, all the Down country is very fairly off for the requisite animal.

x

Tedworth has some nice small coverts about the Park, with a good wood in Ashton Copse, together with a gorse on the hill above, all of which are, it is needless to say, replete with foxes. And about four miles away is Collingbourne Wood, of about fifteen hundred acres, which is in itself a perfect nursery. Wilbury is in the open country, about four miles from Kennels, and has some small plantations, &c.

Tuesday is for the extreme north-west and the Pewsey Vale, which is a deep narrow valley between Salisbury Plain (or more strictly, perhaps, the Everley Downs) and the Marlborough Downs. It is a fair scenting country, with small coverts—none too profusely stocked. Its inclosures are small and divided by narrow banks, often rotten and boggy. Of the meets on this day—Oare Hill, close to Marlboro', is just beyond the Pewsey Vale, and is for West Wood, the property of the Duke of Marlboro', and one of the best coverts in the Hunt. A mile and a half from West Wood is an excellent gorse, called Clinch Common. Savernake Ruins, or Station, with Burbage Wharf are in the eastern continuation of the Pewsey Vale. From these meets, after drawing Ram Alley and Brunslade, they go up into Savernake Forest—a wide fir tract, which foxes inhabit in no great numbers, and beyond which are some other coverts towards Hungerford. Puthall Gate is also on the edge of the Forest; but has, as first draw, a fine covert in Henshood. Woodbridge is in the Pewsey Vale, with small osier beds in its vicinity, and West Wood to follow. New Mill is for the same class of small coverts in the Vale, and eventually for Clinch Common Gorse, which as a covert is quite the pride of the Hunt.

The Tedworth.

Thursday, though on the roughest and most hilly part of the country, is by no means considered the worst day of the week with the Tedworth. At the fixture of Southgrove is a fine wood of the Marquis of Aylesbury's; Oxenwood Village is on the hills by the borders of the Craven; Vernham Gate has a fine covert well kept by Mr. Bevan; Conholt is for Conholt Coverts, excellent places for foxes; and Chute Lodge has small woods and a gorse, where foxes are always found—all these lastnamed meets being in the same rough hilly country. Crawlboys Farm and Collingbourne Shears are for the great Collingbourne Wood, aforementioned—upon which Assheton Smith made his famous experiment of forcing foxes to break, by means of bonfires along the rides. Redenham, Penton Lodge, and Weyhill, when advertised, are for nearly the same district—including the woods of Redenham and the gorse at Penton.

Saturday takes the south-east of the country. About Coombe Wood, which, with Buttermere Wood, is lent by the Craven, it is hilly, flinty and rough; but the foxes are wild and the sport often good. At Faccombe are very large woods: Pill Heath is a fine covert adjoining Doles Wood—Doles Gate and Enham being for the same two draws. Quarley Hill, near Grateley, has a nice covert of moderate size belonging to the Marquis of Winchester. Longstock, on the edge of the country bordering on the Hursley, has a few little osier beds by the river. At Tangley are a couple of very useful woods; and from Clatford Oakcuts, they draw some small, but good, coverts near Stockbridge, on the more level ground.

LORD FERRERS'.*

Of a loan from the Quorn, Lord Ferrers has been able to make a neat two days-a-week country, which, though hitherto little heard of in its separate existence, has by virtue of its sports and capabilities quite as good a claim to a reputation as many a provincial Hunt of note. Lord Ferrers' is, in brief, a plough country of considerable merit—if of inconsiderable extent. Hounds generally have to deal with a scent good enough to put them on fair terms with their foxes; and very often they can run almost as hard as on grass. The plough does not ride deep; and the fences, of moderate size, can be taken much as they come—being an honest description of thorn and ditch. When the Quorn kept it in their own hands, this portion formed their Saturday ground. Sometimes, week after week, they used to come to the grass side on a Monday, full of the smart runs with which they had wound up the previous week—but which, happening far out of the ken of their Meltonian hearers, were accepted, if not with the salt-grain of incredulity, at least with a condescension that plainly

---

* *Vide* "Stanford's Large Scale Map," Sheet 16 also, "Hobson's Foxhunting Atlas."

inferred " Pleased to hear you enjoyed yourselves so much. Very glad *we* weren't there." For they of the hard riding and highly dressed school, except such as had known the Marquis of Hastings' mastership—or even that of Mr. Story—had a vague notion that they were only being told of some rough-and-tumble run in Charnwood Forest. It was never explained that above and beyond this Forest lay a corner where hounds showed a great deal of good and open sport. Nor was it of interest to them to inquire. The scene lay beyond their reach, and—with six days' pastime awaiting them at their doors—beyond their covet. It is the close propinquity of the grass countries that prevents an unpretentious little country such as Lord Ferrers' ever aspiring to fame. It will not bear comparison with its nearest neighbours: and comparison is not likely to be pushed much further for an estimate. And yet it is as a whole a far superior country to half of the main Quorn territory—which, in rock and slate, forest and light plough, offers a contrast extraordinary and appalling, to the pastures upon which that Hunt founds its reputation and its boast. With Lord Ferrers foxes are found, and killed, on fair open soil, where you may ride to hounds all the time, throw your leaps without peril, and see all that is going on. In the Quorn Forest and its outlying woods you are often fain to rest satisfied with the *knowledge* that hounds are hard at work somewhere in the neighbourhood, and that during the many *mauvais quarts d'heure* which you spend without a single sight of them, they are labouring gallantly towards an end. To render this knowledge at all exciting, you concentrate all your interest into their attainment of this end; and, if you have the power to absorb your whole self and enjoyment in sympathy, you may be as delighted as the huntsman himself when the run is over—perhaps a good deal more! But if you can live with hounds, it is always keen delight to *see* them run; and, though holding that the pleasure is more elastic on turf than on tillage ground, you must be hard indeed to please if a clever pack working up to their fox over plough is no treat to you. There is such a wide difference, too, in the scenting properties of various arable soils that it would be as absurd to place them all in one class as to form an opinion of how any country carries a scent from a single day's experience of it. In Lord Ferrers' country alone, for instance, two very distinct conditions of ploughed land are to be found. The Leak Hills on the east are cold unprofitable ground, on which to ask hounds to do their work well and quickly; whereas in the Donington district they can often lay themselves down to a teeming scent, and can almost always hunt their way fairly along. In this latter part foxes are by no means unusually difficult to kill; for, added to the fact that there is generally a steady scent, hounds have the advantage of being free from an overwhelming field on their backs. Except when a meet occurs about Clifton—where his northernmost corner approaches the town of Nottingham—there is no source from which Lord Ferrers can collect a gathering round him. There are a certain number of gentlemen's seats scattered about his country; but there are no towns of any size within its limits. Thus his usual field consists of at most a dozen gentlemen, and as many farmers—the hunting, no doubt, being thus made easier for huntsmen, fairer for hounds, and pleasanter for those of the little company who may prefer their sport without the accessory of society. Loughborough often sends its emissaries over the border on a Friday, rather than condemn them to a better fate and a longer journey on to the grass with the home pack. But Loughborough is not a sporting centre, though a sporting place. People hunt from there; but do not come there to hunt. Nottingham, again, attracts only through its manufactories; and as a home for what the press sometimes terms the knights of the pencil; and, besides, those who manufacture and those who bet have a pack of their own close at hand. In fact, Lord Ferrers' is quite a little Hunt of its own, nestled away in a snug corner, and carrying on its sport in a quiet satisfactory way for its own amusement. It may be reached from Derby, and it may be reached from Nottingham; while Loughborough would join in oftener were not the days of hunting the same as those of the Quorn in their best country—Monday and Friday to wit. If you would pay it a visit from a distance, Trent (where all the Midland trains pull up) would probably be your point. It is 120 miles from London and twenty from Leicester. Or, by a slow train, a ticket to Kegworth would set you down in the heart of the country.

The whereabouts of Lord Ferrers' Country may be defined thus. It begins where Charnwood Forest ends—at, and including, Gracedieu. It thence goes up to the River Trent, along which it runs nearly to Nottingham. The Kennels are at Staunton Harold (Lord Ferrers' residence); and Gillson, the huntsman, came from the Quorn with the draft that formed the nucleus of the pack. It should be noted also that some twenty years ago a similar loan of territory was made by the Quorn to the late Mr. John Story, who hunted it under the name of The Donington Country

The Monday meets are as a rule in the western half of the country. Staunton Harold has the Master's coverts in and about the park—Staunton Spring Wood being the chief of them. A broad ride runs through the wood; and it is a capital place to find, and rattle, a litter of cubs in the autumn. Lord Ferrers has also planted a good new gorse on the hill between Staunton Harold and Breedon Clouds. After drawing Lount Wood, they are likely to get on to the Coleorton Coverts.

Coleorton Hall (Sir G. Beaumont's) is a frequent and favourite meet, with any quantity of covert, rough natural and good, and foxes enough to last out the day. The country round, too, is about the roughest in the Hunt; but carrying a fair scent, and by no means bad for sport. Belton, and Tonge Station, are the next fixtures, and point to Belton New Wood, Tonge Gorse and Diseworth Gorse (only separated from each other by a road, and neither being really gorses but small briar and mixed covert), The Asplings, and Breedon Clouds—the whole forming a cluster, and a fox to be found in one or another. Langley Priory, near by, has also a small covert.

Gracedieu is the outside meet on the southern

Lord Ferrers'.

border, and has much rough covert, through which hounds can often run hard. White Horse Wood is, perhaps, the principal draw; is a good and likely place for a fox; and is easy to get away from. Donington Park (where the late Marquis of Hastings lived) has woods of no great size, but good holding capacity, within its precincts. Islay Walton Toll Gate and Ashby Toll Gate are occasionally advertised; and at Whatton is a gorse and some small spinnies.

Friday has Lockington Hall (formerly the seat of Mr. J. Storey) allotted to it—and gives some of the best ground in the Hunt. From it they draw March Covert, and thence often run fast over the meadows by the river side. But the area is limited in this direction, and the gallop is more frequently a ring back to the covert. Lockington Gorse, on the other side of the Hall, gives more room and very often good sport over a nice line and a good deal of grass. After adding Cavendish Bridge, we cross to the other side of the river Soar, which intersects the country on its way to the Trent, and get to the Leak Hills and colder ground. These hills have been planted by Lord Belper with a prolonged extent of covert, to which foxes take kindly. The meets usually named for drawing them are Kegworth Station, Leak Pit House, Kingston Hall, and occasionally Sutton Bonington. For similar hill coverts are the meets of Thrumpton and Gotham; and at all these wide plantations, though heavily utilised for shooting purposes, foxes are heartily welcomed. In the extreme north Clifton Hall is the nearest fixture to Nottingham, with the covert of Clifton gardens on the hill side above the Trent.

Barton has a wood, and with this we have gone through the country — which, were it not so well preserved, would scarcely afford room for even two days a week. In conclusion, you want a respectable hunter to follow Lord Ferrer's hounds. He need be only half as good as if for the best part of the adjoining Hunt. But he *must* be able to jump fairly; and he ought to be able to gallop when called upon. Yet you need not spend a heavy sum in order to acquire fashion.

THE WARWICKSHIRE.*

THE Warwickshire Hunt has a recorded existence of a century without a break; and it is much further back still that the famous John Warde brought his enormous hounds into the country. But Mr. Corbet is generally looked upon as being the father of the Hunt. He was Master of the Warwickshire for twenty years commencing A.D. 1791. Lord Middleton then purchased his hounds; took the country, and hunted it for the next ten years; after which it passed through various hands till it came in 1839 into those of Mr. Barnard—afterwards Lord Willoughby de Broke, and father of the present Master—who held it for seventeen years. A former Lord Willoughby de Broke was one of Mr. Corbet's chief supporters; and it was his custom to entertain the Master and members of the Warwickshire Hunt Club at dinner on the first Monday every November.

In the palmiest days of the Warwickshire Hunt Club, which I take to have been between the years 1830 and 1840, or thereabouts, Leamington vied with Melton in the quantity and quality of its hunting

---

* *Vide* "Stanford's Large Scale Map," Sheet 15; also "Hobson's Foxhunting Atlas."

visitors. If they did not hunt quite as often as the Meltonians, they had four or five days a week of good sport offered them; on some days they had as fine a country as Leicestershire could have given; and on non-hunting days a great deal more was—and is—to be done at Leamington than at Melton. A Melton man, with the town to himself on a hunting day,—whether from want of a horse or other baneful accident—feels, and looks, as though he were forsaken by Providence and by man. But at Leamington it is very different. It is not incumbent—it is even difficult—to hunt six days a week: there is pleasant idling on the off days; and the wifely sentiment that "men think of nothing but their tiresome hunting" is not so often heard here. An old authority, speaking years ago of Leamington and the Members of the Warwickshire Hunt, set it down that there was " more spirit among them in the way of promoting hunt balls, club dinners, &c., than there is among three-fourths of the hunts in the kingdom." The Warwickshire Hunt Club still exists. The subscription to it is independent of that to the hounds; and is eight guineas a year, six of which are employed in giving an annual ball, alternately at Warwick and Stratford-on-Avon. Formerly there was also an annual dinner; but that has been discontinued some twelve years; and the remaining two guineas go to the Covert Fund. In the days of Lord Waterford and Capt. Lamb, Yellow Dwarf and Vivian, and when Leamington was almost the headquarters of Hunt Steeplechases, the Warwickshire Country included what is now separate as the North Warwickshire,—the division only becoming a recognised fact in 1853. A

The Warwickshire.

separate pack would appear to have been hunting the extreme north of the country for some time previous, but in that year it was laid down that the North Warwickshire Pack should be established, to hunt as far south as the river Leam on the east of Leamington and the two canals which join at an angle at Lapworth on the west. The present boundaries are approximately the same (as shown on Stanford's Map). A few coverts in the Claverdon district have been added to the northern division. And Warwickshire as a hunting county held rank after none but Leicestershire—bracketing itself, as it still may, on equal terms with Northamptonshire.

It would be a great saving of time to me, and an advantage, possibly, to my readers, could I transcribe *verbatim* the account of "Warwickshire as a Hunting Country" as it was printed in the *New Sporting Magazine* of March, 1832. Except in the division of the County into two Hunts, very little change has taken place in Warwickshire since that time; and the remarks are as much to the point for present purpose as anything I can hope to write. Here are a few extracts :

"It comprises a very large tract of grass land, little inferior to that of Leicestershire, and bordering on almost the finest part of Northamptonshire. It is a practicable country to ride over, although a well-trained hunter is essential; it is not subject to be flooded; and though the rivers Avon and Stour run through part of it, foxes very seldom cross them. The Stour is jumpable in some places, and fordable in many; and the brooks not generally wide—the Ladbroke and Walton perhaps the widest. .... The enclosures of Warwickshire are, for the most part, of a fair size; particularly in the grazing districts, which I should estimate at one-third of the whole extent of country. Taking it as a whole, I consider the soil very favourable in scent, as the staple is generally good. A great portion of the ploughed lands, however, are very tender after hard frosts, succeeded by rains; and Warwickshire may be termed a deep country to ride over, and one which requires strong and well-bred horses. A great many such are annually bred in the county, and it always has been the pride of Warwickshire yeomen to have a good hunter or two in their stables, a species of stock that has, on the whole, paid them well for rearing. The fences of Warwickshire are, of course, of various descriptions; but they are seldom placed on banks. Quickset hedges, with a ditch only on one side, are the general obstacles to be encountered; and in the grazing districts, from the richness of the soil, they equal, in thickness and strength, the often-described 'bull-finches' of Leicestershire and Northamptonshire. What are called bullock-fences are also not uncommon in Warwickshire; that is to say, a good stiff rail accompanying a hedge and ditch. Timber fences perpetually occur, either in the shape of stiles, or rails affixed in weak parts of the quickset fences, to which a ditch is always added, as a further security against trespass."

I can add nothing to this, in seeking to give an idea of the country you will cross and the horse you should ride in Warwickshire. Of course the country varies

The Warwickshire.

considerably—as we shall see as we go on to details of its geography. On the Shuckburgh side in the far east you must have as good a horse as you can buy; for a stiffer country (being a feasible one) is not to be found anywhere. Much of the south of the Warwickshire domain too, is a fine grass country, requiring a horse of quality. The poorest part—as riding and scenting ground—is, perhaps, close to the head centre, Leamington. But as your horse, like yourself, must be prepared to take his turn in rough and smooth, and as every mile, south or east, brings you on better ground, you will scarcely be safe at Leamington in keeping an inferior animal for the home circuit. Besides which, as one goes through Country after Country, the fact daily impresses itself more strongly, that if you would be carried *really well*, and go field for field with hounds throughout the day, you want an even better horse for an inferior country than for a first-rate one. You may not require as brilliant fencing qualities—nor perhaps the same turn of speed. But to be galloping continually through the deep, and jumping out of sticky ground, takes twice as much out of a horse as skimming lightly over sound ridge-and-furrow, and "flicking" from field to field upon firm and springy foothold. The question is merely whether the game is worth the candle—the game being bad sport, and the candle no farthing rushlight but a two hundred guinea dip into your pocket. Most of us will decide for a modest half light; lay aside all hope of dazzling effect, and plod steadily on with the certainty of seeing a great deal. But these remarks apply to little of the Warwickshire country.

Leamington is within distance of nearly all the best of that Hunt, as well as the whole of the North Warwickshire. Four days a week are tolerably close at hand; and the Pytchley Wednesdays are easily attainable by train. Its charms apart from hunting are widely sung; and they are dear to the soul of many a dancing man. Leamington is rather more than three hours' journey from London, by way of Euston-square and Rugby, and has house and hostelry for as many as will come, either as residents or as visitors.

Banbury and Fenny Compton are on the eastern border. The advantages of Banbury (which is only about two hours from Euston-square), as a hunting quarter, have been touched upon already under the head of the Bicester. It holds that country, as well as the Warwickshire and the Duke of Grafton's, within its reach. So does Fenny Compton—which (though nearly double the journey from London) is even better placed for choice spots in each of those Hunts, and will give a day with the Pytchley besides. On the west, Stratford-on-Avon (also rather difficult of access from town) lies well within the Warwickshire territory, and offers, too, the Northern Pack, together with the chance of weekly excursions to the Worcestershire, Lord Coventry's, and the North Cotswold. Thus it is evident that there is no lack of quarters for hunting men who would see the Warwickshire. After adding that the Heythrop country runs all along the southern border, it is unnecessary to define further the relative position of the Warwickshire with its neighbours.

The Warwickshire.

The Kennels are at Kineton, and were built by the Hunt forty years ago—the land being given by Mr. Lucy, and the materials for building brought together by the farmers, who (Cecil tells us) combined to the number of 180 and employed between them 553 waggons — completing the whole work during the harvest months. The Hounds, too, are the property of the Country; and no pains has been spared under the present Mastership to infuse the best of blood into the Kennel. At the present time almost all the young hounds are by well-known sires in the Belvoir, Brocklesby, Quorn, Milton, Lord Coventry's, and the Duke of Grafton's Kennels; while among the older hounds a portion of Mr. Chaworth-Musters' late pack forms a leading item. In the same way Lord Willoughby de Broke spares no expense in mounting his men as such country requires; and the Hunt Establishment is done throughout on the most handsome scale.

Four days a week was the agreed number when Lord Willoughby de Broke assumed the Mastership three years ago. But the country having plenty of coverts and plenty of foxes, he is in the habit of advertising for five days. These are Monday, Tuesday, Thursday, Friday, and Saturday; and are arranged as follows: Monday is for the Leamington neighbourhood, though often brought down as far as the Kennels—the country improving much as you move southward. Nearer Leamington it is a cold plough, but gets better as we reach Chesterton and Lighthorne. The best meets for this day are Lighthorne Village, for Chesterton Wood and Bishop's Gorse.

In the latter covert they once found no less than seventeen different times one season. Charlecote Park is for Fir Tree Hill and Oakley Wood—the line from the latter to Chesterton being a good one, mostly over grass, and frequently chosen by foxes. The best run of last season was from Chesterton, after a meet at Charlecote; and, crossing the grass, ended in a ten-mile point at Copredy Station—where, every horse being beat, they had to whip off. The Kennels are advertised with a view to Kineton Holt; and Compton Verney (the seat of Lord Willoughby de Broke) has capital small woods round the Park. The meets of Wellesbourne, Walton Hall, Goldicote and Barford (near Warwick) stand on worse ground. Walton has good coverts of Sir C. Mordaunt's. Goldicote and Barford take you into deep plough, and the former amid much game for the gun.

Tuesday is always given to a wild, but good scenting, district in the extreme south—where but a small field attends, but much sport is seen. Outside the big woods there is a good deal of grass; and foxes often slip quickly over the border into some of the best of the Heythrop country. Wolford Village and Weston House are taken in nearly alternate weeks as the Tuesday fixture. Wolford Village is for Wolford Wood —a large wood belonging to Lord Redesdale. The line from here to Ilmington, in the territory neutral with the North Cotswold, is good and nearly all grass —as also is that to Addlestrop Hill in the Heythrop dominion. Weston House is for Weston Heath and Whichford Wood—foxes are plentiful; but the coverts difficult to get away from. The most desirable points from here are Heythrop Park and other coverts in that country. Other places of meeting are Barton House for Barton Gorse, with Salford Osiers a tempting and pleasant direction for a fox, to carry him over the border. Golden Cross on the Fosse Road has Golden Cross Gorse, a new covert given by Sir G. Philips of Weston House—twelve acres of gorse four miles from another covert, and lying in a good grass country. Brailes is another Tuesday meet, with a good supply of foxes at hand.

Thursday is for the extreme east, adjoining the Pytchley country, and calling in numbers from the Rugby and Daventry districts. Lower Shuckburgh is, *par excellence, the* meet of the Hunt. The coverts to be drawn are those of Shuckburgh Hill and Calcut Spinney—both rare places, the latter perhaps the best covert the Warwickshire possess. From the Hill to Ladbroke, or in the other direction to Braunston Gorse of the Pytchley, are beautiful lines over a stiff grass country; while from Calcut Spinney to Birdingbury, or to Bunkers Hill of the North Warwickshire, make many a splendid gallop. From Birdingbury Hall they have Debdale, and small coverts at the Hall —the former a certain find, and likely for a burst to Shuckburgh or Bunkers Hill. Ufton Wood is the meet for the great, holding covert there—through whose dense thickets there is scarcely a ride. Ladbroke Gorse is probably better famed than any covert in the Hunt; and is generally an afternoon draw from Shuckburgh or Ufton Wood. Watergall is another good gorse; and Harbury is often named to draw it or

Ladbroke, when they are not reserved for the afternoon.

Friday is on what may be termed the Banbury, or the Edgehill side—a sporting country, where the coverts are small and the scent good. A bad Friday was unknown last season. The field is mostly made up of farmers, every one of whom consider it their duty to hunt and to preserve foxes. A fox-killer showing his face in Banbury Market would most assuredly be lynched. Above the Edgehills we meet with light plough that is never hard nor heavy, intersected with grass vales, each holding its little brook. The chief meets are Swalcliffe, for the large gorse of Wigginton Heath; Wroxton Abbey, for Wroxton Coverts and Claydon Hill; and Wroxton New Inn, for Chamberlayne's Gorse. Farnborough, Upton House, Radway Grange, Tyroe Village and Broughton Castle are all good for foxhunting.

Saturday takes in the north-west corner, above the Avon; where large woods and plough predominate, but a very fair scent usually prevails, and in most years foxes are plentiful enough. Charlecote Village, Snitterfield, Red Hill, Billesley Hall, Coughton Court, and Ragley Hall are the leading places—headed, however, by Pebworth, for Pebworth Spring Well, where Mr. Thos. Shekel has a stock of foxes in a square blackthorn covert lying wide apart by itself. To most of these meets hounds have to be vanned.

A few meets come in for any day of the week as may be found convenient—*e.g.*, Pillerton, generally Monday or Thursday, seldom Tuesday, with a fine

The Warwickshire. 303

gorse covert, that is none too certain. Oxhill Gorse, however, was planted and is rented by Sir C. Mordaunt, and is well situated in a fine grass country. Idlicote has lots of foxes, and a pretty twenty minutes from here to Brailes Hill is of frequent occurrence. Ilmington, neutral with North Cotswold, is in a hilly district, and is difficult to get away from. But it is of great service during cubhunting.

A note by the author of an old book on the Warwickshire Hunt is almost worth adding.

"Ladies, singly, and in groups, have often graced the meet of the Warwickshire Hounds, but we are not certain that any of them have ever made a practice of joining in the chase. 'I am not aware' (says a correspondent to a sporting paper recently published) 'of any picture more beautiful than an elegant female on horseback; Lady Grosvenor is a striking exemplification, whom I have repeatedly seen at the fixtures for the Cheshire hounds. I have never observed her cross the country. Her ladyship's presence at the fixture was highly gratifying; it gave a degree of interest to the scene which would not have been derived from any other source. Amidst the busy jocularity of such a meeting, there might indeed be seen the homage which high birth and distinguished rank paid to loveliness and beauty. Lady Grosvenor remains to witness the finding of the fox, and when he goes away, if he happens to take a direction that will enable her to see the run, she rides along the lanes, crosses the inclosures, where gates or openings happen to be convenient, and continues in this way as long as she can. I think I once observed her up at the death of a fox. Lady Grosvenor is an excellent rider. Lady Helen Lowther is the boldest female rider I ever saw. This lady appears in scarlet, completely equipped for the chase. She meets the Earl of Lonsdale's foxhounds, mounted upon steady, superb steeds, and rides uncommonly well. Upon one occasion, when the fixture was at Little Daulby, three miles from Melton, I saw Lady Lowther put her beautiful bay horse along with great spirit and courage.'"

PART III.

THE DULVERTON.*

The foxhunting countries round and about Exmoor may best be dealt with as in connection with the more notable sister sport of Staghunting, which is *primâ facie* the great feature and attraction of the West. The present articles are intended as a guide for the stranger, not as a critique for the native : and the stranger's immediate object in travelling down to Devon or Somerset is more likely to be that he may join in the chase of the wild red deer—much as he will enjoy varying his programme with foxhunting of as crude but genuine a sort as ever fell to his lot. The Dulverton, the Stars of the West, and Mr. Luttrell's are the packs of foxhounds sharing Exmoor and its neighbourhood, and which are most easily available from the quarters a visitor would naturally take up with a view to staghunting. Lord Portsmouth's also, the pride of the west, will scarcely be left unseen by any sportsman who has fixed himself on the Dulverton side of Exmoor. As the staghounds

---

* *Vide* Stanford's " Hunting Map," sheet 19; also Hobson's Foxhunting Atlas.

are only out three times in the week, he will have ample time and opportunity for tasting every variety of sport that the neighbourhood offers.

The west-countrymen hunt every day of the week—and instances exist of their making one horse do the whole. I am within fact in this improbable statement, and unquestionably within the bounds of truth in asserting that the most determined and opulent six-days-a-week man never allows himself more than a trio of hunters. Horses are here never called upon to shake themselves with jumping; and in galloping their effort is always above the ground—the frame is seldom jarred and the sinews seldom wrenched. They come home leg-weary and back-weary, perhaps; but the heart is beating quietly. They eat heartily and sleep well; and the next morning are as fit as ever. And so is the rider. To hurry along a lane involves no great wear and tear of nervous or muscular tissue; and the glorious air of the western coast more than makes amends for any temporary exhaustion consequent on many hours in the saddle—for distance to covert and a late dinner-hour never enter into the calculations of a western sportsman. "The Moor" (a term reserved for Exmoor's most open wilderness) puts a somewhat tougher strain on man and beast; but, bar improbable accidents, the beast of the country can well take his part upon it twice a week—and even be glad of a byeday near home besides. It is a fact that the patriarch, John Russell, for many years hunted a tract of country that included what is at present known as the Dulverton, and most of what is now held by the Stars of the West, with an establishment

The Dulverton. 307

of *three horses,* all told—working the country fairly five days a fortnight throughout, and killing his foxes day after day by fairly tiring them down. It should be explained that at least an hour or two of a staghunting day may be spent by the rider stretching his limbs on the grass that his steed is peaceably nibbling; that in foxhunting you may loiter half the day on vantage points overlooking the valleys which hounds are searching out; and that the requirements for riding to harriers frequently, though not always, extend no further than a safe conveyance to a central hill round which the hare runs herself to death. To reach otter hounds gives opportunity for the stiffest of the stud having his muscles relaxed by a jog to the public nearest the venue; while, should the strain on the stud require easing off for a day, a man who has hitherto been content to go through life without attaining to honours in the gentle craft, may here run a hook through the mouths of as many small fishes as it is worth his while to pull out for the morrow's breakfast. Of a truth it is a sporting country, and a man need never stop at home idle, for lack of opportunity. Horses good enough to carry him with the staghounds are generally to be hired on the spot; on a rough pony he may see much of what goes on with foxhounds, while a pair of strong boots will show him all else when once he has reached the scene. Besides staghounds, foxhounds, and harriers, there are two packs of otter hounds at work in the Dulverton district.

April, which elsewhere is virtually an absolute void as far as the sportsman is concerned, is almost the busiest time in Devon and Somerset. Every branch of hunting (hind being substituted for stag) is carried on through the month: and a hunting-man could scarcely kill the time more effectively and pleasurably than here. In the autumn, again, every pack is here at work by early September, often by mid-August—and where could one who happens to be without taste or opportunity for shooting, employ himself better than amid the varied sport and health-giving breezes of the West? Exmoor may be rough and cold and trying in the winter months; but there can be no healthier, more strengthening air than blows across it in spring and autumn. The scenery is bold and wide,—gorgeous and beautiful in autumn, striking and refreshing in spring. In spring too the great wooded ravines have lost all their under-covert; and as you gain each overhanging headland there is little to prevent your seeing every movement of the busy pack below. On the open moor you can ride with hounds (after fox or stag) where they go: on its borders, or beyond, you must follow a leader (none better than the huntsman), who will guide you by lane and path to where you can command a view and see more of the actual sport than you could in any flat woodland country.

The town of Dulverton, from which the Hunt takes its name, is on the Great Western Railway, about five and a half hours from London; is neat, clean, and picturesque, and offers every facility to the visiting sportsman. The Kennels are at the Master's (Mr. Froude Bellew's) moor residence at Rhyll, within easy walk of Anstey Station, and four miles from

Dulverton. A glance at the hunting-map will show how capitally situated they are for working the country—while the large tract of heather-clad and well-watered hill immediately at their back, is of inestimable value to the Master and his hounds, allowing them to enjoy their summer training and exercise while others less fortunate are kennel-bound by dust and hard roads. Mr. Bellew is his own huntsman; and is essentially a hound-man—in the same sense as his is a hound-country as opposed to a riding-country. He believes and trusts in his hounds, and expects them to work and hunt for themselves, though he is ever keeping an eye forward for the explanation of any difficulty that they may be unable to unravel. Amid the rough precipitous valleys and the impracticable banked-fences of the enclosed parts of his country, hounds can never be ridden over, or hurried, by the field, except it is in the lanes to which the progress of the horsemen is necessarily almost entirely restricted. Thus a mutual confidence between huntsman and hounds is both natural and necessary. Hounds must do their own work; and a huntsman can only take them in hand for a wide bold effort, when theirs has been made in vain and his can be founded on broad reasoning—generally dictated by intimate knowledge of country and much previous experience of the run of foxes. No man can watch hounds at work in such a country without acquiring some useful lessons. It would be a benefit to more than one quick-riding Hunt that we know, if their huntsman, and as many of his competing followers as possible, could be shipped down to the Dulverton country for a month's schooling, on the termination of their own season of feverish galloping. The system of hunting in the one country would not of course be applicable *in toto* to the other, but it would surprise them to learn, first, how often hounds, when not immediately picked up or overridden, will puzzle out a line that at first they seemed utterly at a loss upon; and, secondly, how much they will make out of it when assured that they can take their own time. The frequency of the lanes and byepaths constitutes one of the greatest difficulties the Dulverton hounds have to contend against. It gives the one chance to the field of marring sport; and unless the Master is determined that his hounds shall have time and room, they are only too likely to be pressed at the very moment their hunting powers are put most to the test.

The hard stony surface of the lanes is the most difficult ground on which to carry a line; and for this reason is it a point of paramount necessity in Devon and Somerset to breed foxhounds from such blood as has been known to distinguish itself on the dry and stone-paved tracks. Otherwise, the Dulverton is an exceedingly good scenting country. Both its grass enclosures and its heather carry a strong, almost invariable, scent; and a good pack of hounds—handled by a man who understands them and his country—seldom fail to account for their foxes.

The Dulverton may be said to be an offshoot of the Eggesford—or, as it is better known, Lord Portsmouth's—country. In one way or another it has been hunted for generations. Prior to the year 1826,

Mr. George Templer, of the South Devon, was wont to bring his hounds every spring, and hunted it from Rev. John Russell's house at South Molton. The latter then took to keeping hounds himself; and up to 1852 this territory was worked as neutral ground by his pack and the Tiverton, after which date it was hunted by the late Hon. Newton Fellows, and subsequently by Lord Portsmouth. In 1875 a rearrangement was brought about by Lord Portsmouth receiving from the Hon. Mark Rolle a convenient addition south of Eggesford House, whereupon he relinquished the Dulverton side to Mr. Froude-Bellew —and the Dulverton first became a separate country. The Stars of the West adjoin it on the north and west where it runs into Exmoor Forest; Mr. Luttrell's on the north-east; and the Tiverton—or Mr. Rayer's —on the south-east. Two distinct component parts go to make up the Dulverton country—the one being open moorland, the other strong hilly woodland with a groundwork of grass enclosures fenced and banked far beyond the power of horse to surmount. It is towards the extreme north, where the Barle and other streams take their source from the "Moor" proper, that the best sample of the former is to be found: but commons of more or less extent run down from Exmoor far into the heart of Mr. Froude-Bellew's territory. Of these Anstey (East and West) Molland, Dulverton, Hawkridge, Winsford, and Withypool are the chief. It is only of late years that some thousands of acres have been added to the area of impracticable enclosures. On the Forest of Exmoor itself heather grows but scantily; but on the tributary commons it is found in much greater luxuriance. It is on heath that most sport is found for autumn and spring hunting — the other section of the country forming a great nursery for foxes and an excellent school for cubhunting. It is here that the young entry are taught—or, rather, teach themselves—to work, and turn, and twist, and come to cry. In no country is a silent hound worth more than a yard or two of rope; in Devonshire especially, he can never be tolerated a moment. Throughout the Dulverton country foxes are well-preserved and fairly plentiful. A blank day has long been a very rare occurrence— Mr. Froude-Bellew having only met with three during his seven seasons of command.

The chief landed proprietors in the Hunt are Lords Carnarvon, Portsmouth, Clinton and Poltimore; Sir Robert Throgmorton, Sir Thomas Acland, Messrs. Locke, H. Devon, Jekyll, Llewellyn, Knight, Mildmay, Rolle, Lucas, T. Daniel, J. Daniel, Bere, Collyns, and Beadon —all of whom thoroughly preserve foxes, and support the M.F.H. Amongst the yeomen, who in the West especially deserve the title of the backbone of hunting, may be mentioned the names of Messrs. Lyddon, Chorley, Joyce, W. Halse, Vearncombe, John and James Japp, Westcott, Kelland, Beedle, Moore (2), Dascombe, Baker, &c. The Devonshire chronicles have ever been replete with names ranking high in the world of foxhunting. In late years mark those of Fellows, Portsmouth, Templer, Trelawney, Rolle, Carew, Froude, Russell, and Deacon—all Devon-born-and-bred, and hunting-taught amid the hills and downs of this unrideable, but most sport-loving county.

The Dulverton. 313

The Dulverton advertise for five days a fortnight, viz. Wednesday and Saturday in each week, with every alternate Monday. Many of their fixtures are on the open moor, and on the commons adjoining the valleys of the Barle and the Exe. Lanacre Bridge, Sandy Way, Molland Common, Anstey Barrows, Chippett Post, Windsford Hill, Hawkridge Common, and Withypool are among the most favourite of the "out over," or moorland meets; while elsewhere Tuckers Moor, Stoodleigh, Gibbett Moor, Bullyford Gate, Exbridge, and Knowstone Moor are held in high repute, among those who prefer the neighbourhood of enclosures and civilization. Knowstone Woods and Hayne Plantation—both large holding coverts—are hunted neutrally with Lord Portsmouth's hounds.

With regard to horse and hound most suitable to the country, the same description will apply to both—they should be *big little ones*; thick yet with quality. And it is a *sine quâ non* that every hunter should be a good hack.

The foxes are strong and generally straight running. As there is but little game in the country—except the black-game which abound on the heathery hills, foxes not only get fair play at home but have to travel long distances to find their supper. Earth-stopping is almost unknown (at all events as a source of expense); and payment for loss of poultry is but a slight item. As a return to the farmers for their friendly assistance, Mr. Bellew has always kept a thoroughbred horse at their disposal. At the present time Chieftain—lately the best racing Arab of his inches in India—is standing at Rhyll, his services being gratis to all fox-preservers and well-wishers in the Hunt. His blood, soundness, and quality should be of great value among the draught-mares and ponies of the district—which, for hardiness and endurance, have a reputation quite world-wide.

Mr. Froude-Bellew's pack, consisting mostly of bitches, averages about twenty-two inches in height, is made up of quick, muscular quartered, active hounds—full of drive and strength. They are chiefly bred at home, and walked by the neighbouring farmers who compete keenly for the honour of sending in the best puppy. Crosses of blood are obtained from the Eggesford Kennel—Lord Portsmouth ever lending friendly and well-appreciated help in selection of sires from his beautiful pack.

I cannot conclude better than in the words of one who has had long experience of Devonshire. "The Dulverton country, far west as it is, is most desirable ground for a sportsman—though a sportsman, perhaps, of the old school rather than the new. The man learns the habits, the strength, the endurance of a wild roaming fox, and the instinct, the hunting power, and capability of the hound. He sees the two fairly pitted, one against the other—without the modern interventions of telegraphing, 'hark holloa' and 'yonder he goes,' or the hurry-scurry *melée* which every day tends so much to disorganise hounds and to mar true sport. No Devonshire fox is killed by hustling; the more he is bullied the shorter he turns; and time is more often lost than gained in the hurly-burly. *Let them alone!* is the golden rule for the west country; and it is marvellous the sport a good pack of hounds will show when this motto is thoroughly acted upon. Too many huntsmen are afraid to treat their hounds thus, for fear of losing caste. The alternative is that they lose their foxes instead!"

THE STARS OF THE WEST.*

AN immense tract of extreme North Devon is coloured in the hunting maps as the Country of the Stars of the West. For practical purposes the brush need have touched only about half the area—for, though Mr. Nicholas Snow has undisputed right within the sea limits, of which Barnstaple, Ilfracombe, Lynton and Porlock are the chief points of mark, Exmoor Forest and its immediate environs form an area more than sufficient for a two-days-a-week pack. This is the cream and pith of his country; and to this he naturally and necessarily almost restricts himself. Rough and wild indeed it is: but no country in the three kingdoms carries a better scent. On the great Moor you may gallop to hounds anywhere: amid the barriered slopes adjoining the open Forest you must get about from point to point as you would in the Dulverton country, putting all vaulting ambition under firm restraint, and trusting yourself to the guidance of some one familiar to the roads and paths and gates till, if you stay long enough, you learn them for your-

---

* *Vide* Stanford's "Hunting Map," Sheet 19. Also Hobson's Foxhunting Atlas.

self. I would say of the country of the Stars of the West, as I would say—and in no cavilling spirit—of Devonshire as a whole: Here is where a man may go who—when the pleasures of tumbling about have palled upon him, or when aged bones rebel against the shock of the flying leap—still retains his love of hunting, centred in a fondness for the hound at work. He can no longer compete, or even share, with a crowd: yet, unless he shifts his scene of action, he is altogether debarred from a delight of which he is still as keenly appreciative as ever. He may possess as vivid a sense of the charms of foxhunting as when he pulled on his first pair of tops; why should he give it up altogether because he has to resign to younger men his pride of place in his accustomed sphere? In the wild west country he may hunt nearly all the year round, and daily see hounds at work on a good scent, without his ever being compelled, or even tempted, to ride over a fence. If his previous life has been spent in a flying grass country, his soul may still find refreshment in a brushing gallop across the open face of Exmoor, where foxhounds can dash along as vigorously as over the best scenting pastures of the Shires. Mr. Snow will hunt a travelling fox down on the open Moor in the middle of May, and be rousing the cubs on it again at daybreak in early August—while for summer exercise he will often let his pack work about in the enormous cliff-woodlands of Culbone and Porlock. Cubhunting is a term seldom used—because scarcely applicable—to the autumn foxhunting of this wild country. An Exmoor cub learns to roam as soon as it can see, and requires none of the rattling so necessary to the education of the artificially nurtured animal. Foxhunting once resumed in the autumn goes steadily on for nine months. Each day there is the long wide search for the " varmint," who, once found, is usually followed obstinately to the death. There are generally foxes enough, though they are often difficult to find amid a wide area, nearly *all* of which is covert —though, were it not for the sea cliffs whence the supply is continually recruited, such a drain as is entailed by these many months of hunting could not but be exhausting. Wherever heather grows there is shelter enough for a fox; while, where it has been left unburnt for a few years, snugger harbourage could scarcely be found. On the roughest core of Exmoor Forest, it is true, there is but a scanty growth of heather—rank, bog-grown grass taking its place. But many thousands of acres of the Moor are hidden under the thick purple blossom—amid which a fox may choose a warm dry kennel anywhere. To find him the chief hope rests upon striking his drag, where he has passed in the early morning. The scent then left will remain perceptible for many hours, and give a key to his position that hounds can generally turn to account. In many parts the heather is allowed to grow freely for years—more often as covert for the black game (or heath-poult, as the vernacular of the country has it), which flourish in great abundance wherever preserved. It is easy to understand that a fox passing through this must leave a hanging scent in his passage.

Exmoor altogether is ground of extraordinary scent-carrying properties. The bleak moorlands

retain scent, of whatever animal has passed, to a
degree that is known nowhere else. A deer leaves an
aroma so heavy that, when recent, hounds dwell in
single file to enjoy it, and for hours afterwards they
can follow it without difficulty. The fox can be run
after a lapse of time that would put him far " out of
scent" on any other ground: and the hare never has
a chance of her life when once harriers are laid on.
The sheep and the ponies of the Moor leave as
fascinating a trail as any animal that comes under the
head of game. To discriminate between all these,
and to pursue only the legitimate quest, is of course
purely a matter of education. Yet the older hounds
never waver; and 'tis wonderful how soon the juniors
take example, and hunt only their particular game.
Not only does the virgin surface of the soil catch up
the scent of the footfall; but the heather retains
memory of the passing body even if there has been
no actual touch. For a fox will always follow the
grass-carpeted sheep paths where he can. If hounds
are close at him, they drive him forward. If he has
leisure to stop and listen, he may likely enough branch
off as the wind or his cunning instinct prompts him.
But the neighbouring heather would seem always to
tell a tale. A deer naturally makes nothing of the
high-spreading growth, but plunges through it where
even the great staghounds can scarcely make their
way. A fox cannot act at all in the tall stuff, but is
bound to seek the paths: though, with a pack just
behind him, he will hold his own well enough over
heather of medium age. Mr. Snow's own deer park,
an unfenced waste of four hundred acres on which

not a single sheep is allowed to stray, was a tough sample of high heather—till three parts of it were recently laid bare by fire. Herds of the glorious wild red deer walked about in it, invisible all but their heads and branching antlers. Now they come in double numbers, to feed on the new grass springing from the ashes—and take strangely little heed of the foxhounds drawing across their sanctum.

Shortly, the best and the liveliest sport of the Stars of the West is on the true Moor. The rest is of the point-to-point, hounds-by-themselves, type of Devon and Somerset generally—foxhunting of a kind good for hounds, death to foxes, full of interest to those men who delight in the bare knowledge that the pack are having a "good time," but of mixed pleasure to those who would fain share the fun and the work with hounds from beginning to end. Beyond the borders of Exmoor is, in fact, an unrideable, uncompromising country. Comparisons, always odious, are altogether out of place when the subjects are on utterly different footings; so contrast, rather than comparison, suggests the thought that, whereas in many a country one avoids taking a road lest there should be difficulty in turning out of it quickly enough—in the west you must turn into a road whenever you can, if you would get on at all.

Whence came the name of the Stars of the West I know not. It is sufficient to say that they owe their being and maintenance entirely to the sporting spirit of a leading yeoman, who keeps them for no ostentation, but for his own pleasure and that of his neighbours. The vanities of dress and show are not

The Stars of the West.

formulated for North Devon. Even the Master-and-Huntsman of the Stars of the West does not sport pink. A couple of hard-working whips don the orthodox colour. But an active driving pack know just as well where the horn-carrier is—and what he wants of them—as if he wore a coat of many hues. You will gather that another great point, beyond easy riding, may be counted among the advantages of western hunting—Economy to wit. Not only will a horse come out quite twice as often as in a jumping country; but your own dress requires neither lavish expenditure at starting, nor the assistance of an expensive valet to keep it on a par with the toilets around you. Thus a heavy strain is taken off both purse and mind. The former is called upon to play a very light part; the latter is not distressed between the rival claims of Bartley and Thomas, turns with relief from Tautz to the village tailor, and expands comfortably under the tweed shooting-coat that does duty for the "extra superfine scarlet," with its many other extras of "silk linings, hunt-buttons," &c. And so we arrive at the conclusion that Devon, and its next neighbour, are the counties for sport, economy, comfort, and nerve that is at all doubtful.

Lynton (with Lynemouth), Porlock, and South Molton are the spots on the circumference of the country that a visitor might best choose, to combine stag-hunting with foxhunting and healthy western air. Barnstaple is within reach of the Moor, but is scarcely a hunting quarter; and Minehead is more within Mr. Luttrell's domain. From the three places I have named, all the best meets of the Devon and

Somerset staghounds may be reached, and two days a week spent with the Stars of the West.

The village of Exford, where the Devon and Somerset Staghounds are kennelled, would be another excellent centre for autumn sport—being on the borders of Exmoor Forest, within reach of all the best meets of the Stars of the West, as well as those of the Dulverton and Mr. Luttrell's. Minehead, about six hours from London by the Great Western Railway, is the railway terminus for Exford, Porlock, and Lynton—the two latter being reached by coach, along the picturesque cliff route. South Molton has a station of its own, on the Barnstable line. Besides hunting in every shape, all the places named possess to the full the extraneous attractions of scenery and trout-fishing, on the spot or in close neighbourhood.

The Manor House, Oare, is where Mr. Nicholas Snow lives and has his Kennels. As a place of residence, it is, perhaps, more than all others actually in Exmoor Forest—excepting possibly Mr. Knight's, at Simonsbath. For there is no oasis in the heart of the great Moor. Its barren length is still unbroken by haunt of man, though its width has been narrowed by encroachment wherever tillage seemed possible. A stag may still run from Yard Down to Porlock, some thirteen miles; passing never a dwelling, and being seen by no one but a possible stray shepherd. Oare, with its manor house, its labourers' cottages, its church, and the sparkling trout-stream, lies a mile or so off the main road between Lynton and Porlock, about midway between the two. The Master's deer-park runs into the Moor in the background—while the sea cliffs form a margin line some two miles to the north. Mr. Snow's endeavour is ever to drive the cliff-foxes to the Moor, and to make them look upon it as their safer home. A run from the open to the Cliffs is only too likely to result in the loss of some hounds; for danger will accrue as soon as the cliff coverts open out under winter weather and hounds can press their foxes through. It is for these two reasons that Mr. Snow works the cliffs about once a week during the heat of summer, and fights as shy of them as circumstances will allow during the hunting season.

His days of hunting are Monday and Thursday, with an occasional Saturday byeday. Except in September and October, when the primary attraction of Stag-hunting brings down a number of visitors, his fields are quite small, and his chief and most constant supporters are the sport-loving farmers, who constitute the strength of the west country. The early part of the season is almost entirely devoted to the Moor; and the staghounds may come in for many good gallops after the fox at a time of year best adapted to the open Forest. For, in mid-winter, the dense mists sweeping across the Moor frequently send hounds home; added to which, the cold is often intense on its bare uplands.

Besides the woodlands by the sea, and those of Cloutsham, &c., on the east, there are various big coverts off the Moor on the opposite side of the country hunted by the Stars of the West. Chief among these are the Bray coverts and those of South Molton—deep harbours for red deer or red rover.

Hounds are seldom advertised west of Parracombe; and the enclosed country scarcely represents the domain of the pack that is so closely associated with Exmoor's wild wastes.

The chief landowners—and all of them firm believers in the western creed that hunting in any shape is a sacred thing—are Lords Lovelace and Fortescue, Sir Thomas Acland, Mr. Knight, Mrs. Lock-Roe, Cols. Blathwayt and Wynch, Mr. Clarke, &c.

Some of the leading meets and draws are as follows: From Parracombe we get those coverts and Kentisbury; Challacombe Town is for Challacombe covert, Bratton Down, and Leworthy; from High Bray, both that and Charles Parish—the best district in the hunt—are drawn. Cutcombe and Dunkery form the eastern boundary of Mr. Snow's country.

In conclusion, it need only be said that the most favoured meets on and adjoining the Moor are Malmesmead Bridge, Simonsbath, Alderman's-Barrow, Woodbarrow, and Hawkcombe Head—and that horse and hound for the country should be thick, well-bred, and short on the leg.

MR. LUTTRELL'S.*

ROUGH and hilly as is the ground over which the Dulverton and the Stars of the West pursue the fox, Mr. Luttrell—whose foxhounds work the rest of the territory whereon also the Devon and Somerset Staghounds chase the wild red deer—has a country more mountainous, unrideable, and precipitous than either. The deep valley of the Exe and the rugged side of Dunkery mark his western boundary; whence the rough gorges of Cutcombe run at right angles, breaking in among a succession of other lofty heather clad eminences. The heights of Brendon cross the southern portion of his country; and the isolated range of the Quantocks stand across the eastern edge, where he joins the Taunton Vale. The beautiful Castle of Dunster is the Master's family seat; and his little pack of five-and-twenty couple have their kennel close by. The village of Dunster is two miles from Minehead; and is in itself a favourite quarter for the visiting staghunter, who can thence reach any part of Exmoor and take the field with foxhounds on intervening days. Distance to covert is a point little

---

* *Vide* Stanford's "Hunting Map," Sheets 19 and 20 and Hobson's Hunting Atlas.

regarded in the westcountry—ten, or even twenty extra miles by the way not being taken into account as likely to entail additional fatigue on the horse. And yet that horse is hunter, hack and lounging-chair for the whole day. It follows that he should have good legs and good middle piece, with sufficient breeding to bring him round quickly after such a day's work as he is called upon to undergo. For the rest, it is unnecessary to enumerate any long list of essential virtues. It will be sufficient to say—Get as much as you can in a small frame, and for as little money as possible. As for the rider—if it is necessary for him to choose a pilot with the Dulverton and the Stars of the West, it is ten times more needful here, where you can seldom move half a mile except under the guidance of one who knows each deep cut winding lane, each farmroad, and the points from which some portions of the deep tortuous valleys lie open to the view. So led by the hand, you may often gaze down like the eagle from its eyrie, and mark all the stirring panorama beneath, follow the fox as he winds his way round the hillsides and stops now and again to listen fearfully to the music, which comes welling up so pleasantly to your ears. Thus placidly you may watch each busy member of the pack as he works upon the line—and thus you may, no doubt, take in the whole performance more completely than in the hurry-scurry of riding in hard accompanying pursuit. Reasoning in this way, and content with this view, you may find much sterling enjoyment in such a foxhunt. The fox—or his death—is the object; the hound is the subject; and the horse is only to be regarded as quite the subsidiary means, never as the essential source, of pleasure acquirable. For, in addition to hills that would tax a chamois to surmount rapidly, there are the customary and impracticable banks, most peculiar to the west—higher than a horse's back, steep beyond a horse's power, and fenced besides with double plashing of beech growth. There is only one portion of Mr. Luttrell's country that is not held fast bound in this rigorous form of embattlement. Between the Quantocks and the sea margin, a few miles of grazing district are fenced in with low banks topped with light hedges— the entire fence being amenable either to a flying jump or an easy kick-back.

The range of the Quantocks gives other open riding-ground—the tops of the hills being carpeted with sound rough heather. All the north-eastern side of the Quantocks is a nearly continuous covert of oak copse—foxes being very plentiful, and sport frequent. In various other parts of the country strips of open moorland occur—chief among them being Croydon Hill, Grabbist and part of Dunkery.

Tuesday and Friday are the days of hunting; and Friday is, as a rule, fixed for the Quantock or Taunton side — in which the principal meets are Asholt, Crowcombe Park, Holford, East Quantoxhead, and St. Audries. Willet Hill and Heddon Crowcombe are for the vale between the Quantocks and Brendon Hill—a well-preserved but bad scenting country.

There is more plough in Mr. Luttrell's than in the

immediately adjoining countries; and, consequently, scent is seldom as brilliant. The Brendon Hills favour hounds though they are not altogether too well stocked with foxes. Gorse-brakes are frequent; but rabbit shooting is a study; and broad cuttings are made with a view to its enjoyment, rather than in the interests of the fox who is by nature a recluse.

Of the other meets it is sufficient to name Wick Park—for the covert of that name, and Mr. Daniel's coverts at Stockland, with Hinkley, a gorse close by the sea shore: Nether Stowey for Camerly Brake, Swang Gorse and the Radlet coverts—all good in the early part of the season: Fairfield, for the Great Plantation Honybere and Fairfield Wood: Putsham for Waltham's Brake, Ten-Acre-Copse, and Kilton Park—all good autumn coverts, but from which foxes are likely to draw away during the winter to the Quantock Hills. Then there is Brompton Ralph and its coverts, with Elworthy Combe and Tilsey: Raleigh's Cross, for Leigh Cliffs (with plenty of foxes), and Clatworthy Wood: Woolcot, and King's Brompton for Woolcot Brake, &c.: and Heath Poult for the Quarum and Exton Coverts. Also Williton, for Blackdown, Outmore, and Furzy Ground; Cleeve Hill for a covert on the cliff, whence foxes often make a good point; Withycombe Wood, Langridge Wood (for Slowly Wood, etc.); Dunster Park for the Broadwood coverts; Alcombe and Twington Plantation for Grabbist; Timberscombe, for the chain of coverts reaching thence for four miles up to Dunkery Gate, and for the eastern slope of

Mr. Luttrell's.

Dunkery, on which a good fox is generally to be found.

Chief among the covert owners and fox preservers are Sir A. Hood, Lord Lovelace, Mrs. Carew, Messrs. Stanley, Blomart, Zatchell, Insole, Bouverie, and Col. Wyndham.

LORD PORTSMOUTH'S.*

THE leading pack of the west country is that kept by the Earl of Portsmouth at Eggesford House in the centre of sporting Devonshire. The county has been hunted, on plea of every wild animal it possessed, from time immemorial; and by foxhunters its face has been mapped out and divisioned again and again, till it stands as now. Since 1875 Lord Portsmouth has hunted the area round his house as at present coloured on the maps referred to—a cession from the Hon. Mark Rolle on the west allowing the formation of the Dulverton Hunt on the north-east. His country, as now defined, is a territory of not less than thirty miles in length, its chief breadth being twenty; and to give a rough idea of its general whereabouts it is sufficient to say that it lies between Barnstaple and Exeter. As a matter of fact it does not actually reach either of these towns though it runs up to within ten miles of each, and the kennels of Eggesford are midway on the line of railway between the two. Mr. Mark Rolle hunts all along its western borders: the Stars of the West touch it on the north, the Dulverton and the Tiverton

---

* *Vide* Stanford's " Hunting Map," Sheet 19, and Hobson's Foxhunting Atlas.

on the east, and the South Devon on the south. The Kennels could scarcely be better situated for working the country; though once a week—or at any rate once a fortnight—a long journey has to be undertaken to reach its-south-western corner.

No large town lies within its borders. Exeter is close at hand for the visitor; and of itself always sends out a body varying in strength according to distance of fixture. The staghunter on an off day may join Lord Portsmouth's hounds from either Dulverton or South Molton—both of which, as already written, command Exmoor and the chase of the wild red deer. And to visit Devonshire without seeing this pack would be almost tantamount to visiting Florence without seeing its picture galleries. The stag will no doubt be the primary object of a journey of five or six hours from London; for none but the most ardent seeker of change will be likely to travel so far merely to extend his experience of foxhunting. Yet, being on the spot, here is the opportunity of seeing the latter sport right well enacted according to the requirements of the west.

In the field or in kennel Lord Portsmouth's hounds are, rightly enough, the pride of the west; and for "fashion, form, and fling" are not easily to be beat anywhere. The blood that has so long been acquired in the Eggesford Kennels is, moreover, freely dealt out to the aid and improvement of neighbouring packs, most of whom owe much of their merit to this source. The Eggesford pack derive their chief strains from the kennels of Mr. Parry, Mr. Lane Fox, Mr. Chaplin, Sir Watkin Wynn, and the Belvoir, while of late an infusion has been obtained from the Grove. Smart level hounds, they are built for work, yet with every advantage of appearance. The kennels also, as with everything else connected with the establishment at home and in the field, are neat and businesslike; and the hounds are there seen amid surroundings not only more picturesque but infinitely more pleasing to the various senses than is usually the case—the kennel buildings standing on a sunny, wood-girt, and turf-laid slope behind the Castle. Truly for sport in most thorough form, and for the benefit of his friends, neighbours, and county, does Lord Portsmouth maintain his pack—the cost and trouble being alike his own.

In common with all Devonshire, Lord Portsmouth's is a famous scenting country; and, in common with most of the rest, it seldom allows of riding to hounds. Did it not carry a good scent, the best of hounds would seldom kill a fox; for there is little chance of helping them at a difficulty. As it is, there is little opportunity for over-riding them, and they seldom meet with a difficulty that they cannot overcome of themselves. Yet it was in the west, or Hatherleigh side of the country that in the season 1878-79 they never lost a fox—and this is the district that has been termed "the Leicestershire of the West," the one part where men fond of riding can disport themseves. For the banks are here built of a size within the compass of a horse's powers; and the South-Western Railway never fails to bring a cargo of aspiring spirits to take advantage of a meet in this neighbourhood. A stiff clay soil is not the most elastic material to jump off; and an occasional bog is apt to fetter the leap or interfere with the safety of landing. But it is a treat to get across a country at all—rather than *round it*, as must be the almost universal rule of action in Devonshire. There is much less moorland, or open common, in Lord Portsmouth's country than in those of his neighbours towards Exmoor and the north. The land is everywhere inclosed as stiffly as steep bank and stout hedge can make it; and roads, lanes, and gates must be the study and the means of getting about. So for this country, as for Devonshire generally, your mount should be one that can make his way quickly along a road, scramble over and through rough places, and carry you safely home at night, after having been out of his stables for as many hours as would often suffice for two days' hunting in some more fashionable parts of England. For want of this—by far the most suitable—class of animal, the visitor need never find himself unable to go out. They are not only grown in the country, but are to be hired everywhere, with much less cost than—and none of the risk of—bringing expensive horses a long distance by rail, on to ground to which they are unused and unsuited.

Throughout the west country good sportsmen and stout foxhunters are freely scattered. They are especially plentiful where Lord Portsmouth holds sway —for instance, Mr. Robert Luxton, who for many a year has been quite a right-hand to the Hunt, ever ready to settle any damage or smooth any dispute, to rear his share and more than his share of cubs and puppies, to turn a hound or read the Riot Act over a young-one; Mr. Henry Churchill, who for more than twenty years has kept a special keeper to watch, preserve, and feed fox cubs, to the entire disregard of hares or pheasants; Mr. Holley of Oaklands; Mr. John Cobley, who would as soon see his table without dinner as his best gorse without a fox for "my Lord;" and Mr. George Tucker of Hill, another of like sort. The church are also very staunch in support of the chase. The late Rev. P. Johnson of Wembworthy, though he never took the saddle in person, was as good a preserver and neighbour to a pack of hounds as could be desired. He was wont to say, "I will have foxes on my property—in fact I put it in my leases." His son, recently M.P. for Exeter, follows worthily in his father's footsteps. The Rev. Nathaniel Hole of Broadwood Kelly was an active friend to foxhunting as long as weight and health would let him. No one ever worked more heartily in the cause of the noble science than has the Rev. John Luxton for twenty years; and few whips of the present day can view Reynard away, or turn hounds, quicker than he. Sir George Stucley of Afton Castle owns considerable property and many coverts in the Eggesford country, and well supports the Hunt. The large Preston property close to the Castle has just passed into new hands, the present possessor is a very keen sportsman and as kind a friend to the Hunt as were his predecessors for so many years.

All through Lord Portsmouth's country foxes are found in plenty. Immediately round Eggesford they positively swarm; and last year no less than fourteen litters were laid up in the home woods alone. No doubt the universal support accorded to the Hunt is due in a great measure to the personal popularity of the Earl of Portsmouth and his Countess. The latter or one of her daughters is always to be seen taking active part in the hunting field.

A great feature of the Hunt in the days of the Hon. Newton Fellowes, father of the present Master, was the Chumleigh Hunt Week; but this ceased to exist some thirty years ago. At South Molton in after days a similar happy réunion was held under the name of the South Molton Club Hunt, when the Eggesford, Mr. Russell's, Mr. Trelawney's, and the Tiverton Foxhounds would hunt turn about for a fortnight. "There is wine in the Club cellars still; but the spirit of the club is missing, and its doors are closed."

Lord Portsmouth's days of hunting are Mondays, Tuesdays, Thursdays and Saturdays—subject to occasional necessary change. The River Taw, alongside whose bed runs the South-Western Railway from Barnstaple to Exeter, nearly bisects the country, with a chain of overhanging woods—chief of which are those of His Lordship at Eggesford. The special district for each day is settled by no fixed rule. Perhaps Monday and Thursday are more often in the western half of the country. The new extension in the Hatherleigh and Ashbury direction has been productive of much capital sport on good ground. There is more moorland hereabouts than in the rest of the country: foxes often find themselves obliged to take to it for their lives; and hounds have seldom any difficulty in pressing them hard. Lying as it does at a great distance from Kennels, it necessarily receives most attention in autumn and spring, when the days are long—and when, moreover, the ground rides firmer than in midwinter. Both landowners and tenants are enthusiastic in the cause of sport—and the latter appreciate keenly the determination to kill a fox when once on his track and the success with which it is so frequently — nay generally — accomplished. Mr. Holley's coverts at Oaklands, Mr. Woollcombe's at Ashbury, Mr. Harris's at Beaworthy, Mr. Coham's at Black Torrington, those of Messrs. Veale and Oldham near Hatherleigh, and of Col. Arnold at Iddesleigh are all staunchly preserved. A run over Broadbury is by many accounted the finest thing of the west, rarely failing to scatter the field or even lose many of them for the day.

Among the leading meets on the west of the Taw are North Tawton Station, whence Barton Moor, Blacklands, and Crook Plantation may be drawn; Sampford Courtney for New Plantation, Star Brake and Babbicleave; Brightley Bridge for Oaklands; Inwardleigh Village for Northwick Wood and Mr. Riddaway's coverts; Hatherleigh Moor for the Jacobstowe coverts, Hatherleigh for Pascoe; Golden Inn for Brakes and Bremridge Wood; Ashbury for Mr. Copp's brake; Halwell Station for Stowford and Foxholes Brakes; Black Torrington for Coham Woodlands; Stafford Cross for Stafford Brake and Brimmacombe Wood; Leckington Cross, Winkleigh for Lewesdon Moor, Holeacombe and Chubhouse; Bondleigh Moor for Ven Cohoe, Honeychurch, and Brewsland Brake; Tawbridge for Taw-green Plantation and Brake; Lymington Arms for Abboskham Moor and

Brushford Wood; Ashreigney for Riddlecombe, Ash Wood and Coldharbour Brakes; Portsmouth Arms for Gratley Wood and Northcote Coverts. Nearly all these coverts are of natural growth and workable size.

East of the Taw we have Thelbridge Cross near Witheridge, a very favourite fixture, whence hounds nearly always find in Mr. Thos. Strong's Gorse close by, or in the coverts of Mr. W. Cornish Cleave, who may be said to have purchased his estate (with Brown's Wood in the centre) chiefly with a view to assisting the hunt in that direction. Pedley Wood is one of the leading draws: and Kennerleigh Wood, the property for generations past of Sir Stafford Northcote's ancestry. It is told that a Northcote won both the wood and the manor of Kennerleigh from a Dowrick of Dowrick (in the parish of Stanford) at a game of piquet. The Northcote of that time was considered but a poor hand at the game by his neighbour, who, again, fancied his own play so highly that he did not hesitate to wager the manor of Kennerleigh (some 2000 acres) against a comparatively insignificant sum of money. The Northcote won the game and the manor—whereupon the Dowrick had the hands of cards and even the markers passed down to posterity, by causing a facsimile of them in Italian marble to be inlaid in a stone table. The table is still to be seen—a warning to reckless gamblers—at Dowrick House (Mr. Ireland's). Not very long ago two maiden ladies, relatives of Mr. Ireland's, entertained an old woman of the parish one Sunday afternoon to a cup of tea, served on this very table. The servants asking the old dame afterwards how she had fared—she answered "Oh, I never should have thought it of them, such nice ladies too! Why, if they wasn't a playing of cards on a Sunday!"

Three Hammers is another old fixture of the Eggesford, and in days gone by the cottage was notable for Mr. Drake's quaint yew trees cut into design of a peacock and other devices. Bromsmead and Heatherfield are the usual coverts to draw. At Worlington (East and West) are two good yeomen, Smith father and son. Ash Moor and Creacombe have a collection of small gorses, and are held in great esteem, being on most favourable ground for scent and sport. These are Lord Portsmouth's farthest fixtures towards the Dulverton. Knowstone and its woods are neutral; but seldom visited by his lordship, except after a travelling fox.

To shorten the tale of meets and coverts it may suffice to note that Castle Hill is for Lord Fortescue's wide and well-preserved coverts; Meath Gate for Warkleigh Wood; Head Bridge for Head Wood and King's Nympton Park; Chumleigh Beacon for Horridge Moor or Lakehead Moor; Stone Moor for The Plantations or Cheldon Brake; Beauly Court for Mr. Cobley's Coverts; Puddington for Mr. Eland's Coverts; Morchard Bishop for those of Mr. Churchill or Mr. Tucker; Morchard Road Station for Wales Brake or Braddiford Brake; and Ashridge Manor for North Tawton Woodlands and Cottles Wood.

Between the Morchard Road Station (near which lives a sportsman of note with hare and otter, and yet ever in full support of the fox—viz., Mr. William Cheriton) and the Portsmouth Arms Station are various meets for Lord Portsmouth's home property—in itself quite enough for one day a week. Lapford, Nymett Wood, South Molton Road, Coleridge Mill, &c., are all named for the picturesque woodlands that branch forth from Eggesford.

THE ESSEX AND THE ESSEX UNION.*

IF you must hunt from London, the Essex packs are as easy of access as any others, and will give you quite as much sport as is to be had anywhere near. To the City-man they offer unusual advantages; for the Great Eastern Railway, starting from the midst of the money-making quarter of the metropolis, will set him down at points within riding distance of hounds every morning that he can wash his hands of work, or delegate someone else to do it for him. He can either hunt from his work, or work from his hunting-ground. Half an hour—to an hour—from Liverpool-street Station will bring him down, with comfort and the morning paper, to Romford, Brentwood, Ingatestone, or Chelmsford—allowing him to breakfast at a comfortable hour before starting. By a man of business habits the breakfast-hour may possibly be held as little or no concern. But the sternest devotee of the gold-god can surely never have tutored himself to such a pitch as to prefer taking his relaxation by candlelight—which a fox-hunting merchant must do, each morning that he would travel from Euston or

---

* *Vide* Stanford's "Hunting Map," Sheets 16 and 17, and Hobson's Foxhunting Atlas.

St. Pancras to join a fashionable pack at a greater distance. Living in town, he may take train to the Essex or Essex Union at 9 a.m., reach any of their meets, and make a full day's hunting before returning to dinner. Or he may reverse the system; and, taking a snug box in a district that is undulating, well wooded, and picturesque, use the train to London on working days, while giving to his household all the advantage of fresh country air in summer, to himself all the luxury of being in a hunting quarter in the winter. For it is the Benedict and the busy man who will chiefly affect Essex. Ambitious youth, with time and energy to spare, may probably elect to go farther afield, and join the rush on greener fields and pastures that to him are still new. Mayhap he will return unrewarded, possibly shaken—personally or pecuniarily —and content in future to take his pleasure amid scenes less trying and more easily accessible. It will not always happen so; and of this he may be sure— that, if disappointed in his pictured Elysium, much of the shortcoming will be due to himself rather than to the scenes he visits. But this by the way.

Essex, it is true, is purely a county of plough—but *good plough*—plough that holds a scent, and yet does not hold a horse with half the tenacity of grip belonging to some grass. Over most of Essex you may gallop to hounds, and hounds will often go fast enough to furnish the chance. Under certain conditions of weather, part of it—the Ruthins—becomes a flying country; and all of it is rideable in one fashion or another. Of the two representative packs nearest to London, the Essex takes the northern side of the

Great Eastern Railway, the Essex Union the south; and the places we have named as hunting-quarters are on the line between the two, Brentwood being the most central spot of all. At the latter place a man may hire something fit to ride, if it happens to suit him to do so rather than keep his own on the spot; and, both here and at Chelmsford, the week's programme can be varied between two (or even three) packs of foxhounds, and Hon. H. Petre's staghounds. The staghounds—the kennels for which are at Springfield, close to Chelmsford—are out (in the best of the Ruthin country) on Tuesdays and each alternate Saturday; the Essex on Mondays, Wednesdays, Fridays, and Saturdays; and the Essex Union on Tuesdays, Thursdays, Saturdays, and alternate Mondays. Thus the man of business has a holiday provided for him on any, or every, day he may choose to take it. The chances are that he will not confine his attentions solely to one pack; and thus he should be mounted so as to suit the requirements of each. For, though divided only by a nominal boundary in the shape of the London-and-Chelmsford High-road, the countries of the Essex and the Essex Union differ considerably as riding-ground. The horse that is good enough to go well with the Essex pack over their Ruthins ought to be capable of conveying you in tolerable comfort and safety with the Essex Union. It does not, of course, *necessarily* follow that a horse that goes fast, and jumps wide at a low hedge and broad ditch, will drop his legs on to a bank; but the chances are very much in favour of its being possible to teach him to do so. On the other hand, a sticky jumper will never be a comfortable conveyance over the Ruthins—the latter being the pith of the Essex country and almost entirely free from banks, which are the chief feature of the Essex Union. Strength and stoutness—especially in the form of jumping power—are required in the Ruthins; and a horse possessed of these may easily, unless his temperament is of the hottest, be taught to land on a low bank, guarded on one side only by a moderate ditch. True, this ditch is often blind, and the bank is often half hid in ragged growth. Creeping then becomes a necessary accomplishment; and there is no reason against a horse that can jump learning to creep quite as well as a malformed animal with neither spirit nor spring—any more than it is out of the question to ask a Leicestershire horse to walk through a gap.

The Ruthins form the heart and core of The Essex Hunt, and furnish an arena such as is not given to the other packs of the county. The name is a corruption of Roding, a term that was brought to apply to the whole property of the Earl of Roding. From about Great Canfield to Willingale embraces the best of the Ruthins; and in this tract a whole string of villages will be found, with the distinctive appellation Roding subjoined to their other name—the most northern being High Roding; the most southern, Beauchamp Roding. The Ruthins as a descriptive term, and for our purpose, point to a fine flat and open hunting ground, with small fences and wide ditches; light arable carrying a good scent and fairly easy for horses. The coverts are small; foxes run well; and over the low hedges you may see all that hounds are doing.

On a tolerable scenting day you have every chance of a gallop, and, as has been already remarked, the indulgence may generally be accepted without unfairness to your horse. Yet, it must be confessed, the steamplough is rapidly, and sadly, changing the face of the Ruthins, and robbing them of their chiefest merit. Where it used to be thought enough that the mere crust of the sound firm soil should be disturbed, the steamplough now tears through to the depth of a foot—and to a difference of pleasure and possibility of riding that may be imagined. Harlow (which is the site of the Essex Kennels) and Bishops Stortford are other points that command the Ruthins. They are about the same distance from Town, and start from the same base, as the other quarters we have named; and for variety they have the Puckeridge instead of the Essex Union, with the same opportunity of a gallop with the stag. We are now engaged upon foxhunting; but it is no heresy to say that a burst after a stag in dusty March is not the worst item in sporting Essex. You may, and must, ride hard from beginning to end; for—as you who have hunted the deer must know—the scent never fails and hounds are seldom baffled. The chase of the carted deer is but a spurious pastime, granted. But it is productive of much merry fun; and they do it comfortably—heartily—in Essex, breakfasting *à la fourchette et Perrier Jouet* at some hospitable centre, till the broadest ditch in the Ruthins has no terrors for local or Londoner. Saturday is the great day upon which Essex rejoices in a field, and makes its best show. Saturday is a home meet of the Essex Union,

The Essex and the Essex Union.

with an alternate choice of The Hon. H. Petre's Staghounds.

The leading, natural, divisions of the Essex are the Ruthins, Takeley Forest, the bank country in the north, and Epping Forest in the south-west. The first-named is the type on which the Hunt builds its fame; and the neutral wastes of Takeley Forest are a source from which both The Essex and The Puckeridge ever aim at driving a fox forth on to the Ruthins. About Thaxted and Bardfield every farm is more stiffly enclosed, usually with stout banks. At the south-western end, again, we come to the almost hopeless depths of Epping Forest (best considered as sacred to Easter Monday and the Annual Benefit of Her Majesty's Buckhounds) and just short of this is Nasing Common and its adjuncts, whereon a run may be carried for miles on open grass. Along the southern-most border of the Essex—from Brentwood past Romford towards London—is a rich wooded district of park and enclosure, beautiful to the lover of scenery, precious in many senses, but not altogether best fitted for the pursuit of bold Reynard.

The Essex are under the popular Mastership of Sir Selwin-Ibbetson, M.P.; and his leading meets are much as follows : For Monday, Passingford Bridge, with its good Gorse, and General Mark Wood's well-tended coverts; Navestock; Shank's Mill; and Kelvedon Common, Havering, whence a fox is always to be found in the late Mr. Macintosh's Gardens; and Purgo Lodge for Purgo Big Wood, where General Ffitch looks well after the foxes.

The Wednesday meets are the best of the week;

and among them are High Easter in a good open country, whose chief coverts are Garnett's and Old Park, both made sure and safe by Mr. Barnard; Willingale for Whitney Wood (a sure find) and Screens (preserved for foxes and pheasants alike); Hatfield Heath; Matching Green (the Kirby Gate of The Essex), whence are drawn Brickells (which the Master ensures ever being full of foxes) afterwards probably Man's Wood (an equally certain find) and Down Hill (the Master's seat and a source of supply to much of the country round), with still another good draw in Row Wood. Hatfield Windmill is also a favourite meet, generally leading to a run into Takerley Forest.

Among the chief Friday fixtures are Stebbing-Brand-End and Radwinter. Fox's Wood is a stand-by for the former; while from Radwinter is drawn Langley's (invariably with good result), and then on to the Bendish Coverts and Hempstead Wood (the latter being one of the finest strongholds in Essex). Spains Wood is neutral between The Essex and the East Essex.

For a Saturday are the meets of High Ongar, for the coverts of the Rev. F. Fane, who supports the Hunt both by preservation and presence; Swallow's Cross for Thoby or Park Wood (both very favourite); Toot Hill for Sir Charles Smith's coverts, and Ongar Park Wood (carefully preserved by Mr. Capel Cure); Taylor's Cross, to draw Galley Hill (where Mr. Colvin cares well for the Hunt), and on to Ongar (Capt. Hall's) where the hounds were formerly kennelled, thence to Epping and the Forest coverts. From

The Essex and the Essex Union.

Hare Street they work round Parndon Hall (the seat of the late Master, Mr L. W. Arkwright), and are safe to find quickly near the Hall. The Harlow meet takes place at the Green Man Inn, where Mr. Bambridge will house man and horse, and let worthy specimens of the latter. From this meet Moor Hall is always equal to the occasion. Leaving the open country, we get to Blackmore and the enormous coverts of the High Woods, whence it is a difficult task to persuade foxes into the Ruthins beyond. The stations of Epping and Ongar should be added as offering access to the centre of The Essex.

Turning to the Essex Union we find that their Tuesdays are usually spent in the direction of Tilbury and Mucking, and likely to tempt men across the Thames from the Gravesend side. First mention should be made of Belhus, the seat of Sir Thomas Lennard (than whom no more liberal fox preserver is to be found in Essex, or England). Sir Thomas keeps a pack of draghounds of his own, which are mostly out on Thursdays and more often in the Ockendon district. The Essex Union have meets at Mucking, Langdon Hills (coverts of great size), Dunton Blacksmith (in a good open country), East Horndon Mill, Upminster Bell, and Stifford.

On a Thursday (which, with Saturday, covers their best ground) the Essex Union are towards Southend, under order for the following meets, among others— Hadleigh has an enormous wood from which it is no easy matter to get away; Runwell (belonging to Mr. T. Kemble, one of their best preservers); Wickford, with coverts of considerable size near by; Purleigh

Wash, close to the Thames, and whence foxes are bound to go for the open (by many people, indeed, considered the best meet of the Hunt); Rayleigh and Southminster, the pick of the country in spring and autumn.

Saturday is essentially for the home district, and for the Londoners—Brentwood being the best starting point. Hutton Railway-Arch; Billericay Street (Billericay being the site of the Kennels); Stock Street for "The Forest" and its many foxes. The "Fortune of War;" Burstead Clockhouse; and White's Bridge are the most prominent meets; and the last is for a wide open country.

THE HERTFORDSHIRE.*

ANOTHER of the home countries is the Hertfordshire. And if munificence of expenditure could have raised it to the top of the tree the Hertfordshire would be one of the uppermost shoots of foxhunting growth. It aspires, however, to no prominence as a "fashionable" country. On the contrary, it rather aims at obscurity, by declining to advertise beyond the columns of a local paper. It is near enough to London to tempt a crowd, and it prefers that the crowd should find scope elsewhere. But if it suits you to hunt with the Hertfordshire, few obstacles are likely to be put in your way. With fifty-three couple of hounds in kennel, they take the field four days a week, viz., Monday, Wednesday, Friday and Saturday; and are easily reached from St. Pancras on the morning of hunting—the Kennels at Luton (in the very centre of the country) being less than an hour from London. You have the option of disembarking also at St. Albans; or of taking the Great Northern to Hatfield or Hitchin; or, again, of quartering yourself at Leighton and varying your time with Mr. Selby-Lowndes and the Baron.

---

* Vide Stanford's "Hunting Map," Sheet 16, and Hobson's Foxhunting Atlas.

A deep, muddy, country you will find when you get there, it is true: but a country well cared for, and with an establishment long ago set on a superb, almost princely footing. The Kennels at Luton too, two miles from Harpenden Station, are a sight for anyone to whom the care of the foxhound is a matter of concern—unless, indeed, the unattainable magnificence of the buildings bring a too reactionary sense of disappointment to the ordinary beholder. The Kennels at Luton are as far removed from the ordinary structure in which the foxhound is housed, as a farm homestead is from Buckingham Palace. Through the entire length of the hounds' building runs a broad flagged corridor, on either side being the various kennels with their offices. Thus in cold or wet weather the pack is to be seen without any of the discomfort so often attendant on an ordinary "day on the flags." Feeding houses, washhouses, &c., are all on a commensurate scale: and the stables are to match—no less than twenty loose boxes being ranged in a continuous double line under one roof. The "grass-yards" are of several acres apiece; and separate ranges (fenced and kennelled) are provided for the needs of the matrons of the pack. It is to be questioned, in short, if the Kennels built by the late Mr. Gerard Leigh, at Luton, have a rival for completeness and costly grandeur anywhere. The hounds are quite worthy of their residence—being of old blood, and very striking in appearance. As a pack they go back fully fifty years, for most of which time they were in the hands of Lord Dacre and Mr. Leigh. A glance at their Kennel-List will show how purely

The Hertfordshire. 351

their blood has been for many years maintained. The Belvoir and the Fitzwilliam had much to do with their original stock: and now they have turned to their neighbours, the Oakley, for a fresh strain. The present management is that of a Committee—an alternative method generally forced on a Country by want of a Master, and seldom to be resorted to except under such pressure. However, there is no reason to believe that in this case it works otherwise than well. The committee, no doubt, find that various strings that have for so many years been pulled by their veteran huntsman move well enough in his hands; and things go on evenly enough. "Bob Ward" (originally christened Charles, by the way) is the institution of the Hertfordshire Hunt. Like Carter and Treadwell, his natural instinct has been so developed by long practice that he can almost kill a fox by himself. Most of our readers must have seen his giant frame pourtrayed and exhibited a few years ago as a presentation picture from the hunt; while in the mind of every Hertfordshire man his colossal figure exists almost in the light of an impersonation of the chase.

The situation of the Hertfordshire may be taken roughly as stretching from London to Bedford. On leaving London you first get on huntable ground near Potter's Bar (on the Great Northern Line); and from thence northward, for nearly thirty miles, the duty of harassing the foxes amid arable and woodland devolves upon the Hertfordshire pack. For, from end to end, there is scarcely a blade of grass grown in Hertfordshire Country proper; and the plough is worked to the bitterest depth by the aid of steam. The fences are made according to requirement—the most that is aimed at, beyond mere landmark, being hedge sufficient to keep sheep from straying from a turnip-field. This does not apply to the Shillington district in the north, or to the Woburn corner on the west (until lately lent by the Oakley, but now reclaimed by them). Here the fences are strong enough for a glutton; and the former area has a succession of wide bottoms to swallow man and horse. But in most of the country there is more to scramble over than to jump: and your horse must be steady and clever rather than brilliant. Above all, he must be able to travel stolidly through dirt for many hours in succession: and have hocks and quarters to lift himself, and you, out of the mud, when called upon to cross a fence. As a hound-country, again, it seldom carries anything like a bursting scent: but hounds can generally make their way over it, and there is a good deal of sport to be seen with a pack like the present. The Woburn neighbourhood was, perhaps, their best scenting ground. This included most of what is coloured in the map between the main lines of the North-Western and the Midland and above the Great Northern branch from Leighton to Luton—Chalgrave Gorse being still drawn by the Hertfordshire.

The four days are generally carried out somewhat thus—Monday is for the eastern side, on the borders of the Puckeridge; Wednesday is for county Beds and the north; Friday is on the west—or rather south-west, as the boundary now stands; Saturday

The Hertfordshire.

takes in the home district, and, in the words of the natives, is the "loose-off for the Londoners." Willion is one of the leading Monday meets, and usually takes them into the woods of Bush, and Box, neutral with the Puckeridge (Mr. Stanford's colourer is requested to note this point). There are many other strong woods in this district; for instance Wain Wood (a sure find), West Wood and Westbury (equally good): and at Knebworth is another, further celebrated for the depth of its rides. From Welwyn commences a great chain of woodlands, stretching far beyond Hertford, which Mr. Abel Smith of Woodhall and Lord Cowper at Panshanger are admirably situated to preserve. But the hunting is of a somewhat limited description. Hatfield, too, is a Monday meet; and Lord Salisbury is seldom without a fox on his preserves. Symonds Hyde is a good fox-covert, and well cared for.

Of the Wednesday meets and coverts—Hexton is the residence of one of the committee (Col. Young), and is a good and frequent meet. Silsoe, or Higham Gobion, are for the gardens at Wrest Park (Lord Cowper's place in Beds) and Maulden Woods. Farthest north is Hawnes Park, generally leading to the woods neutral with the Cambridgeshire, of which Exeter Wood, with Great and Little Warden Woods are a leading trio. All these are sure finds, as is Wilshampstead Wood; and from any of them a stiff run over the border may be looked for.

In the now curtailed Friday country, Ashbridge (Lord Brownlow's), Gaddesden (Mr. Halsey's), and Cheverell's Green are prominent meets: and the

Beechwood Park coverts have always held high character. Another good Friday's meet is Colney Heath for South Myms—the coverts at which run into the county of Middlesex. Saturday as stated above takes in the centre of the country, round Luton, The Hyde, Wheathampstead and Harpenden, with many large and well-stocked coverts in their neighbourhood, and a great acreage of riding-ground such as is given to central Hertfordshire. Mrs. Leigh takes care that the welfare of the foxes round Luton Hoo is still attended to: Mr. A. Flower is a good supporter at the Hyde: and Lord Dacre, so many years Master, takes as deep an interest in the Hunt as ever. Two or three times at the end of the season the hounds are taken to the Hertford Heath Woods, a large tract of woodland country at a long distance from Kennels. The coverts are very deep, with few if any rides, and the land between the woods is uncultivated. It joins the Essex country. Though the wildest it is the best scenting ground in the Hunt, and a fox found there is sure to be a good one. The meets there are Bayfordbury, Balls Park, Hertford Heath and Northam. The coverts, Brickenden Woods, Balls Park, Hertford Heath, Haileybury Woods, Box Wood, Broxbourne Woods, Cow Heath, Wormley, Northaw and Black Fan. These are all large coverts and in a very wild country.

In Lord Dacre's time the run of the season took place from Cow Heath, they killed in Enfield Chase. There was also a famous run from the same covert in Mr. Leigh's time—the kill near Harlow in Essex. Another good run was also in Mr. Leigh's time, the last day of the season, when they did not kill before seven o'clock, leaving off thirty miles from kennels, which hounds did not reach until twelve.

The Hertfordshire, in short, is a country into which little of the *poetry* of foxhunting enters. Its prose is solid, and often pleasant: but it aims at no lofty flights, and bases its chief merit on treating a difficult subject in a liberal and thorough spirit.

THE WHADDON CHASE.*

A SWEET little country is the Whaddon Chase, offering Londoners two days a week on the grass at no distance from their home. They can run down from town on the morning of hunting, leaving Euston Square at the comfortable hour of nine; a slip carriage drops them at Leighton, or the train sets them down at Bletchley, in time for all meets; while the up express stops specially for them in the evening, and brings them back in time for dinner. These two places are the best resorts for the man who can only afford twelve hours at a stretch for fox-hunting. The town of Aylesbury is thoroughly situated to command the Vale; but, standing as it does off the main line of railway, is most frequented by those who can station themselves on the spot, and give fuller fling to their appetite for sport than is allowed to the man escaping for the day from his business. The same remark applies to Winslow; as well as to Stony Stratford and Newport Pagnall, which hold good also the Duke of Grafton's and the Oakley.

The Vale of Aylesbury is the Londoner's Leicester-

---

* *Vide* Stanford's " Hunting Map," Sheets 15 and 16.

shire. He may slip down for a gallop over the grass almost any day of the week that he finds himself, or sets himself, at liberty. He will get his hunting here much as he did in his college days—snatching it according to his keenness and his conscience; often putting weightier matters aside, if he is a weak man or an enthusiast—persuading himself, perhaps, that health and nerve bid him take the saddle and breathe the open air. We have even heard instances whispered of barrister or city man being seen sailing over the Vale when sympathetic relatives imagined him to be poring over musty law books at Gray's Inn or slaving over invoice and ledger in Cornhill. Knotty law-points or trade depreciation were the subjects they brought home to dinner, while inwardly they chuckled over that brilliant twenty minutes from Christmas Gorse, gloated silently over the way they had left the Addington brook behind with the Baron, or hugged themselves as they toasted "the Chase" under their breath.

The Whaddon Chase hunt Tuesdays and Saturdays (with occasional Thursdays devoted to the hills and woodlands adjoining the Oakley and Herts countries) while the staghounds are out on Mondays and Thursdays, and the Bicester, with the Oakley, the Hertfordshire, or the Duke of Grafton's on various sides, may be reached on other days. The whole of the Vale, with the exception of Lord Carington's property, and a few minor freeholds, may be said to belong to Mr. Selby Lowndes or the Rothschild family; and it is needless to add that in these hands it is as complete a hunting-ground as the New Forest was to our Norman kings, with an invitation to the sporting commonwealth of England that these latter were never disposed to offer. "The Baron" (as represented by Sir N. de Rothschild) defrays all the expenses of the sport he proffers you. "The Squire's" is a subscription pack; and, as is only fair, you are expected to subscribe when you hunt with him. Have your cheque written before you start for your first day's hunting; present it to the secretary at the covertside (or, better still, post it to him beforehand), and your way is smoothed towards being considered a friend of the Hunt at once.

Mr. Selby Lowndes (or, as he is best known in the Vale, "The Squire") has kept the Whaddon Chase Hounds altogether some forty years—a break of five years occurring, when he assumed the mastership of the North Warwickshire, and immediately afterwards of the Atherstone. This was previous to 1862; and during that period his country was held by Lord Southampton. Whaddon Chase itself, where the pack is kennelled, and whence the country takes its name, is the squire's property and residence, and is a truly beautiful place. Until late years the Chase was an almost continuous woodland; into whose depths, it is said, fifty couple of hounds were sometimes thrown at a time, on the chance of enough of them forming a pack on one fox, among the swarms that they were sure to open upon at once. Now, like most other Forests and Chases of modern England, it has been cut and uprooted till there remain only detached woods on the wide acreage that still bears the name. One day of the week (Saturday) is generally devoted to the Chase and its neighbourhood, while the other (Tuesday) is spent in the Vale proper.

The Vale of Aylesbury is, *par excellence*, The Vale of England. Its turf, its fences, and its soil are sounder, fairer, sweeter than even the Vale of Belvoir, or the Blackmore Vale. It has more extent than the Berkshire Vale; and has more character than the Vale of White Horse. The Catmose Vale alone can rival it—and that is a name scarcely recognised, even among the Cottesmore Hunt, who look upon their hills as more typical of their Country than the lower flat, between the old Tailby-grant and the woodlands, which bears the title of the Vale of Catmose.

The Vale of Aylesbury is one great dairy farm—rich pasture from end to end. Comparison between grass land and plough is worn-out and odious; but the fact must ever assert itself that, whether for hounds or for horses, turf underfoot is a *sine quâ non* for brilliant performance. Without it, each may be hardworking, steady and solemn; but without it there can be little dash, no enthusiasm. They have it in the Vale of Aylesbury to a perfect, heart-stirring degree—till the wet falls, to choke their flippancy, and suppress their *elan*. For the Vale holds water shockingly; and in a deep winter becomes a nightmare slough. One week a springboard, the next it is a treaclepot. At its best it represents a lovely succession of sweet-scenting meadows, from whose elastic face a horse bounds easily and gladly on to sound firm banks, to light with equal safety on turf renewed beyond—while hounds spread out at their fences and carry a broad head from field to field.

Mind, the doubles of the Aylesbury Vale require a horse; and, above all, they require a horseman. Often a double ditch guards a bank and its double wattle-growth atop. Courage in a horse (want of it in the man must never be hinted at); skilful handling by the rider; are the requisites. The first can be attained if your income, your horse dealer, and the size of your family allow it: the second is to be achieved by a few falls, innate ambition and a real love of the sport. Some good men have it that the Vale of Aylesbury is *too* stiff. Others equally good (perhaps less self-depreciative) say it is practicable enough. The mean truth is, I fancy, to be found in the opinion that it is sufficiently rideable to allow of hounds being at all times commanded by a good couplet of horse and man though now and again they may have to diverge a trifle from their direct path. For there are, undoubtedly, many welded upbuilt fences that appear unwarrantable to a rider of discretion, however well mounted. Yet, again and again—and somehow—these terrors get dispersed by the passage of a leader bolder than others; and his example soon brings on a following that lays a breach for the season through. Thus, by means of stag and fox, the Aylesbury Vale is very different ground in spring to what it is in autumn. A well-horsed waggon might almost cross it at a gallop in April; but "a mon is a mon" who can carve out twenty quick minutes on its face in November. You will not so often as in Leicestershire be checked and hindered by a crowd all aiming to reach and take their turn at a few certain feasible points. The Vale occasionally has its multitude, but after all a limited multitude. But, apart from numbers there is more room at a fence—because most of its fences are alike from end to end. If you can have a fence at all—before it is gapped as above; you can have it anywhere, and may ride at it in good heart as it confronts you. Neither horse nor rider must rake-and-tear. Quick between your fences, and a "steady" at them is the rule in the Vale—and is not the same rule absolute *anywhere*—if you would not make a fool of yourself at the end of one field. Get the way on *before* you settle for the jump is no Maxim: it is the means by which the best of our elders (Lord Wilton and Mr. George Grey of Northumberland) set their juniors year after year; leading the latter either to hustle at the critical moment of the jump, or else to believe that big fences were to be had without pace. In the Vale it is not only to cover height and width that a steadier must be taken. Often and often a first spring is only preliminary to a second bound for a second fly. You are on to the bank over stout wattle, with just room enough to take ground for a launch over the second and the ditch beyond. That ditch is probably blind and dark; and the double hedgerow is all one growth, up to Christmas. But you are not all, and always, going best pace at such obstacles: and you are not, every day, riding an animal new and untangled to the work.

The brooks of the Vale form another distinguishing feature, and supply the prettiest water-jumping in England—almost every stream being a fair clean jump, with sound banks and the water almost level. The Addington Brook is the only doubtful one:

for, though practicable in many places, it swells out here and there to unjumpable proportions; and the Hunt regard it with wholesome awe in consequence.

The Vale calls for all the best essentials in a hunter. He must gallop, he must jump and he must stay. He need not be an absolute flier; but he can't be too good: and it is noticeable that a man tutored in the Vale is not only likely to ride well over the best of the shires, but generally brings thither a stamp of cattle that can do him credit. Stoutness is a main feature in a Vale horse. Hocks, quarters and backs are the main points—depth of chest and ribs indispensable. The length of one type of Leicestershire horse is out of place. But there are two sorts for Leicestershire; and the thick one is the better. This is the Aylesbury horse.

Now for a few items of geography—Tuesday, as above noted, is for The Vale proper; and among its meets are Shipton for the Winslow spinnies, on the edge of the Vale, or for Christmas Gorse. The latter lies well in the lower ground, belongs to The Squire, is full of foxes, and replete with recent memories of good gallops. From the Gorse to the Claydon Woods (Bicester) is a fine and constant line. Hogston may also be for Christmas Gorse; and Dunton is a great meet held at the house of Mr. Mead, who makes Lord Carington's covert of High Haven his special care and treasure. High Haven is a square mass of gorse and Blackthorn mixed; and is the Ranksboro' of the Whaddon Chase. A common and beautiful line is from High Haven to Christmas Gorse — eighteen minutes at fastest, with no water but many good doubles on the way. In the other direction they may run out to Aston Abbots, another fine gorse near Leighton—for which the meet is at Mr. Straw's place or at Wingrave Cross Roads. Mentmore is a beautiful meet, with the shrubberies to draw and frequently a fox at home; while near by is Baron Rothschild's new gorse at Puttenham, on the edge of the country, and with the Rousham Brook running just below it. By the way, it may here be noted that Mr. Stanford should have shown Puttenham as within the Whaddon Chase boundaries: and also that the Oakley have retained that strip of their country by Woburn, which they had lent to Mr. Selby-Lowndes. At Ascot Mr. Leopold Rothschild has planted a new covert. On the other side we come to the meet of Creslow Great Ground, with small patches of covert near; and Hardwicke (the rendezvous being Mr. Casenove's place, The Lilies), whence they have little to draw but thick hedgerows — no strong covert existing between here and Christmas Gorse. For Mr. Monk's Gorse they meet at his house; and thence you may likely enough find yourself in the Addington coverts —possibly in the Addington Brook.

The three chief woods still remaining to mark The Chase itself are College Wood, Oak Hill, and the Thrift: all of which are a thorough home for foxes— the meets being Nash, Whaddon and Furze-in-the-Field. Outside these we find Saldon Wood from Saldon Windmill, which may also take you into the Vale—Saldon down to Aylesbury Town being about the extent of the Vale hunted by these hounds.

Newton-Longueville is for Mrs. Villiers' Gorse; Liscombe Park or Soulburys mean Hollingdon Gorse or the Hop Garden in the Park. North of The Chase is a stretch of mixed plough and grass; wherein Shenley New Inn is named for Shenley Wood, and Bradwell for Linford Wood. In the extreme north of the country, near Newport Pagnall, is Willen Gorse, usually drawn also from Bradwell.

THE VALE OF WHITE HORSE.*

BEYOND the bounds of a day's outing, yet well within visiting reach from London, the Vale of White Horse offers excellent ground and plentiful sport to the travelling foxhunter. He may select Cirencester, Swindon, or Malmesbury for his base; and the Great Western Railway will see him there in less than three hours from Paddington. The respective advantages of the places named are that Cirencester is close to the kennels, and lies at the point of junction with the Cotswold and the Duke of Beaufort; Malmesbury commands all the Duke's country; while Swindon gives further opportunity of taking the Old Berkshire and the Craven in turn. Or again, on the upper side of the country, he may fix upon Fairford or Lechlade; and vary his programme by the help of the Heythrop and the Old Berkshire.

A very sporting country is the Vale of White Horse throughout—honest and practicable to ride over; fair, and generally favourable, for hounds; liberally and thoroughly managed; and, as a rule, well preserved. The latter point proves itself by the fact that, on an

---

* *Vide* Stanford's "Hunting Map," Sheet 15, and Hobson's Foxhunting Atlas.

area by no means over-extensive, hounds can be out five days a week, afford to kill nearly sixty brace of foxes, and leave a better prospect than ever for the forthcoming season. Mr. Hoare's agreement with the hunt only extended to three days a week; but by the help of the Cirencester Woods and the Swindon side, he has been enabled to advertise and hunt five—Monday, as market day at the principle town, being the off-day. Even on Mondays his hounds were last season not always at rest; but, by the Duke of Beaufort's invitation, were often taken into the Lower Woods in the adjoining country. It is not surprising, then, that sixty-eight couple of hounds are required at the Cirencester Kennels.

The Vale of White Horse (a title, by the way, that it takes from off its neighbour's ground—the White Horse being cut on the slope of the Old Berkshire's bordering down) is by no means of one class and calibre through length and breadth. Along the north it has wolds and stone walls similar to those of the Heythrop and the Cotswold, is oftentimes cold and discouraging, at other times ravishing, for hounds. After much rain the wolds will carry a burning scent; while the light soil remains firm and easy, and men can flutter over the walls as fast as they choose to ride. This is favourite ground for Cheltenham and Oxford; and a capital let-off for the energies of both, *when* there is a scent. When there is *not*, the "let-off" might, with a different temperament, fairly be the Master's; for the temptation of the stonewalls is so irresistible that visitors and natives alike are apt to get out of hand, to the sore discomfiture of hounds and

The Vale of White Horse.

huntsman. In curious contrast with the above-named condition for scent on the wolds, is the fact that in a dry and dusty March hounds frequently fly from find to finish, at times almost hidden in the cloud they raise. A cold easterly wind must, no doubt, be the agent and the explanation then.

The centre of the country, taken diagonally from Cirencester by Cricklade to Swindon and · beyond, is chiefly a vale country—a continuation, in fact, of the Berkshire Vale. Its fences are, with the exception of a few doubles in the neighbourhood of Swindon, plain, fair, hedge-and-ditch, requiring but not overtaxing a hunter; most of its surface is grass; and its coverts are of a nice handy size. In a wet season it may ride a trifle deep; but can scarcely be said to have a pronounced failing in that direction. In and about Braydon, however, the ground will often be found deep and holding as a snipe marsh. Amid its woods you must plunge about sticky yellow rides that threaten to take you in bodily; and outside it is often all you can do to make way across a field before coming to a hairy uncut fence, whose thorn-growth has never been thinned or trimmed and whose ditch has never been freed of the long rank grass. Visitors speak with no affection of the Braydon Woods. The Hunt pin their faith strongly to them; asserting, with good reason, that they find the stoutest foxes there; and that thence come many of their longest and best runs. As it is with the Claydon Woods in the Bicester country, and the Launde and Owston Woods in the Cottesmore (with similar examples all over England), so it is with the Braydon Woods in the Vale of White

Horse. Once clear of them an excellent country is met with; and foxes will go as far again as those bred and tendered in small artificial coverts. Towards Charlton and Crudwell is a capital district, of grass riding, pleasant fencing and good scenting country. The Sapperton and Oakley Woods (which though coloured by Mr. Stanford and Mr. Hobson as exclusively the Duke's, are regularly drawn by the V.W.H. —and, indeed, the Kennels of the latter are beyond the painted margin) form still another feature of the country; and besides being invaluable for cub hunting and teaching hounds, are at least a fortnightly resort throughout the season.

You must ride quite a hunter with the V.W.H., if you would be with hounds. A lighter type of horse may do on the northern, and higher, ground: but all through the Vale, and more especially in the Braydon district, he must be stout and strong and full of condition. Wherever the fixtures draw in the Duke's men, or the train brings its cargo from Cheltenham and elsewhere, you will find a strong field—at times almost Leicestershire-like in its proportions.

The Kennels, which are given by Lord Bathurst and built on his property, Oakley Park, close to Cirencester, are somewhat wide of many of the meets, though well situated for cubhunting and the woodlands in the north-east. The Master's hunting residence is Hill, at a stone's throw from the Kennels.

The country is hunted, day by day, much as follows, though no unbending rule is laid down for weekly routine.

Tuesday is the day chosen for the north (the Cotswold, Heythrop and Cheltenham side of the country), with its light plough uplands, but often leading to lower ground and grass, as hounds draw or run, into the Fairford neighbourhood. Among the meets are Arlington Cross Roads, with a wide choice of draw between a number of small coverts—Bibury, for instance, being a likely direction; Barnsley or Ready Token, with capital holding for foxes (which are plentiful enough all round). Ampney Riding is a favourite place, with two small coverts adjoining each other—now looked after by Capt. Dansey but owing all earlier reputation to the care of the Messrs. Daniel. And Tuesday has generally the largest field of the week.

Wednesday and Friday share the centre of the country, from corner to corner, between them. Once a fortnight, at least, hounds work the home woods—Sapperton, Pope's Seat, and Ten Rides being the usual fixtures for the Sapperton and Oakley Woods. Hailey Wood—though at one time under a ban, appears now to have recovered its prestige—both Mr. Hoare and the Duke having lost hounds there by poison. Lord Bathurst is the mainstay and best friend of the Hunt at Oakley and its neighbourhood —doing everything possible in the interests of foxhunting. In the open country Siddington and Down-Ampney are popular meets; and the name of Mr. Bowley should here be written down as an excellent sportsman. Cricklade, with Tadpole to draw, is also a place of mark; and the same may be said of Hay-lane Wharf, for Lord Bolingbroke's coverts and for

Binall. From Swindon hounds are generally taken to Major Calley's coverts (Birdrop). Hannington has some of the best of the country, with the Hannington Brook running through it; and Highworth and Stanton worthily complete the district for the days mentioned.

Thursday usually points to the Malmesbury side, and brings many of the Duke's Hunt over the border; and most of the country hereabouts belongs to Lord Suffolk, who also is a true friend to fox-hunting. Braydon, as above-noted, is the deepest part of the district, and has great woodlands, from which, however, foxes are generally readily forced. Charlton, Red Lodge, Ravensroost, and Webb's Wood, are leading meets. Brockhurst is looked upon as almost the best covert in the Hunt—always producing a run, often a clinker; and Oaksey and Crudwell complete the tale of Thursday.

Saturday is more often for the Alvescot corner, where the Hunt stretches into Oxfordshire with a mixed reach of grass and plough—the Thames Valley towards Bampton being a strong wet lowland. Lechlade, Alvescot, Southrop, and Fairford are the best known meets; and Kempsford may be told off for any day at the latter end of the week.

THE CHESHIRE AND SOUTH CHESHIRE.*

When without verdure the woods in November are,
  Then to our collars the green is transferred;
Racing and chasing the sports of each member are,
  Come then to Tarporley booted and spurred;
      Holding together, Sir,
      Scorning the weather, Sir,
      Like the good leather, Sir,
        Which we put on.
      Quæsitum meritis!
      Good Fun how rare it is!
      I know not where it is,
        Save at the Swan.
(*Tarporley Hunt*, 1833, by R. E. EGERTON WARBURTON.)

TILL three years ago, the beautiful county of Cheshire was hunted entirely by Mr. Corbet—with five and six days a week over its grassy surface. On Mr. Corbet's succession to his present place at Adderley, in the extreme south of the shire, he made arrangement with the committee that he should retain a two-days-a-week pack for this southernmost corner—Capt. Park Yates undertaking to work the wider residue in the north the four other days, with Kennels

---

* *Vide* Stanford's "Hunting Map," Sheet 8, and Hobson's Foxhunting Atlas.

as hitherto in Delamere Forest. And thus came about the present division of the county and the present distinctive titles of The Cheshire and the South Cheshire—one Committee still representing the shire and the ownership of the two packs.

Cheshire is indeed worth a visit—if to be always on grass, and to see hounds ever running well, where the fences are easily flown, where the field is not too swollen in size, and where anyone and everyone may ride his own line—if such a state of things in any way represents enjoyment. It is not unlike Meath— easy flying fences being substituted for the "narrow banks." It is altogether like the best of Derbyshire —its hedges, perhaps, of lesser height and more readily to be cleared than those that bound the meadows of the Meynell.

Cheshire, briefly and generally, consists of flat grass inclosures of a few acres apiece, fenced with thorn hedges that are trimmed but never "laid." The grass grows freely on the meadows, and lavishly in the ditches and hedges. Thus, in the wettest seasons, you splash along the surface rather than sink deeply into the ground—save in certain well-known holding districts. And, again, you are more likely to tumble about in Cheshire, especially before Christmas, than you will in Leicestershire—though there are no top binders to catch you tripping, and scarcely any timber to turn you over. You may, and probably will, come to grief occasionally through the misplaced confidence of a young one or the carelessness of one that has grown too clever. But in neither case are you likely to meet with the concussion that so

The Cheshire and South Cheshire. 373

often involves a collar-bone or a loss of nerve. A fall does you either harm or good. In Cheshire it will likely enough do you good—up to a certain time of life; enabling you to pick yourself up with renewed confidence, under the grateful discovery that a fall need not be such a terrible thing after all. On the theory of chances, too, you run a double risk of a tumble in Cheshire; for are you not twice as often in the air as you could be anywhere else—unless it be Derbyshire or the stonewall section of Gloucestershire? And, in the last-named, there are no blind ditches to ensnare the hunter, already overtaxed by continued jumping. There is scarcely a gate to be seen, and, to cross the country at all, you must have the fences as they come. Jump and twist and turn, and mind you are never in front of hounds! "The fence that gives a moment to the pack," is your temptation in Cheshire. It comes too frequently and too temptingly; and a field should be under command enough for an advance by squadrons. A solid rush gives no time for the scouting party, represented by a too often over-ridden pack. Yet, taken all in all, hounds (and foxes, too) have a rare chance in Cheshire. There are few commanding points from which a fox may be seen, and a clever man (oh, how fatal is a pointrider in many an open country!) has few chances of meeting a fox in his path, and sounding a damning yell to lead hounds astray or turn the fox from his point. A good fox in Cheshire may go where he will, and never be viewed on his journey till he becomes food and trophy. Hounds and huntsman must work unassisted. The former have their noses down as long as the master can keep them untrampled; the latter need never look wide afield with uplifted cap for extraneous help, or hope to make brilliant cast to a forrard signal. The practicability of the fences, and the galloping grass, may induce men to a virtue of valour that is almost exuberance; but it is seldom that hounds cannot almost hold their own—and he is a notable demon that can over-ride them every day in the week.

The line of railway from Crewe to Chester, or rather that part of it which reaches from Crewe to Beeston, cuts off the corner which now constitutes the South Cheshire, and which Mr. Corbet hunts on Tuesdays and Fridays—leaving the remaining days for The Cheshire proper. For twelve years previous to the new arrangement he lived near the Kennels in Delamere Forest; hunted the whole country; and was accustomed to bring hounds by special train once a week to Wrenbury. Some twenty or thirty years ago there were supplementary kennels at the latter place; and hounds were taken there over night. A special train still runs every Tuesday from Crewe to Wrenbury (in conjunction with the ordinary trains from Liverpool and Chester, from Manchester and Warrington), and waits to pick up for the return journey. Thus all Cheshire, and others from the great cities, can join Mr. Corbet on a Tuesday; and *very* many avail themselves of the chance—tea at Wrenbury before re-embarkation being a recognised part and ceremony of the day. Mr. Corbet's present little country is allowedly the pick of all Cheshire—better even than the Chester Vale—for there is scarcely an acre of bad ground in it; and the whole rides firm and sound in all weathers. The fences are light and easy, though improving agriculture has of late given considerable attention to deepening and widening the ditches. This charming district has its chief pillar in Lord Combermere—who, living at Combermere Abbey and owning a great property round, lends all his energy towards the support of Mr. Corbet and his Hunt. And he, together with Lords Cholmondeley and Tollemache, has greatly improved and opened out this beautiful part of Cheshire by throwing three or four of the small enclosures into one, and substituting wide sixty acre pastures for the limited meadows that are the distinguishing feature of the county generally.

The Peckforton Hills, a great rough range running into Wales, are neutral between Mr. Corbet, Capt. Park Yates and Sir Watkin Wynn. Precipitous, rugged, and full of holes, still they are ground not at all unsuitable for hounds to learn their work; and they send many a good fox down into the Vale, to be chivvied back to his fastnesses.

The Chester Vale is generally held to be the best of The Cheshire (Capt. Park Yates')—at least everyone makes an invariable point of being out when hounds are in the Vale. From Tarporley to Chester about defines the Vale; and comprises an area where nothing but grass is grown. Deep it often is, as the season goes on. In autumn the turf is at its best, but the fences at their worst; and so, perhaps, spring time brings the pleasantest riding. The Chester Vale, though, is seldom out of tune; and Margery's Almanack, in which autumn, winter and spring each in turn, is "pleasanter than all," might often be sung with truth among these goodly green meadows. For its coverts the Vale depends almost wholly on artificial gorses, which are freely scattered, and carefully tended, throughout its length. Its fences are nearly all rough, ragged, hedges, with ditches always deep and often perpendicularly cut—and a struggling horse is as likely to follow his hindlegs as to pull them out after him. In the neighbourhood of the elegantly-named covert of Saighton, the hedges grow out of low banks (in Cheshire termed cops); the fences require more covering; and it must lie between your mount and yourself as to whether you get foothold for a second spring, or go at them with a rush. The Gowy is the terror of the Vale—a black, sedgey, sluggish stream, with boggy uncertain banks, and only possible to be jumped in a few favoured spots. Its bridges are none too frequent; its fords are foul and treacherous; a ducking in it is a dirty and dreadful thing; and altogether its presence is very hateful to the Hunt. Yet it winds its slimy way across the country from Beeston to the Mersey: and you must often encounter it as best you may.

The River Dee runs down the extreme west of the Vale, and through Eaton Park, the seat of the Duke of Westminster. During the mastership of the latter, then Lord Grosvenor, and about twenty years ago (the 13th Light Dragoons being at that time quartered at Manchester) a strong section of the field had the temerity to follow hounds into the river. The Dee was running a great pace, and overflowing its banks, "as swift as a torrent, as deep as a tank;" and most of the adventurous ones (numbering in all nearly a score) were swept on to an island in mid stream, thence to be rescued by boat. Lord Grosvenor had to leave his horse and swim ashore as best he could— a rope of whip lashes assisting his sinking efforts. Of the rest, the late Mr. Cecil de Trafford, who was first to take water, was one of the first to reach the farther bank, with Col. Starkie (at that time a well-known steeplechase rider), Mr. Bolton-Littledale (still one of the best preservers and the hardest worker for the Hunt), and the doctor of the 13th L. D. The death of the fox was a fitting and satisfactory sequel. Only three men were up at the end; and these had great difficulty in inducing hounds to follow them home. Col. Starkie still possesses either head or brush—a memento of this memorable day.

The Tarporley Hunt Club is an institution cherished and maintained as stoutly as ever in Cheshire. It was first formed in 1762, and its yearly celebration has been carried on ever since, with mirth and song and good cheer, as each November comes round. For the first week of that month the club assembles at Tarporley to hunt and dine together. Its number is limited to forty; and year by year vacancies are filled up by ballot among the landowners of the county—the elected ones receiving the green collar, as the distinguishing badge of the honourable company into which they have been admitted.

Beyond the little town of Tarporley the ground rises towards Oulton Park, the seat of Sir Philip Egerton, the leading veteran of the Hunt, and a grand type of sportsman. Though now over seventy, he still rides, and walks, with all the vigour of a young man. Not only are his coverts of the greatest service; but hounds are constantly exercised in his park, amid the deer and game. On this point (and on a much wider one) both sections of the Cheshire are especially fortunate; for all over the county are scattered large parks and friendly neighbours. Foxhunting is the county pastime; and the county families maintain it religiously. Round Oulton the ground is deep and undrained (though right good country, especially in spring); hounds can nearly always run well; and their field follow as best they may. Fortunately, the fences are small; so riders can struggle on, without having to diverge from the direct wake of hounds. The Weaver may possibly come in their way; in which case they must look for the best ford at hand. For the river, running frequently through deep gorges is not to be jumped. Along its banks are the Minshull Dingles, a belt of excellent covert. Following the stream thus, we come to Middlewich, where the country becomes sounder—as, indeed, it is towards Crewe, Capt. Park Yates's farthest point on the edge of the North Staffordshire. And here, too, the soil is chiefly laid down in grass: and some artificial gorses have been set to assist the natural coverts.

Delamere Forest, though much reduced from its erst magnificence, still boasts of some thousands of acres of woodland; and, backed by the Mickledale Hills and their rough, gorse grown ridges, presents an invaluable sphere for cubhunting. Capt. Park Yates has a hunting box close to the Kennels, as

The Cheshire and South Cheshire.

being more convenient during the season than his place at Ince. The northern, or Knutsford, side of his country, again, is of a wilder—and so to speak more natural—description than the south. There is, perhaps, more plough in it, but this rides firm and well; foxes have much increased in numbers of late years, and are stout and wild. Between Knutsford and Warrington, however, are large tracts of ground devoted to potato growing; and the presence of wire proclaims that foxhunting is not the first object of the native mind. Otherwise this is a fine district, with good coverts in its midst. Many large park-properties—or, as they term them in Ireland, "demesnes"—mark all the upper portion of the country, and the plantations and woods round these constitute the chief coverts. Among such is Arley Hall, the residence of the Cheshire poet of sport and kindly-fellowship, Mr. Egerton Warburton—now alas, stoneblind, but still keenly anxious as ever for the welfare of the Hunt, and delighted to hear of their daily doings.

Mr. Corbet's chief meets and coverts are much as follows (Tuesday and Friday being his days of hunting). It may be said that two Tuesdays out of every three he meets at Wrenbury, not far from which is the famous Baddeley Gorse (Mr. Wickstead's). One season especially he had a wonderful succession of fine gallops from here, running the same old fox many times across a superb country up to the Peckforton Hills, some eight miles away. Wrenbury-Mosses, The Yeld Covert, Hall o' Coole (Mr. Tomkinson's), Court's Gorse, and Broomhall are all good strongholds of gorse or thorn, with Lord Combermere's fine coverts to follow.

Other Tuesdays he is usually at Wilkesley, drawing from it probably Kent's Rough, a fine holding covert of Lord Combermere's bordering on the Master's Adderley property. Mr. Corbet's own coverts and those of Lord Kilmorey at Shavington are within the North Staffordshire territory, permission being given by that Hunt that he should draw them.

Mr. Corbet's best known Friday meets are Cholmondeley Castle, Ridley Tollbar, Worleston Grange and The Rookery, with Wistaston occasionally for the distant Crewe side. Hurleston Gorse is a very celebrated covert in this part of the country, with Poole, Spurstow, The Breeches, Wardle, and large plantations round Cholmondeley Park and Norbury Mosses.

Capt. Park Yates works his country in the following order, subject of course to necessary variations. On Monday he takes the Knutsford, or northern, side. Lord Egerton's seat, Tatton Park, is a place of considerable note—the park itself being the largest in England. There are plenty of foxes in the coverts, and deer and every description of "riot" in the park, which is consequently much favoured in the preliminary summer and autumn work. Lord de Tabley's place at Tabley is also notable, with Mrs. Brook's at Mere Hall and Withington and Joddrell Hall adjoining. At Peover is Sir Philip Mainwaring—whose grandfather was for twenty years Master of the Cheshire; and Arley Mr. Egerton-Warburton, whose eldest son is one of the M.P.'s for the County. Rud-

The Cheshire and South Cheshire.

heath (part of which belongs to Rev. Armitstead, is a rough heathery moorland.

Wednesday is, as a rule, the day for Delamere Forest—among whose wooded depths horsemen must keep to the rides, but where hounds can work vigorously and foxes are very plentiful. Vale Royal (Lord Delamere's) and Delamere House (Mr. George Wilbraham's) are two of the more usual meets.

Thursday is for the Chester side, alternately in the Chester Vale and the Oulton, or Crewe, district. Among the best Vale meets are Tattenhall Station, Stapleford Mill, and Tarporley Town End. From the first-named hounds will probably begin work at Handley or Crow's Nest: from Stapleford they have Cotton Gorse (a fine stronghold of briar and gorse) or Waverton Gorse: and from Tarporley Town End they will perhaps commence with Huxley Gorse and Clotton Hoofield. From any Vale meet they may draw the covert of Saighton. Occasionally, too, they meet at Saighton Grange; and perhaps draw Eaton Drives.

On the alternate Thursday there is a meet at Oulton Park for the coverts round Darley, The Adjuncts, the celebrated Oulton Low and Philo (all the property of Sir Philip Egerton). From here they get on to the Calveley neighbourhood, where are the coverts of Page's Wood, Calveley Old and New Gorse, Hill's Gorse, Wetenhall Wood, Darnall and Blakeden—all good places. Calveley, for seven years under the guardianship of Capt. Kennedy, was during that period continually highly tried, but never tried in vain. The chief coverts towards Crewe are Braidby,

Foxholmes, Groby, Warmingham Wood, and Brereton (Mr. Howard's); while on towards Middlewich (by the way, this ultimate syllable, so common in Cheshire nomenclature, is pronounced wiche, to be translated salt) we find Manor House and its coverts (belonging to Mr. Court), Union Gorse, Bostock (Col. France Hayhurst), and further on the celebrated Whatcroft Gorse. The meets of Crewe and Bradfield Green embrace most of the above coverts.

Saturday is likely to take in the rest of the country towards the north. On the Appleton Hall, High Legh, and Marbury, near which meets are some capital gorses—The Cobbler, Newton Whitley and Stretton Moss being all likely for a good fox. Norton Priory Sir Richard Brook's) is the farthest meet in this direction. Along the Mersey is Ince (the seat of the Master). With a meet at Dunham a gallop is frequently had from Dunham Gorse (Lord Shrewsbury's), which may lead across the Ince Meadows, and their wide and difficult ditches. And thus we may conclude the geography of the Cheshire.

For hunting quarters Tarporley is one of the best commanding points within the boundaries of the Cheshire packs. Chester and Whitchurch give thorough access to both sections of the country and to Sir Watkin Wynn's as well; while Crewe is not only well placed for hunting in Cheshire, but commands the North Staffordshire also, and is the nearest point to London besides. From Euston Square to Crewe is a journey of some four hours.

It will easily be understood from what has been written above that a quick-jumping active horse is

The Cheshire and South Cheshire.

wanted for Cheshire. A short strong-backed animal, with plenty of breeding, is perhapt the most suitable. Though there is a good deal of work to do, and a horse is constantly galloping and jumping, the fences do not knock him about to the extent that happens in many countries that in themselves are not more trying to cross. And so it comes about that a man does not require an overgrown stud in Cheshire; and will find a second-horse more of a luxury than an absolute necessary.

The fields have certainly diminished in strength of late years, with the depression of trade in the adjoining great manufacturing centres and shipping bases; but still there will often be found a muster of two, or even three, hundred on the most favoured ground; though in the north, again, the numbers frequently dwindle down to some forty horsemen.

Only members of the Hunt subscribe to the maintenance of the hounds. But a visitor will probably contribute to the Covert Fund, and receive cards of the meets. These are issued a fortnight in advance (advertising in the papers having been discontinued); and the six days, as set down for the two packs, are printed on one card—another point in proof that Cheshire is virtually an undivided Hunt.

THE BLACKMOOR VALE*.

ANOTHER fine grass country is that of the Blackmoor Vale, at present hunted—well and worthily—by Sir Richard Glyn. Three to four hours of a westerly course from London will set you down in its midst, whether by means of The Great Western from Paddington or the London and South-Western from Waterloo. Yeovil is the junction point of the two railways; and, once there, you may please yourself as to whether you settle self and horses on the spot, or move back to Sherborne or Henstridge.

The Aldershot men as a rule choose Sherborne, where in their interests, and entirely from a fox-hunting light, an hotel has been specially thrown up by Mr. Wingfield Digby, who, at one time hunting the Blackmoor Vale at his own expense, is now only able to get about on wheels, yet still retains to the full the respect in which his name has so long been held. All the world, within reach, takes train to Yeovil for the meets in its neighbourhood. For the Blackmoor Vale is a half-way house between the brown acres of Hampshire and the unrideable enclo-

---

* *Vide* Stanford's "Hunting Map," Sheet 20, and Hobson's Foxhunting Atlas.

sures of Devon and Somerset. Here you are offered the oldest of turf and richest of scenting ground. The lines of earthwork that form the fences of the far west are here modified to practicable enjoyable proportion; and, stiff and deep though it be, the Blackmoor Vale bears a character as a sporting and riding ground that makes it the Queen of the West. Deep—undeniably deep—it is, let the season be what it may. And the deeper it rides, the faster hounds go. The man and the horse that can consistently and conscientiously live with hounds over the Blackmoor Vale must both be good, and determined.

Men come out of the far west glad to launch into a sphere wherein horse and rider have more to say to the game than amid the rough coombes and impracticable enclosures, which, however favourable to hounds, leave all the fun in the hands of the latter. There is joy in the spectacle of hounds on a scent; but there is other, and to very many a greater, joy in taking an active vigorous part in the *mêlée* and life of a foxhunt. The soldiers think so too; and many of them gladly leave the weak-scenting plains round Aldershot for the more lively country presided over by Sir Richard Glyn.

The Blackmoor Vale Country is in reality, a succession of vales separated only by slight undulations of so little elevation as to differ but in a very slight degree from the lower ground on either side of them, except that they begin to dry up earlier in spring than the other. They represent, indeed, little greater difference of consistency than is perceptible between the furrow and the ridge of old Leicestershire grazing ground.

The extreme north-west is the exception to vary the features of the country: which there is rougher, more hilly and wooded. Of the rest we have the Sparkford vale, the Stalbridge vale, the Pulham vale, besides the Leweston-and-Caundle Marsh district; and all these differ more or less in characteristics of soil, scent, and fence. But before specifying further, it must be set down as an order distinct and irrefragable, that wherever you would follow Sir Richard's hounds with credit, you *must* be on a strong, shortbacked, horse and a stayer. In the stiffest part of the Blackmoor Vale he must be able to take off well away from his fence, light on the bank like a cat, and shoot himself forward again without dwelling. To effect this thoroughly and cleverly, many good judges assert that a certain amount of pace is requisite. Others have it that you can best afford to go slow. The truth, as I glean it, lies between the two. No one would argue that for such an effort it can ever be permissible to rattle a horse off his legs—to put it in stableyard Anglo-Saxon. Yet a horse with a certain amount of way on, yet fully collected, must surely be able to combat the height and distance with greater ease to himself than if called upon to rear and scramble out of deep ground at a walk. For many of these banks, apart from the hazel and thorn growth on the top, are five and six feet—or even more—almost sheer; and a horse that can cleverly top them and cover a wide ditch beyond as he changes his legs, would seem to leave the fence behind him more neatly and with much less labour than if a slow triple effort were exacted from him—let alone the fact that while he is

The Blackmoor Vale.

jumping hounds are running, and running as they can in the Vale.

A welter-weight rides at comparatively little disadvantage in the Blackmoor Vale—always supposing he is mounted according to his weight and the requirements of the country. As a matter of fact, his weight will often give him a pull, enabling him to force his way where a lighter man and horse would be entirely checked. For the hazel and thorn are frequently matted and stiff, to a degree that calls for no common momentum to make a passage through. There are very few fences to be met with in the Blackmoor Vale that are not to be pierced and surmounted at some spot in their length; but it takes a good eye, much experience, and a horse fitted for the country, to mark and take advantage of these assailable points as quickly as hounds demand. Timber is freely found—and freely avoided; for the approach to it is too often spoiled and poached by the cattle, who work the ground into a quagmire wherever they can thrust their heads through post-and-rails.

The Sparkford vale is undoubtedly the choicest ground of the Blackmoor Vale country. It is firmest riding of all; carries as good a scent as any part; its banks are low, with a ditch on a single side, and every obstacle is to be taken in the stride. You may sail along as quickly as over the easiest part of Leicestershire; and hounds will generally give the opportunity. Now and again a wider ditch than common is met, but a little extra pace should annul the difficulty. The Sparkford vale is almost all grass, though a trifle of plough has crept in of late years; and it is safe to repeat that you may slip over it at speed. It is a more difficult matter to lay down a rule as to what day of the week by custom holds a particular district of country. Agricultural dinners and various other considerations materially affect Sir Richard's programme. The Sparkford vale, however, is more often taken every alternate Monday; and its chief meets are Sparkford, Marston, Mudford, Babcary, Pudimore, and Lydford. Annis Hill is a fine wood; and Babcary has a very good blackthorn covert planted by the Master — and forming an exception to the rule of the country, where thorn coverts are little known, though gorses are frequent. Other Monday meets are likely to be The Kennels (Charlton Hawthorn), Compton Castle, Creech Hill, Redlinch (Lord Ilchester's), and Stourton Woods —leading us into a worse country as we go on. The largest fields come out on the Yeovil side—though, after all, what is a field of 100 to 150 as compared with the attendance with many a Hunt elsewhere. Were it only better stocked with foxes the whole of the district north of Yeovil would be charming. The enclosures expand while the fences dwindle. But the farther north we proceed the less is Mr. Reynard a favourite—till at length fox hunting lapses for want of him and of coverts to draw: and Sir Richard's almost outside meet of late has been Lydford. By the way, it is worthy of mention, that in Mr. Farquharson's time the whole country now occupied by five packs was hunted as one, to wit—the present Blackmoor vale, the Cattistock, the South Dorset, the East Dorset, and the greater part of the South-and-

The Blackmoor Vale.

West Wilts. Now there are fifteen days where there used to be five, and many more foxes now than then. For, with the exception of the Upper Sparkford vale, the supply is fully equal to all demands; and Sir Richard is never at a loss where to draw. The present Master has hunted the Blackmoor Vale for the last sixteen years. Leweston House, near Sherborne, is his residence; and the Kennels (built by Mr. George Wingfield Digby, originator of the present Hunt) being quite in the centre of the country, he is enabled to turn which way he pleases, and orders his meets and draws to suit circumstances.

The rest of the country is very varied. The Stalbridge vale (extending, perhaps, as far as Fifehead Magdalen and Temple Coombe), wherein many of the Tuesday meets are fixed, is not so deep as further south; the enclosures are small, and the banks strong and high. Double fences are not as frequent here as in some other parts. The drainage is mostly above ground both here and in the Pulham vale, and intersecting drains, four to six inches deep, cross most of the meadows, and render progress difficult for bad shouldered ones, or horses unused to such traps. In such a country you soon learn to gallop over the drains at an angle, a subterfuge which will generally keep you on your legs. The Chetnole neighbourhood may likely enough come in to Tuesday meets; and so may Compton House and Pointington (a moderate country, with some light plough — but always the chance of getting into a vale), though the two latter are perhaps more often chosen for a Monday. The leading meets of the Stalbridge vale are Five Bridges,

Fifehead-Magdalen (for Nyland and the Fifehead coverts), the latter belonging to Mr. Merthyr Guest; Henstridge Ash for Stalbridge Park and Inwood.

Wednesday is an off-day; and if you are at Sherborne or Henstridge, you may employ it with Lord Portman and the East Dorset—as that is the day he usually fixes for his Manston Vale.

Thursday is more often told off for the district comprised in the names Leweston (with the Master's coverts and Honeycombe to follow), Holnest, Caundle Marsh, Haydon Lodge, and West Hill Gate. Holnest Pound has a most popular draw near at hand, in Butterwick, the property of Mr. Drax of Holnest House. Butterwick Wood is quite a historical name, being linked with many great runs in Mr. Farquharson's time, with Treadwell as his huntsman. It is six miles from the hills, and a fox must fly for his life. And Thursday may bring you on to somewhat firmer ground than that of the morrow.

The fourth hunting day is Saturday, and is in the deepest but perhaps the most sporting of all the Blackmoor Vale. Your strongest and best horse should be kept for the Pulham Vale; and he must be clever as well as stout; for the fences are chiefly blind big doubles, with a high bank as their base. *Pewy* is an epithet frequently and aptly applied to the Pulham Vale. The best known meets are the Green Man, or the King's Stag, Pulham, Thornhill, and Fifehead-Neville. Near the latter place, which immediately adjoins Lord Portman's Country, you find yourself in the stiffest ground of all. But it carries a great scent, and a great deal of sport has ensued during the last two seasons from Deadmore (which is well looked after by Mr. Connop of Fifehead-Neville, and may be drawn any day towards the end of the week)—running across to Lord Portman's hills. Humber Wood is a very favourite draw in the Pulham vale; so are Pulham Gorse, and Pontin's Gorse (called by Mr. Digby the "Ranksboro'" of Dorsetshire). Byde's Gorse is another well-known place.

It must not be left unsaid that a brookjumper is a most desirable acquisition for the Blackmoor Vale. For instance the Pulham Brook, the Buckshaw Brook, and the Annis Hill Brook in the Sparkford vale, are frequently to be jumped, but demand a bold horse.

Grange Woods (Lord Digby's) is a great field for cubhunting in the Blackmoor Vale; and Ven for the Ven Woods (Sir W. Medlycott's) is a meet omitted above.

One or two of the principal fox-preservers beyond those already alluded to are Mr. Dendy of Lattiford, Hon. Sec. to the Hunt, who looks after the interest of the Wincanton country, and Mr. Bell of Gillingham, who preserves all that neighbourhod.

Now that Lord Wolverton has relinquished his bloodhounds (which on most Fridays were in the vicinity of Hentsridge), the sixth day of the week, from Sherborne to Hentsridge, will have to be sought with the Cattistock or Lord Wolverton's harriers.

THE CAMBRIDGESHIRE.*

A COUNTRY of considerable extent — and all that extent a cold plough flat — is the Cambridgeshire. The summary is not a flattering one. It is true, but imperfect. For there remains to be said, that, with a cold scent, there is yet plenty of sport to be seen here — and it is a right good school for either hound or horseman. You will scarcely be led to visit the Cambridgeshire country with foxhunting as the immediate magnet; but finding yourself there from whatever cause, you are bound to acknowledge that in making the best of things you reap a reward, and you will hunt on with content if not exactly with enthusiasm. Again, you may make a worse start in your foxhunting life than by graduating from Cambridge. The hot blood of youth is under a cooling steadying influence while hounds are picking their way over fallows — quite in contrast with the fevered enthusiasm springing from contact with the grass vales of the Bicester, or the choice pickings of other hunts that surround the sister University. Oxford men are constantly under temptation to ride — as near

---

* *Vide* Stanford's "Hunting Map," Sheet 16, and Hobson's Foxhunting Atlas.

The Cambridgeshire. 393

hounds as their good sense, and a master's forbearance, will let them. Cambridge men on the contrary must either watch quietly and patiently the instinct and science of the hound at his work, or else turn quite aside from his track to find a loose off for their own superfluous spirits. In other words, Oxford has taught many men to ride to hounds and some to hunt. Cambridge has taught hunting to many; and riding to a few. From Cambridge the fieriest youth that ever donned pink for the first time will seldom find excuse to gallop; from Oxford he may often go out expressly for a " flutter "—and get it to his heart's content. As for the hound, he must always have his nose down, and must learn to depend upon that only—which he has a much better chance of doing in that the scent upon which he has to work is seldom sufficiently exuberating to lead him out of bounds. He must be kept in hard and constant work, though; or for very spirits he will decline to stoop and toil at his work, to that degree that alone can gain him his object. He must go out full of condition, but sober as a horse that is fit to run; or he will underrate his task and be very flashing over the mark. Power of nose is his first essential quality; perseverance and stoutness are the two next.

These virtues have been cultivated for many years in the Cambridgeshire pack, chiefly at the hands of the families of Barnett and Lindsell, with the result that sport has been obtained wherever, and whenever, possible. It was as huntsman of the Cambridgeshire that " Bob Ward " first made himself a reputation. For seventeen years he killed foxes there in his peculiar and inimitable style—which, like Charles Payne's, has been copied by many a man, only to entail on him total loss of caste for ever. Both of these famous huntsmen may often be said to have caught their fox themselves, and merely taken their hounds with them to run into him at the finish. Indeed, Ward did more than that on one occasion with the Cambridgeshire. He galloped on and met his tired fox in a lane, jumped off to seize him by the brush as he crawled up the bank, and held him till hounds came up.

Unlike its neighbour "The Fitzwilliam," the Cambridgeshire country has been ploughed from time immemorial, whereas the other was rank deep grass less than sixty years ago. The saving clause of the Cambridgeshire was contained in the grass headlands, which, till removed by "high farming," gave every field a border of ten to twenty yards in width. These headlands were not altogether pleasant riding, for they were constantly intercepted by sharp-cut open drains, which in the earlier months of the season were more often than not completely hidden in rough herbage. But they carried a tremendous scent; hounds flew along them at a pace that frequently distanced pursuit, and foxes always took them for choice, as against the draggling fallows alongside. And, besides robbing the soil of this advantage, improved cultivation has brought further damage by means of the steam plough, which is now as generally used in the counties of Cambridge, Hertford, and Beds as elsewhere where the vain struggle to grow wheat at a profit is still maintained. Consequently certain parts of the Cambridgeshire Hunt are in a wet season traversable at no quicker pace than a walk. But it is when wettest that the ground carries the truest scent; and then it is that hounds are often quicker than horses over the country. The fences are not sufficient to stop either, being merely light and low thorn hedges, with perhaps a ditch on one side. Though true, this ditch is often well hid in grass and weeds, and constitutes the chief difficulty in the path of a rider in the earlier half of the season.

Economy is another strong point of recommendation that must not be left without mention in any analysis of foxhunting with the Cambridgeshire. You require few horses—and those need be of no extravagant type. Like the hound for the country, one of his chief essentials is endurance. A good barrel is his best feature, and an easy disposition his fittest temperament. With these in his favour he will take you out and bring you home more often, and farther, than a more expensive conveyance in most other countries.

You may easily reach the Cambridgeshire from London. Biggleswade is little more than an hour from London (the Great Northern from King's Cross) by the best trains; Cambridge an hour and a half (by the Great Eastern from Liverpool-street or St. Pancras); and either destination may be attained in time to show you a good pack of hounds, whenever advertisement points to their meeting near these places. Huntingdon (about an hour and three-quarters from King's Cross) commands them in their favourite country, and gives full access to the Fitzwilliam and Oakley too.

The Cambridgeshire take the field three days a week —the district for each day having its distinctive shade of variety. Monday is in the south-west, as *vide* below. Tuesday is their favourite day : for it gives the Huntingdon woodlands and the chance of a run over the choicest of the Fitzwilliam country. This is the north-west corner; and the woods in it are in some instances of considerable size—*e.g.*, Brampton Wood being fully three or four hundred acres. Good wild foxes are bred here, and seldom hang in covert, but once on foot will move on for many a mile before being hunted down or lost. There are also various woodlands of some extent in other parts of the Hunt— Potton, Hatley Buff, and Haley Woods for instance, with many of a hundred acres apiece. The above named come in of a Friday, together with those of Wimpole and Waresley—all large natural coverts. But from all these it is comparatively easy to get away; and open country lies round their borders. As we get more into the centre of the country—into the shire of Cambridge (for the Hunt is as much in Beds as in the country from which it takes its name), the coverts are much smaller, though still what are termed " natural " as distinct from coverts planted purposely for the fox and the pastime of which he is the leading hero. As a rule, he finds plenty of refuge and due care throughout the greater part of the Cambridgeshire territory. Beyond Waresley is a very sporting district—open, with small coverts which hold well up to Christmas, when the undergrowth dies down, and

The Cambridgeshire. 397

it is difficult to lay hand upon Reynard's whereabouts. The largest fields come out on the Friday side—Cambridge sending out a strong division and Newmarket a contingent, the whole often amounting to a couple of hundred.

The following are further particulars of the hunting of the country, according to the adopted custom of Mr. C. S. Lindsell, the present Master. Each alternate Monday is told off to the Warden neighbourhood, which, belonging to the Oakley Hunt, is hunted on sufferance by the Cambridgeshire. Here are several large coverts—Shearhatch, Ickwell, Palmer's Wood, Warden, and Southill; Rowney Warren, and Chicksands are neutral with the Hertfordshire. The leading covert-owners are the Duke of Bedford, Sir G. Osborn, and Messrs. Harvey, Whitbread, and Shuttleworth; and foxes have every encouragement. Meets for this side are Morhanger, Ickwell Green, and Warden. The rest of the Monday meets are on the side of Potton Wood, a large covert belonging to Sir John Burgoyne, a keen preserver of foxes. Hatley Buff and Haley Woods follow this, with Gillrags, Rowsers, Sandy Warren, Sutton Plantations, and Morden Osiers. Farther east are the Wimpole coverts. All those above-named are sure finds, and the leading owners, besides Sir J. Burgoyne, are Lord Hardwicke, Messrs. Evans and Peel. A considerable property belongs to Downing College, whose Bursar Dr. Perkins, is secretary to the Hunt. Meets for this district are Potton Wood, Downing Arms, Hardwicke Arms—Waresley, and Sandy Warren.

Tuesday, as above mentioned, is for the corner of

the country that runs into Huntingdonshire. The chief of the chain of large woods hereabouts are Brampton, Graffham, Calfer, Perry, Gaynes, Agden Green, Midloe, and Paxton, owned mostly by the Duke of Manchester, Lord Sandwich, Mr Duberley, Mr. Thornhill (to whom also belong Knapwell and Boxworth on the Cambridge side), Mr. Reynolds, and Lord Overstone. The latter, however, leaves the control of Paxton Wood entirely to the farmers; and it is never known to be drawn blank. These woods hold a very stout race of foxes; which frequently give capital runs into the Fitzwilliam and Oakley countries. Pheasants are held of little account by the covert owners; who one and all are determined friends to foxes and enemies to keepers who cannot show many a litter. The usual meets for the Huntingdon Woods are Buckden Tower, Diddington Park, Gaynes Hall, and Megre.

Friday being for the Cambridge side, the chief meets are Waresley, Eltisley, Caxton, Childerley Gate, and Oakington—whence they draw the coverts of Waresley, Eltisley, Toseland, Swanley Grove, Papworth, Childerley, Madingley, Knapwell, Boxworth, Long Stanton, Oakington, Hardwicke Wood, Harston, Newton, and Harlton Spinnies. Mr. Newton is a good supporter and leading member of the hunt on this side. Mr Cheere is a good friend; and so is Mr. S. Linton, who purchased Long Stanton Covert to prevent its being grubbed up, and out of it sixteen foxes were viewed away one day during last cub hunting season. Besides these there are Mr. Linton, Mr. W. Hurrell, Mr. H. Hurrell, Messrs. Rowley, and others, all of whom take great interest in the welfare of the Hunt, and keep foxes for it.

The Kennels of the Cambridgeshire are at Caxton, near Cambridge; and the hounds are the property of the Hunt.

THE DUKE OF GRAFTON'S.*

To be reached from anywhere, and especially accessible to the Londoner—a good country, managed liberally, smartly, and practically—no wonder the Duke of Grafton's is a popular and a leading Hunt. It has a great deal of fine ground of its own; abuts on some of the choicest of the Bicester, the Warwickshire, and the Pytchley; and is backed up by the Whaddon Chase (or, as it is better known, Mr. Selby Lowndes'). You may hunt at most of its meets by means of the morning train from Euston-square; you may run up to it from Rugby; or down from Leighton, &c. You may be one of the few lucky soldiers quartered at Weedon; or you may find it convenient to establish a small stud on the spot, and eke out the week by work or play in Town. It is not a country to which many men bring a long string of horses for a solid six days a week. Such gluttons are more often found just over the border; they accept his Grace's liberality once or twice a week; and make up the rest from the varied fare spread around. For the northern corner of the Duke of

---

* *Vide* Stanford's "Hunting Map," Sheet 15 and Hobson's Foxhunting Atlas.

The Duke of Grafton's. 401

Grafton's country dovetails into what is almost a common junction-point of four hunts; and a man who plants himself anywhere near this point can secure an almost daily change of scene and surroundings.

The finest runs of the Duke of Grafton's hounds have more often been across their neighbour's ground; and this was remarkably the case last season—when their most notable run of all (from Canons Ashby) was, after the first three miles, entirely over Bicester and Warwickshire country, till it culminated at Shuckburgh. But it is the Duke's country in itself that we have to consider, and this contains everything from light plough to strong deep grass, and from small artificial coverts to dense woodlands and forest ranges. In some parts the fences are light and easy; in others they are as formidable as even those of the Pytchley. Their favourite fixtures lie along their northern border—many of those in the north-west being on ground similar to the stiff grand country across the boundary; others nearer Towcester are on arable; while some of those in the north-east, on the Bugboro' and Weedon side are on the same stoutly bullfinched ground that extends across the Pytchley to Shuckburgh and beyond.

Through the centre of the country run two good grass vales, somewhat cut up, unfortunately, by the lines of railway which thread them: while to the south are the great glades of Whittlebury Forest and Wakefield Park; and on the east the rough acreage of Salsey Forest. The fences throughout the country are of a simple hedge-and-ditch type; but range between the extremes of insignificance and impracticability. Open water is met with once or twice in almost every run — and, though not as a rule of formidable width, call for a horse that is ready to jump without dwelling whenever he is asked. And, in short, a thorough hunter is needed for the Duke's country—if you would take him over all parts of it. There are several places that hold out advantages as quarters within the limits of the Hunt. Buckingham and Brackley (the former two hours, the latter twenty minutes more, from London) supply a good proportion of the fields in the south of the country; and are on the borders of the best of the Bicester. Towcester, which it takes you also a couple of hours to reach from town, is right in the middle of the country. Weedon is not only the elysium of the military fox-hunter, who by good luck or management is established there by Royal command and at the expense of a nation that pays little attention to the desirability of teaching its officers to ride across country; but is much in favour with the ex-militaire, who, having tasted its sweets during his term of service, continues to indulge himself with them in after life out of his own pocket. Indeed, it would be difficult to point to a better situation than Weedon, for a man who would hunt with first-rate packs and in first-rate country, who yet is unable to afford himself the whole of his time, but must be always within easy journey of London. For Weedon lays the map of the Pytchley at your feet; has the Duke of Grafton's on the other side, and the Bicester and the Warwickshire, at their best, running close up—while it is less than two hours from Town. The Londoners (*i.e.*, men out for the day from London) come down to the Duke of Grafton chiefly in the spring; disembarking either at Blisworth, Wolverton, or Weedon.

The Duke of Grafton's hounds are out three days a week—his country being by no means an extensive one, and only a moiety of that formerly hunted by Lord Southampton. These days are Monday, Wednesday, and Friday: and are distributed much as follows. Monday is alternately for the northwestern, or Fawsley side, where you get both grass and plough, and every chance of a gallop into the Bicester territory towards Boddington or Griffin's Gorse, or over the stoutly-fenced pastures that intervene before Shuckburgh can be reached: These meets are always attended from Weedon, and frequently from the Pytchley dominion. The other alternate Mondays are for the Towcester and Blisworth district, where plough and small fences prevail throughout.

The chief Monday meets on the north-west are Preston Capes, whence the usual draws are Church Wood and the Fawsley coverts (owned by Sir R. Knightley), or the deep Badby Wood, a neutral covert with the Pytchley. All these are full of foxes and prolific of sport. From Woodford they get to Hinton Gorse—quite on the outside of their own territory, and bordering on a grand spread of country, belonging part to the Bicester, part to the Warwickshire. The great deep grass fields and the dense bullfinches of this region call for the highest and boldest qualities on the part of the horse—only to be employed to the full at the hands of a high-class rider to hounds. Close to

the above covert is another, Charwelton Osier Beds.
Canons Ashby has two nice coverts of its own; while
Stowe-Nine-Churches has Stowe Wood, which is
neutral with the Pytchley (mark this and Badby
Wood, Mr. Stanford !), besides Everdon Scrubbs.
Foster's Booth is usually for Drayton Osier Bed and
Ascot Thorns—falling back from there upon the thick
gorse Bushy End, close to Grub's Copse. From the
meets of Tiffield Toll Gate and Shosely Grounds follow
the draws of Tiffield Allotments (a very thick thorn
covert), Blisworth Gorse, Nun Wood, and Plane
Woods—rather large woods near the London and
North-Western Railway. Foxes are also well preserved at Easton Park (once inhabited by the Empress
of Austria); but the coverts are not of a very holding
type.

Wednesday is, by custom, considered the woodland
day; and is held alternately in the neighbourhood of
Wakefield and in the Salsey Forest district. Wakefield Park, with Whittlebury Forest and coverts give
the perfection of woodland hunting (amid open rides
and hollow glades); and it generally happens that
hounds eventually work their way into the open. For
instance, they often get out to Wicken Spinnies (Lord
Penrhyn's), adjoining which is some good country,
while only the river close by which separates them
from Mr. Selby Lowndes' is often crossed for a trip
over nice ground beyond. Salsey Forest, in the
alternate weeks, furnishes rough but sporting ground,
beyond the L. and N.W. Railway on the east of their
country, adjoining the Oakley. Of the meets in the
southern woodlands—Stratford Hill is for a wood of

that name, with Shalston Spinnies and afterwards the great woods of Wakefield, Whittlebury, Stowe, &c. Meeting at Wakefield Lawn they occasionally trot off to a nice little covert in the open, and by the Canal side, known as Friary Furze (well preserved by a good old sportsman, Col. Fitzroy). After this they probably go on to Stoke Park. Wicken Park is a good place on the southern border, with the forest to fall back upon. The meet of Tilehouse is for Tilehouse Wood and other coverts where foxes are well cared for by Mr. Robarts. In Salsey Forest the most familiar fixtures are Keeper's Lodge and Ranger's Lodge; and those whose taste points to good rough woodland hunting may here indulge it to the full.

Friday is the most popular day of the week, with the men of the Hunt; is in the north centre of country; and on ground pretty nearly equally divided between grass and plough. Some of the Bicester men frequently attend; and, as the season goes on, the train brings numbers from London, Leighton, &c. When Brackley or Whitfield are advertised, the likeliest draws are Brackley Gorse, Halse Copse, and Whitfield Spinnies. Whistley Wood is a meet, as well as a very large and first-rate fox covert. Some three seasons ago they had an extraordinary fine run from here—fifty-five minutes with an old dog fox. Hounds were never cast; and ran right into their fox in the middle of a grass field. From Astwell Mill they take Weedon Bushes, a nice but not altogether a sure covert; or go to Allithornes, which by many people is held to be the best place in the Hunt—being a certain find with a good country all round. Braddon is for Braddon

Spinnies and Kingthorne Wood; Blakesley for Seawell Wood and Grimscot Heath. To draw Plumpton Wood, a favourite covert of considerable size—they meet at its outskirts.

Once a year hounds are run through Huntsbury Hill, near Northampton—once a good covert, but now almost—if not entirely, wiped out.

Among the chief covert owners and fox preservers of the country are the Duke of Grafton, Lord Penrhyn, Sir R. Knightley, Mr. Robarts, Mr. Loder of Whittlebury, &c., &c.

The kennels are at Wakefield Lawn near Stony Stratford; and His Grace has had the hounds quite a score of years—during which they have always been maintained on the most liberal scale, and, as now, well hunted and whipped-in to. As a pack they have attained a very high degree of excellence, both in field and on the flags.

THE HOLDERNESS.*

The horse and the hound are the pride and delight of every Yorkshireman, are a subject with which he has been familiar all his life, and a topic on which he is always eloquent and enthusiastic. High class horses and high class hounds are apparently the natural product of the county; and men ride a better average of hunter amid these northern ploughs than we see bestridden even in the midlands—certainly if we confine the comparison to animals indigenous to the two localities. Lincolnshire and Yorkshire alike are mostly given up to cultivation; but they stand apart from the bulk of other plough countries, in that they decline to admit that foxhunting may, under such condition, be carried on in a more plebeian style than on fashionable galloping ground. They meet the facts of cold plough and deep plough with the argument that the colder the scent the cleverer the hound required, and the deeper the plough the better the horse must be to live with him. So their packs have for generations been cultured from the best blood in England; and the farmers breed and ride nothing that cannot lay claim to both quality and strength.

---

* *Vide* Stanford's "Hunting Map," Sheet 6, and Hobson's Foxhunting Atlas.

The Holderness does *not* come under the head of a "cold-scenting country." For a plough country it carries an exceptionally good scent; and hounds can generally work their way well whether on the lower area of Holderness proper or on the Wolds—the two sections offering very distinct descriptions of ground, as will be shown below. The late Mr. Hall, who had the pack for nearly thirty years, was most particular about legs and feet; and the hounds could stand any amount of work—coming home sound and comparatively fresh, even after being twelve or fourteen hours out of kennel. He got his blood entirely from three packs, viz., the Belvoir, Brocklesby, and Burton. The season immediately following his death, they hunted one hundred times with only fifty-one couple in kennel; and notwithstanding the long distances were never short of hounds. And cubhunting did not begin till the last week in September.

The Holderness country is, perhaps, larger in extent than any other in England; and the Hunt has been going uninterruptedly for more than a century—having been first established by a Constable, an ancestor of the present Lord Herries. Hull is its chief present source of support; Beverley is the best resting place for the visitor. By road or train every meet can be reached from these places; and the Humber crossed occasionally for a day with the Brocklesby. From London you are landed at either town in four or five hours. Etton near Beverley is the site of the Kennels—Mr. Arthur Wilson last season assuming the reins of government.

For practical purposes the country may be treated

of in two divisions—the Eastern and the Western (or, rather, Holderness and the Wold)—each of which might, indeed, well form a country of itself. The Eastern portion, or Holderness proper, runs along the sea border, is quite flat, and holds a capital scent—being a rich soil, only reclaimed from sea and swamp some sixty or seventy years. The enclosures are very large; and the chief obstacles encountered are large open drains—some few of which are far too wide to jump, and must be forded where practicable. The other fences are small and of an easy description, except in parts of North Holderness; and nowhere is much timber to be met with. There is little—but *very little*—grass to ride over; but the plough is well drained.

The coverts of Holderness proper are almost all of gorse (or, as it is termed in the vernacular of the country, *whin*) the sole exception being at Rise and Burton Constable (Sir T. Constable's). The most famous of these gorses, and the one which is credited with perhaps as many good runs as the rest put together, is Dringho. It has always been noted for an expecially stout breed of foxes; and belongs, together with all the credit due to its excellence, to Mr Bethell of Rise. There are also good whin coverts at Catfoss, Wassand (Mr. Constable's), Barmston, Owstwick, and Humbleton, with Blacksmith's Whin, &c., and stick heaps here and there that are very tempting to foxes. Hounds have every chance in Holderness proper; for the enclosures are large, there are very few hares, and the coverts are often six or seven miles apart, while their field is a small one and gives them plenty of room. The farmers of Holderness are a thorough race of sportsmen. They go out to see all the sport they can; and besides the consideration which they are naturally ready to pay to hounds, they do not forget that their one horse has to last them the day, which may be a long one and may moreover end in a twenty-mile ride home. Consequently they watch hounds without riding too close on their backs. Some of the chief meets for Holderness proper are Brandesburton (from which Dringho Gorse is drawn, and whence sport is always had), Fordingham Bridge, Rise Park, Wassand, Hatfield Station, and Danthorpe Hall. The above are all situated in the best part of Holderness proper; and the most favourite coverts are drawn from them. Burton Agnes must be added as a good meet and sure find in North Holderness. It belongs to Sir H. Boynton. And Lowthorpe, too, is another popular fixture for the same day of the week.

Monday and Thursday are the days for Holderness proper; Tuesday and Friday for the Wold district. On Mondays and Thursdays hounds generally have fifteen to twenty miles to go to covert and frequently still longer distances to return. On Fridays, too, they often have very long journeys.

Taking Beverley as about the point of division, on the other side of it is the wold section of the country; which is very different—being very hilly and light, though also all plough, with the exception of several steep grassy dales, not unlike the declivities of Brighton Downs. As scenting ground it is very inferior to Holderness proper; though in spring and autumn hounds occasionally run hard over it. The inclosures are of great extent; the fences of little magnitude—being low quicksets without a ditch. But on such days as hounds run, only a strong wellbred horse can climb the hills quick enough to live with them. Indeed, there is only one qualification that a hunter for Holderness need not possess. Timber-jumping is an unnecessary accomplishment. Water-jumping, on the contrary, is a virtue that is absolutely indispensable. You may put it, indeed, with regard to Holderness as to many and many a country that aspires to no higher than Class II. in the list of foxhunting countries—it costs as much to buy a first-rate horse for such a country as to find a suitable animal for the cream of the Shires. Is it worth doing? Of course it is; if your foxhunting lines lie in such places. If you are obliged to be there, you will naturally like to be as well mounted as you can. You are not likely to select an inferior country of your own choice: but if you are looking about for a sphere in which to spend money upon horseflesh, you will in all probability choose a part of the world which seems to you to offer most in return for the investment. That taking part with the Holderness is viewed from this light is proved by the fact that very often not more than two or three red coats reach the covert-side—and these do not invariably accompany hounds in their search for an afternoon fox. The landowners of the county mostly preserve foxes, because it is according to the spirit and custom of Yorkshire so to do (and it is said the stock of foxes is increasing rapidly with the Holderness). But they are by no means all open to the soft impeachment that they are rabid foxhunters. On the contrary, the farmers are the men who chiefly ride and hunt. With them it is a sworn principle and practice, inherent and maintained, and they are the truest friends of the Hunt.

The coverts of the Wolds are of a much larger description than those found in the lower ground by the sea, and there are many woods of considerable size—some of the principal ones being Lockington Wood, Neswick and South Dalton Woods, the coverts about Londesborough, the Bygate, Bentley, and Bishop Burton Woods. Mr Christopher Sykes has large woods at Brantingham Thorpe, and Colonel Broadley the same at Welton. Lord Herries always has plenty of foxes at his coverts at Everingham. Houghton Wood is never without one; nor are Mr. Burton's coverts at Cherry Burton: and there is a good wood at Etton near the Kennels. The Raywell Woods are generally tenanted; and in the hilly country of Kilnwick Percy Admiral Duncombe has large coverts. There are also good coverts at Arras: and a fine wood at Holme.

Among the best Wold meets are those of Sunderlandwick, Neswick, Arras, and Etton Kennels, with Everingham Park, which is amid flat low ground and in as good a country as any part of Holderness. Beverley Grand Stand is occasionally advertised as a kind of holiday-meet for the people of Beverley. There is, however, nice country near Beverley and Scorboro', where Mr. Hall lived for so long.

Between the foot of the Wolds and Howden is a

large tract quite equal to any part of Holderness proper; but more difficult to ride over, as the fences grow much stronger. This district, though, has hitherto been but little hunted, and foxes have been by no means too plentiful.

THE OAKLEY.*

FROM Bedford to Wellingboro', and from Kimbolton to Newport Pagnell, Bletchley, and Leighton Buzzard, gives an approximate idea of the extent of the Oakley country, as at present hunted. A large strip along the southern border has long been on loan to the Whaddon Chase, the Hertfordshire and the Cambridgeshire, and the greater part of this has recently been reclaimed. Thus, though Mr. Stanford's map was practically correct at the time it was coloured in, it by no means shows either what is the range of Oakley territory, nor the boundaries to which the Oakley limit themselves at the present day. Briefly, then, they now hunt down to their limits at Bletchley, Leighton, and Toddington, but still lend Silsoe and Chicksands to the Hertfordshire, Northill etcetera to the Cambridgeshire, and Southill to both packs. This renewal of their right of country became necessary on the alteration in the management of the Hunt, as arranged four years ago. Mr. Robert Arkwright, who had for six and twenty years so ably carried on the Hunt, wielded the horn so successfully, and

---

* Vide Stanford's "Hunting Map," Sheet 16, and Hobson's Foxhunting Atlas.

brought the pack to so high a standard, found himself unable longer to sustain the strain of four days a week, and accordingly tendered his resignation. Not unnaturally, it was found difficult to hit upon a successor at all adequate to fill his place. At length the gap was bridged over by Mr. Arkwright finding a collaborateur who would share the work with him: and, since then, he and Mr. T. Macan have, with the help of a committee, kept things going as smoothly and satisfactorily as ever. Mr. Arkwright hunts the lady pack twice a week in the northern, or woodland, part of the country, while Mr. Macan, with Whitmore as his huntsman, works the more open country of the south and east with the dog pack two other days. Mr. Arkwright continues to superintend his Kennel, with Whitmore as his kennel huntsman (and as first whip on the days Mr. Arkwright hunts). Mr. Macan sees that the stable is kept up to service pitch.

The present series of sketches does not aim at touching more than passingly on the packs of the different countries; but, were it permissible, too much could scarcely be said about the Oakley hounds. At least fifty yéars ago the pack existed as the property of the then Duke of Bedford. Next they belonged to the country, who sold them to Mr. Arkwright. The latter added to them large drafts from the Belvoir and Brocklesby, and, by dint of a quarter of a century of skilful breeding, built up a grand pack—which, on his proffering his resignation four years ago, the present Duke of Bedford purchased from him, and generously presented to the hunt. They are remarkable for true symmetry, thorough working qualities, and striking fashion. The Kennels are at Milton Ernest, near Oakley Station, about half a dozen miles from Bedford.

A fair notion of the Oakley Country—or at least of its more open portion—may be gathered from the window of a railway carriage as it bears you from Bedford to Wellingboro'. Pay the extra shillings for a seat in a Pullman car, and you may almost dwell at the fences and give time for the pack to feather over a fallow. A quiet undulating surface of tillage, glorious in summer, dull in winter : cut and partitioned by easy thorn fences with ditches that, like all others, look delightfully insignificant from the cushioned seat of a train, but that vary up to unexpected width when under trial from the pigskin—this is the view presented. You see nothing of the woods; and your soul, unless mated to agriculture, is not likely to be deeply stirred as you whisk through the corn-fields. There will be none of the blood-rushing that, after four summer months of London and with the Sundays half through Trinity, makes you rise to the gleam of the Harboro' pastures, and may even tempt you to frighten a sleepy fellow-passenger out of his wits with an unmuffled view holloa. But there is honest prose about the view. It looks like steady foxhunting— noses down and sterns waving, a fox to be wearied down, and a pack to be marked and watched for the work it is doing. And such is truly the Oakley country. It is mostly flat; it is very mostly plough; and the rest is woodland. But it is a right good hound-country; and a fair horse must be ridden there.

The Oakley. 417

The steam plough has been driving its villanous grooves through the soil of late years—perhaps to the benefit of hounds, certainly to the discomfiture of horses, and—with the sad experience of two wet seasons—apparently to the disadvantage of farmers, who in many cases will have no more of it. So, when a scent rages, horses cannot live with hounds—though, truth to tell, scent does not rage here more habitually than on other well-tilled ground. The woodlands have the better scenting soil, at all events in early autumn and late spring. And the woods of the Oakley are everywhere well-rided. It is always possible to get about them. They are of no great width, and only a stranger need ever be afraid of getting lost.

It is only in the lately reclaimed Woburn district that anything like a real hill is to be seen. Here the soil changes to a sandy description, and rises and falls in some stiff slopes. Just north of this, again, we come to the only part of the country that lays claim to possessing more than the thinnest scattering of grass. Round Newport Pagnell there is a good deal of nice meadow land. But, it may be repeated, the Oakley country as a whole is flat plough, containing very many coverts. These coverts are, generally speaking, excellently preserved—and so, though it is always easy to find a fox, it is often equally easy to change on to a fresh one, as hounds bring a line through a covert.

The fences are much the same throughout—except that round Thurleigh are a certain number of doubles. The ditches are often blind and often wide. Water in a jumpable form is seldom met with. The horse, like the hound, for the country, must possess both strength and breeding; else he will tire in the long days in deep ground, or fail at a pinch, when called upon to gallop and jump under difficulties. The shorter his legs and the stronger his back, the more serviceable is he likely to be.

From London you may easily see the Oakley for yourself. From St. Pancras (Midland) to Bedford is but little over an hour, and will put you in reach of most of the open country on that side. Bletchley Junction (by L. & N. W.) will do the same for you on the west, while Sharnbrook, some eight miles farther on than Bedford, is the best landing-place for the woods in the upper portion of the country.

The line of division marking that part hunted by Mr. Arkwright in person and that worked by his *confrère*, runs at about right angles with the Midland Railway, cutting it at Sharnbrook, reaching to Kimbolton on the one side, and following the River Ouse to Olney on the other.

Tuesday and Saturday are the days for the woodlands—of which those in the extreme west, viz., Easton Wood, Yardley Chace, and Horton Wood, are neutral with the Duke of Grafton. These all possess excellent grass rides, that even in mid-winter are scarcely too deep. They hold a capital scent; and are of the greatest value for autumn and spring hunting, but are not now so well stocked with foxes as formerly. No absolute rule for distribution of days and meets is followed; but Tuesday is more often in the Harrold district, of which some of the leading fixtures are—Dungee Corner, a very favourite meet, for the

The Oakley.

Harrold Woods (Lord Cowper's), whence they get on to Strixton, where are some nice, and smaller, coverts of Lord Spencer's. These last are looked after by some very sporting farmers and produce many a run. Nunn Wood is another good draw hereabouts. Odell is named for Odell Wood, and Colworth for Mr. Magniac's coverts. Knotting Fox is the Duke of Bedford's and a great stronghold. Easton Wood is generally advertised when The Chace (the property of Lord Northampton) is to be scoured; and round the outsides of these great woods is a good deal of grass, which also extends to Brayfield and on by Newport Pagnell, as above-mentioned, and to Northampton on the north-west.

Saturday is almost always for the Kimbolton side, where perhaps the best sport is had, and a run over the most favoured of the Fitzwilliam country is frequently looked for. Risley Toll-Bar is one of the best-known meets, and commands Melchbourne, Keysoe Park, or Shelton Gorse. Melchbourne itself is often advertised. It belongs to Lord St. John, who, though not riding himself, is an excellent friend to the Hunt. Keysoe Park is Mr. Crawley's, and well-cared for in the interests of foxhunting. Shelton Gorse is the only artificial covert in the Oakley country, and lies close to Stanwick Pastures, the well-known Fitzwilliam covert, just over the border. For the Kimbolton Woods themselves Kimbolton and Swineshead or Peetenhall are the fixtures. The Duke of Manchester not only has his coverts always full of the stoutest of foxes for the Hunt, but he and all his family take an active part in the field.

Mr. Macan's days for the lower, or open, portion of the country are Monday and Thursday. Monday is usually told off for the south and south-west of the town of Bedford—*e.g.*, Bromham, for the coverts of Hangers, Bromham Spinnies, and Salem Thrift; Wootton, for a good covert of Sir C. Payne's; Cranfield, for Marston Thrift (where the Duke of Bedford has always plenty of foxes); Moulsoe Village for Moulsoe Wood and Drake's Gorse (the latter planted by Lord Carrington, who owns all Moulsoe, and is another right good friend to the Oakley Hunt); Chicheley (Mr. Chester's) for the fine covert of Thick Thorn and on to Sherrington Woods (Mr. Tyrringham's); and Turvey, round which Mr. F. Higgins has many foxes.

Thursday is for the Thurleigh side, where the coverts are smaller and the country more open than anywhere else. From the White Lion, Ravensden, they may draw the coverts of Ravensden Grange or Putnoe; from Renhold Capt. P. Turner's good wood is adjacent. In the St. Neot's neighbourhood are the meets of Roxton, Hail-Weston (where is a good covert), Bushmead (on the borders of the Cambridgeshire), Little Staughton and Thurley Windmill.

No Hunt is more staunchly supported by its members, and the country generally, than the Oakley. Foxhunting is actively upheld throughout its breadth by preservation, and, if need be, by purse. And conspicuous among the leading supporters are the Dukes of Bedford and Manchester, Lord Cowper, Mr. Whitbread, Mr. Magniac, Mr. H. Thornton, and Lord Charles Russell. The last-named has taken the greatest possible interest in the Hunt for nearly half a century, and maintains it to the utmost still. In former days he was a celebrated rider, and though now over seventy years of age, he still stays out with hounds till they turn for Kennel, and will ride longer distances to meet them than will most younger men—while their breeding and kennel-management is ever a source of keen enjoyment to him.

THE NORTH HEREFORDSHIRE.*

MUCH excellent foxhunting is enacted all along the border of Wales—and even as far up the sides of its rugged mountains as is by any means practicable. Herefordshire is a county of apples and bullocks, hops and cereals. Orchards and meadows, hop gardens and cornfields succeed and intermingle with each other in curious confusion; and the hound throws his note among them all, every time he leaves covert on a scent. Herefordshire is cultivated as carefully, as miscellaneously, and almost on as miniature a scale, as a poor-allotment garden. The same red clay apparently serves equally well for all purposes. Doubtless it has its degrees of virtue, or why should the grazier often be called upon for four pounds rent per acre, the tiller of the soil but twenty-five shillings for his oatland, while the cider maker pays heavily for his orchard, and the hop grower a fancy price for a snug corner? But, for all that, each

---

* *Vide* Stanford's "Hunting Map," Sheet 14. Hobson's Foxhunting Atlas has a patent, and therefore unimportant, misprint in entitling the country in question the *South* Herefordshire.

The North Herefordshire.

occupies the said red clay—a cold, unscenting soil, differing of course according to what is grown on its surface, and differing also according to the weather of the moment, but never offering more than negative assistance to the efforts of the foxhound.

The North Herefordshire Country undulates more gently than some of its near neighbours. It is not so rugged and hilly as the Ludlow, nor broken with such heights as cross the face of the Ledbury. It has more than an average of grass along its river sides; corn is grown on the top of every rise, and hops and apples crowd in wherever they are best sheltered and the soil is suitable. A hill rises here and there, and its sides usually offer footing for a large covert, or chain of coverts. The most notable of these is Dinmore, which stands up alone in the middle of the country, and bears several good woods on its shoulders. Round its base winds the River Lug, which runs down the middle of the Country, and whose valley is the greenest, the most open and the best scenting, district in the Hunt.

The position of the North Herefordshire with reference to London is a point that need scarcely be touched upon: as a five hours' journey (by Great Western) is likely to require some attraction more powerful even than foxhunting (be it of the purest as well as of the simplest type). You know where the city of Hereford lies; and it is sufficient to say that between it and Leominster (some twelve miles due north) lies the bulk of the North Herefordshire Country, bounded on the east by the River Froome, and having some recognised but intangible boundary line to divide it on the west from The Radnor and West Hereford.

The Kennels are at Whitecross, close to the town of Hereford, were built by Mr. John Arkwright, and are now lent by him to the country. The present Master is Col. Heywood; and under his care the little pack has risen to high proficiency and is built of the best of blood.

How the Hereford, whole and undivided, came to be formed into two separate Hunts was briefly as follows. Some years ago Sir Velters Cornwell and Mr. J. H. Arkwright, as partners, hunted the Herefordshire Country in its entirety—the former working the southern portion with half the pack, Mr. Arkwright the northern with the other half; and the hounds being kept at the Whitecross Kennels. This led eventually to Mr. Arkwright building other Kennels at his place at Hampton Court, and to the Country being divided into North and South. Capt. Helme afterwards reunited it for one season; but it soon relapsed again into a division. Mr. F. Platt bought a pack of hounds of Mr. Villebois for the North Herefordshire Country; and the ladies of these, with additions made by Col. Heywood, have formed the present pack—which is said to have worked an improvement in sport, commensurate with the trouble that has been taken with its development.

The fertility of the soil of North Hereford extends its influence to the growth of timber as well as to the varied and lighter assortment already enumerated. Every hedgerow is set thick with spreading trees; and, as the inclosures are, as a rule, of very narrowed

The North Herefordshire. 425

dimensions, the whole surface of the country is more or less draped with foliage. The bearing of this upon foxhunting is that the range of sight is consequently very limited; and a sinking fox is never to be viewed till he is handled. And, what is still more to the point, the small size of the enclosures is all against hounds—as they are debarred from flinging wide or carrying a steady head for any distance, while their fox is constantly tempted to dodge down the hedgerows and seldom even runs the middle of the field.

The hedges are of thorn, hazel, and what-not—of no great height, but ragged and thick. Sometimes they are set on a low bank, but more often rest on a level surface, with a ditch on one side, whose depth may be probed, but is seldom apparent to the clearest vision of horse or man, owing to the veil of grass and "rough stuff" that generally shrouds it. The fence that most often impedes the way of the North Herefordshire sportsman is one that is most dangerous to the daring; but, while really safer to the timid man, cannot but prove a trial to one who has in any way lost his nerve. He who is rash will hold light such an easy fence; and may fall in his careless hurry. He who fears a fall will give his horse plenty of time to pick his way, but will find it impossible to forget that this is the trap that caught him so often in hot youth. It is not a country that I, for one, should select for my declining years and nerve. Each veiled fence would then be as a jog to the memory of mishap, and each blind ditch would seem a pitfall set to bring one's hunting career to a miserable close. To secure safe conveyance over it at *any* time, your horse should be steady, cautious and clever—one that will stop for some seconds well away from the brink of the half-hidden ditch, examine it carefully with eye and nostril full-extended, and be ready at the word "Come Up!" to spring far enough to light in the middle of the hedge, and finally to bore his way through. It is, perhaps, advisable to give a friend a mount before committing yourself to a late-purchase, of whose capacities, as above defined, you are not quite certain. In most Hunts you will find some unsuspecting man, who is fond of a ride and thinks he is being mounted for charity's sake. Failing such a personage ready to hand, it will be as well to send your groom (who has already learned a little too much to volunteer for the saddle) with a lungeing rein and an assistant, to lead the new acquisition over some trappy places.

As regards other requisites for the horse for Herefordshire, it must be borne in mind that he has to be a good deal in stiff clay that is always tiring and often deep. He may not be required to go a great pace over, or through, it; but he has got his journey home to perform afterwards; and it is just as well for your sake that he should not be tired before he sets about it. So let him have strength enough for the day's work: and to bring you back without endangering your joint safety. For the rest—if you want "appearance" you must of course pay for it. Appearances are, no doubt, as much a matter of moment in Herefordshire as elsewhere: but if you can afford to set them at naught, you can further afford to mount yourself with tolerable economy to ride to hounds there. Many horses of high-class used to be bred in the county; but of late years it has become an axiom that bullocks pay best, and the nobler beast—though not entirely set aside—has lost much of his nobility.

There is one difficulty to straight progress over the country in question which has yet to be described. This is what is known in local parlance as a " dingle," and is much equivalent to the "nullah" of India, and the "bottom" of Leicestershire. The latter answers most closely to it; as, with the watercourse, it gives in a guard-hedge on one side or both. It is seldom to be jumped; and can only be scrambled through in places where the stream runs over sound ground, where the banks are not too deep and steep, and where the overhanging hedge can be bored through. Frequently your passage may be entirely stayed by one of these dingles; and you may wander up and down its banks for half a mile without a chance of crossing. A knowledge of the country is the only means that will avail to keep you clear of such a difficulty; and till you have acquired this you must be content to rely upon others for warning and for guidance.

The North Herefordshire hunt twice a week—Monday and Thursday to wit. The former day is for the Leominster side, the latter for that of Hereford.

Among the Monday meets are Berrington for Lord Rodney's preserves on the hillside above Leominster, the chief covert being the Long Wood. Docklow is for Marston Firs, notable for good runs, and Bilfield Gorse another favourite draw. Hampton Court, the seat of Mr. J. Arkwright, the late Master, is a very leading fixture, and his home-coverts always provide sport for the Hunt—the Kennel-covert, Hell Holes, and Wig Wood all being full of foxes. Fordbridge or Hope-under-Dinmore is the usual advertisement for the great woods on and near the Dinmore Hill. These and the coverts round Brierley constitute the chief woodlands of the Country—the names of the most important items being Ivington Camp, West Hope, Burghope, and Wellington Wood (under which last runs the railway tunnel). From Edwin's Wood (the property of Mr. Childs) they go on to draw Bredenbury Plantations, which belong to Mr. H. Barneby, and which are always a sure find, though the owner takes no part in the chase. From England's Gate they draw the wood of Tankard's Walls, with Dewdale Hope to follow. Pencombe is often named; and Ullinswick for Brox Ash and perhaps Duke's Wood. From the Trumpet the draw is likely to be Hennor. Burton-Court and Dilwyn are two meets in the north-west.

Among the Thursday meets are Sutton Walls, for the fringe of rough covert round the edge of the old Wall Hill Camp, where a fox is generally to be found early in the season. Burley Gate is the probable meet for Morton Wood. Ocle Court is the seat of the present master; and from it they draw Cowarne (belonging to a good fox preserver, Major Bourne) and Whitwick. These are two celebrated coverts in the best country in the Hunt, and furnish many good runs—often to Hall Court and Cannon-Froome, which last is also a good meet and is the property of Mr.

John Hopton. Hall Court belongs to Major J. Browne, Master of the South Staffordshire, who always has a good fox at home—giving frequently a run back to Cowarne. West Hide is a great wood of perhaps three hundred acres in all, clothing the side of a steep ridge in a semicircular course, and is a great stronghold. Ashperton is a meet with some good coverts; while to the south-west again are other extensive woods—e.g., Credenhill, Badinage, and Garnons (Sir H. Coxwell's). Lugwardine Court is the seat of Sir H. Croft, and is always the scene of the meet following upon the Herefordshire Hunt Ball—an old and well-sustained institution. The coverts drawn are usually Swanley Wood, Moorend Covert, and eventually, perhaps, West Hide Wood.

THE DUKE OF BUCCLEUCH'S.*

PART of Northumberland, all Roxburgh, part of Berwickshire and all Selkirk go to make up the territory now hunted by the Duke of Buccleuch's hounds—forming altogether an area some forty-five miles across, either way. The Holderness is a big country; but the Duke's leaves it in insignificance. At first sight it would appear marvellous how a five-days-a-week pack can deal with such an extent of ground. But steam power, if it cannot, like electricity, altogether ignore distance, can at least modify it; and a handy railway offers covert-conveyance to the more remote points. It is only this year (1880) that his Grace has added English ground to his Scotch dominion—the dissolution of the Northumberland and Berwick Hunt having led to that country being absorbed in three sections, by the North Berwickshire, Lord Percy, and the Duke respectively.

The basins of the Tweed and the Teviot virtually form his present hunting-ground—which, in its main characteristics, will be found much alike on either

---

* *Vide* Stanford's "Hunting Map," Sheets 1 and 2. Also Hobson's Foxhunting Atlas, and Rutherford's Border Map.

side of the Border. Waves of rich, undulating, arable form the ground-work, broken here and there by detached off-shoots of the mountain ranges looming on the outskirts. The soil, though fertile and highly tilled, is never deep, and carries a scent as it carries a horse—firmly and steadily, almost uniformly. The in-country hills are steep but rideable; and breed a race of foxes that can travel like wolves. When winter weather, or a hill-pack, has driven them down from their upper fastnesses, they are often to be found at great distances from their former home, and will give fine sport in their efforts to return. A blown fox can no more mount a steep ascent than a blown horse; and so, if pressed at first, they will scarcely do more than skirt the hillsides or turn down again as soon as he reaches them. The ploughed land of these open vales possesses a stronger combination of the essentials for enjoyable sport than are often credited to cultivation and crop-growing. The five-years-system on which it is tilled gives two years to grass, one to turnips, and two to corn. A foxhunter need not be a farmer to know that even new grass will carry a scent on most soils, or that turnips generally speak strongly to a fox's passage. But he must accept the testimony of the natives that, whether in Northumberland or just over the border, hounds can almost always bring a fair head across these northern fallows. Again, the grass—which a mind of very ordinary mathematical capacity will understand to be at all times two-fifths of the whole—is of course sound going; while the same evidence vouches for the fact that turnips and fallows may be galloped over more readily than deep grass elsewhere. The steam cultivator has had its turn at the land, is generally considered to have played its part for the present, and the soil has been allowed to settle again—to be subjected only to the milder combing of the horse plough. The fact that the soil is but a kind of decayed "whinstone" lying on the top of the stone itself, will account for its riding so light under all conditions.

Each field is from twenty to fifty acres in extent— more of them, perhaps, being near the latter size than the former. There is nothing, therefore, to hinder a fox if inclined to a straight course—which, to do him justice, he generally is, at all events if a member of the hill breed. In Northumberland there are but few trees in the hedgerows; and the undulating slopes lie open to the view for miles—all to the advantage of the huntsman, and all against the fox. Over the border, frequent belts of trees break the view, and tempt foxes to run their length. Hounds can press them then more readily than in the open; and horsemen, galloping freely outside, can keep pace readily enough—till, perhaps, a sudden turn throws them a field to the bad, and sends them round to seek an outlet. In Northumberland the Hunt is entirely dependent on whin (gorse) coverts—all of natural origin, but in many instances now civilised into the category of rent-producing property. In Roxburgh there are two fine woodlands, Long Newton and Beaumont, each of which is dignified by the inhabitants of its neighbourhood with the title of The Forest. These, with Ancrum and the Eildon Hills, are not only valuable for cubhunting, but, when well rattled, serve as a source of supply to the surrounding country. Within the borders of Berwickshire again are the Hirsel Woods (Lord Home's) which answer the same purpose.

The kennels are at St. Boswell's, on the line of railway which joins Berwick-on-Tweed, Kelso, and Edinburgh. The pack has been in the Ducal family for some generations; and has long been noted for speed and stoutness. The present hounds, whose breeding has, until quite lately, been confined almost entirely to home resources, retain these qualities in a remarkable degree, can run all day on hill and plain alike, and drive as closely at the end of a long run as at its commencement. The fences of the Duke's country are, at least on the plains, much the same throughout—viz., chiefly thorn hedges, mended with light post and rails, and many of them with a ditch on one side. Sometimes the hedge is planted on a low bank, with width enough to make it obligatory for a horse to take it in two. These hedges are never laid (*i.e.*, stake-and-bound), seldom even trimmed; but stand up ragged and thin, to form partial shelter for cattle and sheep in the chilly winter. In many places you may force your way through them; or, again, by steering somewhat to the right or left as you approach, may hit off a spot where timber has been employed to fill up a gap. Thus your horse should be ready to face thorns, pop over timber, or double on-and-off. He will seldom be called upon to fly water; but should be able to creep in and out of any complication. It is especially a country in which to make a hunter clever;

and it is a school through which a young rider may graduate with the greatest advantage. A big loose-made horse is altogether out of place here. He must be compact and well bred; and, with strength to go up hill and shoulders to come down, had better be on a small scale than on an exaggerated one. In fact, a sturdy clever thoroughbred is the best mount with the Duke of Buccleuch's hounds.

As a rule, but small fields go out in the Duke's country; but on Mondays and Thursdays, when the railway brings in recruits, and Northumberland, Berwick, and Roxburgh all supply their forces, as many as sixty to a hundred horsemen muster for the fray—and hard riding may be witnessed in fully due proportion to the numbers.

The country, as at present constituted, is arranged to be hunted much as follows—the days of hunting being, Monday, Tuesday, Thursday and Saturday. A Friday is given once a month to the rough country up the valley of the Gala; and once a month the same day to the extreme north corner of Northumberland (hunted in common with the North Berwickshire and Lord Percy's).

Monday is for what is known as the Kelso country, south of the Tweed and Teviot to the Cheviots, and takes in much of the Duke's best and most open ground. Some of the principal meets are Crailing, Eckford, Blakelaw, Lurdenlaw, and the famed Hadden Rigg, from which so many great runs took place in days gone by—when men used to come even from Edinburgh by coach to meet hounds at Hadden Rigg.

It was immortalised by the famous run from thence

—more than forty years ago—to Middleton Hall, two miles south of Wooler, where they killed their fox without a check. The hounds found in Hadden Rigg old plantation and went off in a moment, running fast eastward for two fields, and then turned sharp to the south and never put nose to the ground again, the late Sir David Baird riding as usual alongside of the pack got half a field's start of everyone else and was never caught till they reached Kirknewton Tors although he was closely pressed by the huntsman Old Williamson, the whip Hugh Burns, Lord John Scott (the Duke's brother), young George Grey of Milfield Hill, Mr. Spottiswood of Spottiswood, Mr. Todd of Drygrange, &c., &c. Out of that gallant field, Mr. Grey is perhaps the only survivor.

On a Tuesday they go north of the Tweed, as far as Greenlaw, West Gordon, Spottiswoode and Mellerstain—a rougher country than the previous days. The fences of this district are frequently faced on the one side with stones, on the other with railings—making it necessary for a horse to drop his hindlegs quick-and-clever. Gorses and plantations constitute the coverts of this neighbourhood: and the ground rises a trifle deeper than elsewhere.

Thursday is given to the new Northumberland portion, south of the Tweed and west of the Till—Wark Common (with a gorse of such size, that only a third of it is maintained up to mark at one time, the remainder being cut as occasion requires), Pallin's Burn (Mr. Askew's, a former master of the Northumberland and Berwickshire, and who provides an unfailing gorse near by), Milfield (Mr. Grey's)—with its gorse coverts and plantations, and the wood of Flodden Hill, the property of the Marchioness of Waterford. Mindrum is another meet, from which the covert of that name is drawn, and afterwards perhaps the gorses of Downham, Pawston, and Kilham.

Saturday scatters itself over a very wide area to the west of the Kennels. Hounds may be taken by train to Hawick, and thence reach a considerable tract of country on the banks of the Teviot and the Borthwick. Here they get into a hilly grass district abounding in stone walls, the coverts being chiefly plantation. Minto, nearer home, is a leading meet, as also is Drinkstone. The Kennels, St. Boswell's, is generally named with a view to Long Newton Forest, or for the Eildon Hills, whose three peaks rear their heads as a landmark visible over the whole of the Duke's country. Far away, again is The Haining, near the town of Selkirk, where there is also much hilly moorland. Round his Grace's residence at Bowhill, too, are hills covered with coarse grass. And, as we get higher into Selkirk we come upon more mountainous ground, fit for fox-hunting only when spring has driven it from elsewhere.

The occasional Friday, when given to the Gala water, takes us into a wild, often precipitous, country, where sheep find a short herbage and the fox hunter climbs as best he may—his progress constantly stayed by stone walls whose height is proportionate to the number of stones to be cleared off, rather than to the requirements of fence-making. The other Fridays when made use of, lead to the neutral corner of Northumberland above mentioned—viz., east of the Till and south of the Tweed as far as Ford and Lowick—which is not only good as a tillage country, but also includes some thousand of acres of old grass. The chief coverts to be drawn by the Duke's hounds will be Riffington and Newbiggin (gorse coverts), and the wooded banks on the east of the Till to Etal and Ford (where the late Lord Fred FitzClarence for many years resided and hunted). At Ford are Lady Waterford's well-preserved coverts. Bury Hill Gorse and Wood End Wood (about 500 to 600 acres, and the only wood of any size in the neutral territory) are both good coverts.

Some other leading fox preservers, besides those already mentioned, are the Duke of Roxburgh, Sir William Scott of Ancram, Mr. Charles Cunningham, Sir John Majoribanks, Mr. Sprott of Riddell, Mr. David Henderson of Abbotrule, Mr. Robert Oliver, Mr. Baird of Stitchell, Lord Dunglass of Newton Don (now Earl of Home), Lord Haddington (to whom belong the Mellerstane woods), Sir George Douglas, Lord Polwarth, Sir Hugh Campbell, Mr. Paton of Crailing, besides many others.

Great tracts of land throughout his country belong to the Duke of Buccleugh himself; and it is needless to say that on these, as on his Grace's other properties in various parts of Great Britain, no effort is spared to secure the wellbeing of the foxes.

THE TYNEDALE.*

THE first association that, in the mind of a stranger, would naturally enough associate itself with the Tyne, is coalmining rather than foxhunting. To ask him to believe that the Tynedale is the best hound-country in the North of England would probably startle him as something altogether incongruous. "Canny Newcassel, where arle the coals come frae" keeps itself, comparatively, " to itself ; " and interferes with hunting but little beyond the scope of its own smoke-drift. Taking train on the Newcastle and Carlisle Line, you are very soon free from black dust and tall chimnies; and, running along the southern bank of the beautiful woodgirt Tyne, are shortly in as purely a rural scene as even the river Exe could offer. From the railway you will not see the pick of the country—in a hunting sense. For that you must disembark before you get opposite the Kennels ; and strike northwards—the Kennels being at Stagshaw, some three miles from Corbridge Station, and about eighteen from Newcastle.

Taking up your map, you will easily follow me in

---

* *Vide* Stanford's "Hunting Map," Sheets 1 and 2; and Hobson's Foxhunting Atlas.

dividing the country into four parts, all of which are of distinct character, and in accordance with whose variety the system of hunting the country is alone regulated. Tyneside is one division, comprehending the light valley and the coverts along the northern bank of the Tyne—which it will be seen flows from west to east along the southern edge of the Country. Another division is the Eastern, with Stamfordham as a centre. The third is the Western; with the kennels as the base. And the fourth consists of the rough, wooded, strip of the south bank of the Tyne.

The peculiarity—and superiority—of the Tynedale among its fellows lies, however, in the fine grass of its Western district, where for miles the hills are covered with firm crisp turf, and the valleys with equally green, but ranker, herbage—stretching westward while the hills grow gradually steeper and the turf wider and wetter, till the rugged moorland is no longer fit for foxhunting. Nothing could be finer than these splendid grass slopes, were they not marred by a drawback that neither valour nor horseflesh— nor the happiest combination of both—can avail to efface. Were it not for this, there would be a rush to the Tynedale that would at once ease much of the pressure off the Quorn, the Cottesmore, and similar suffering, overpopular, packs. This one imperfection, so detractive as regards the country, and deterrent as regards visitors, is found in the presence of stonewalls such as a stag might turn from. Designed purposely to pen in the black-faced mountain sheep, no wonder they are beyond the wants of the veriest thruster that ever loved a fall. Varying from four to six feet high, they owe their build in many cases to the "expert" with lime and trowel, rather than to the simple labourer who merely piles stone upon stone with a guileless indifference to how soon he may be called upon to be paid to do the same work over again. Their tops are coped with angular pieces of rock, more often cemented together with plaster, and whose sharp edges will cut a horse's legs as readily and deeply as an operator's knife. Frequently a wooden railing lends further assistance to the stone coping, and laughs at the approach of anything with less power of flight than a bird—or a foxhound. Consequently, riding to hounds on the Tynedale grass is little more than a *façon de parler;* and in actual fact is limited to watching them, with awe and respect, in the more or less remote distance. While they are glancing over the greensward and flinging the wall behind them, you and others (luckily not many) are taking your turn in single file at the bridle gates, and regarding their doings the more intently that you can have none of the fun of riding over them. In this way men have an open page laid quietly out before their eyes, and from it they may, no doubt, learn better than from page after page hurriedly skimmed. They cannot devote talent and energy to "brilliant horsemanship" here; so there is nothing for it but to watch and study hounds. This they fully recognise—and claim to carry out. In a word, the cream of the Tynedale is a *hound* as opposed to a *riding* country. If you know your way about, or are content to follow some one who does, you may see a great deal of what hounds are doing. Go beyond that, attempt to ride to them, and your career will soon end in mortification and a return to the ways of the more modest. The latter (perhaps with scorn in their glance) have been working along the upper ridges, taking advantage of gates where they offered, or, failing these, of gaps now, or previously torn down in the stonewalls. All the time they avoid as much as possible the lower and deeper ground, trusting to their knowledge of country, and of the run of foxes, to keep them on sound going and on some sort of terms with the pack. As above noted, all the Tynedale country is of a very undulating character; but as you get westward it becomes more and more confirmedly hilly, and the valleys attain a softer consistency. That they may cope with the hills and walls, it follows, naturally, that hounds must have the strongest of backs and quarters to carry them up, and the best of shoulders to bring them down, in their jumping and galloping. Mr. George Fenwick's pack possess these essentials in the highest degree. And another requisite, to which they have been bred and schooled, is to be as much as possible independent of extraneous help. As a matter of necessity they can receive little or none in their strong-scenting stonewall country; and they are educated to look for very little elsewhere. Lest the power and pace of the grass should tend in any degree to induce flightiness, it is made a rule, for each division of the pack, that a day on the grass shall be succeeded by a day in the East Country or the Valley of the Tyne, where they must work hard and "turn short." Mr. Fenwick purchased the foundation of his present pack about a dozen years ago from Mr. Allgood, who held the country for two seasons after the retirement of Major Bell, who established the Tynedale pack and hunted the country thirteen seasons. Since then he has added the best and oldest of blood from whatever direction it could be obtained.

The East, or Stamfordham, country (except that the soil is more akin to clay) is on the other hand of the ordinary Northumberland type—to wit, undulating tillage ground with a certain intermingling of old grass, and fenced in the same crude untrimmed fashion as prevails further north. It is not to be supposed by this that the fences can be galloped through for want of repair. The Northumbrians are too good farmers to allow of that. Every fence is carefully mended up at once, with either fir-strips or dead thorns. The latter by the way, though equally efficacious in stopping the way, and much more disagreeable, one would imagine, for either horse or bullock to force his way through, are in Northumberland looked upon as betokening a much less refined and intelligent soul on the part of the farmer. The fir-strips, though puny-looking indeed as compared to a Leicestershire ox-rail, have quite virtue enough in them to turn a horse over, when, as is generally the case hereabouts, he has to meet them at a walk or slow trot, or finds them erected on a bank where he can only reach them in a second spring. The term unkempt merely refers to the growth of the hedges themselves. These, partly for the sake of shelter and partly because it has never become the custom of the country to *lay* them, are allowed to grow as high and ragged as they please—except in some few favoured

The Tynedale. 443

localities, where their top-twigs have been trimmed annually. The fences of the Stamfordham district also vary a good deal, especially where this side begins to merge into the western. Stone walls appear by degrees; double ditches are frequent; and banks are common. And this is the side most in favour with the members of the Hunt; for here they can ride with hounds all day and be present at all that goes on. The whole of the Tynedale may be said to be good scenting-country; and this, the open ground, is well-favoured in this respect. Foxes are not only well preserved and sufficiently plentiful; but, being a mixture between the native-hill breed and Scotch importation of some years ago, are very stout travellers, and very long runs have been registered during the last few seasons. Many of the Newcastle division of the field keep their horses at Stamfordham, and the Master himself finds it convenient to lodge a couple there for his own riding. It is in this neighbourhood that by far the largest attendance prevails.

So far we have been speaking only of the higher ground of the Tynedale. The third division, the valley of the Tyne—or Tyneside—is lighter soil. From its woods, which are individually small and in which foxes never hang long, the upper country is very soon reached, and a run may carry you anywhere.

Fourthly and lastly, across the Tyne is a rough deep woodland strip—most useful for cub hunting and spring hunting and for disciplinary purposes at all times—and touching on an indefinite area of hill and moorland to the south. The Tynedale territory, as a matter of fact, reaches in this direction much farther than is credited in the maps referred to.

For a visit to the Tynedale you would probably go to Newcastle, whence you may find yourself at Stamfordham, or may avail yourself of the Newcastle-and-Carlisle Railway and be dropped at Corbridge or other stations along the line.

The Tynedale hunt Mondays, Wednesdays, and Fridays, with a frequent byeday on Saturday. No particular district is told off for any one day of the week—the requirements of the hounds being chiefly studied in the selection of locality. The chief meets along Tyneside are Horsley Wood, Whittle Dean, Bywell Hall (the residence of the Master), Styford, Aydon Dean, Beaufront, and Brunton backs—all of which are for the nice woods along the Tyne. It is a maxim in the country that no fox ever hangs in covert north of the Tyne.

Among the fixtures in the east of the Country are Dissington (the nearest meet to the town of Newcastle), Stamfordham (for Stamfordham-Heugh, a famous covert). Belsay (near which is the good Bitchfield Gorse, the property of Sir Arthur Middleton), Shafto (Lord Decies), Matfen (Sir Edward Blackett's), and Capheaton (Sir John Swinburne's) Plantations form the chief covert in this—the most open—part of the country.

In the west there are more gorses; and the best-known meets are as follows—Stagshaw Kennels (with a whin covert on the common close by), Swinburn, Bavington, Chipchase, Countess Park (quite on the

The Tynedale.

edge of the country hunted), and Little Harle (Mr. Anderson's). Dunsmore should be mentioned as a covert of great note not far from the Kennels. Over the North Tyne on this side are Chesters and Nunwick, beyond which hounds are seldom taken, for, though practicable for them, it would be next to impossible to follow on horseback.

Finally, on the south bank of the main river the meets for the woodlands are Bromley and Minster Acres (Mr. Henry Silvertop's)—and behind these you soon come upon grouse ground.

LORD PERCY'S.*

On the maps referred to you will find, under the denomination of Major Brown's, an approximation of the country now hunted by Lord Percy in Upper Northumberland. A part of that set down as "the Northumberland and Berwickshire" was in his hands even previous to the demise of that Hunt; while of late a considerable further addition has accrued to him by the apportionment of the territory of the deceased between its three nearest neighbours. Belford and Wooler were already on his northern boundary. Now he goes as far as Ford and Lowick, and has a joint right (with the North Berwickshire and the Duke of Buccleuch) to the topmost corner of England. The Cheviots on the west, and the North Sea on the east, are his lateral boundaries—and serve to denote his general whereabouts. A mixed and various country is Lord Percy's. Some of his best will take rank with anything that is under tillage; some is rough and mountainous; some is soft and sedgey; and a strip of it is a neat pretty vale. Foxes are strong and plentiful; and whatever ground

---

* *Vide* Stanford's "Hunting Map," Sheet 2, and Hobson's Foxhunting Atlas.

they run over, they seldom fail to leave a scent—while here and there they can scarcely get away from hounds on a day at all favourable to the latter.

The river Coquet, which cuts Northumberland into its two divisions of North and South, acts as the southern boundary to Lord Percy's country. The simplest plan—if the driest—of giving some idea of the latter will be to take it in longitudinal sections as Nature has laid it out, and call them respectively A, B, C, and D, with E as the new acquisition from the late Northumberland-and-Berwick.

Section A, then, is the sea border, and forms about the best of the country. The railway from Newcastle and the South to Berwick-on-Tweed runs along this; and introduces you to a very fair view of it—except that it picks out little but the best of the grass for its route. From Belford by Alnwick, down to Felton—and between the sea coast and the Old North Road (Newcastle to Edinbro') defines this section, which, as a tillage-country, is as good as anything in England. At least such was the verdict of old Treadwell, who came to hunt it after long experience of crack Hunts, and laid it down that hounds carried a better head over the plough here than over many vaunted grass countries. It is a stiffer soil than that of the former Northumberland-and-Berwick; and its enclosures, while equally extensive, are less undulating than there. With a considerable sprinkling of old grass, the bulk of it is employed in growth of turnips and corn, which—at all events before the stubbles are once again under seed and the turnip roots ploughed in—carries an extremely good scent, and is always firm enough for galloping. The fences —throughout Lord Percy's country—are light and various with characteristics much the same as belong to the best of the Duke of Buccleuch's (already described)—and the horse that will do for the one will do for the other. The foxes of the country, throughout, are of stout hill stock; and take a great deal of killing.

Section B may be the title of the rougher district of Chatton, Chillingham, Eglingham, &c., which lies immediately west of the Old North Road just alluded to. Here broken moorland alternates continually with soft mossy ground, unfavourable for riding, but carrying by no means a bad scent.

Next, as section C, we have the narrow vale of the Till, or, in its earlier course, the Beamish—a pretty but very limited strip. It is nowhere much more than three miles broad; and at any point a fox is likely to run out of it either to the moorlands or to the western hills.

Section D is still more to the west, and takes in the lower spurs of the Cheviots—ground that only just runs short of being absolutely mountainous. For all that, it is better riding than is offered by section B— for, though hilly, it is grassy and firm, while the latter is constantly robbing your horse of his shoes and condemning him to overreaches in its treacherous sloughs. Ilderton, Ingram and Aluham denote where this hilly district begins : and it stretches away in a rideable form to Biddleston and the woody crags of Thrunton. What is known in the north as a hillhorse (Birth, shape, and education must be combined to meet the definition) can travel about this part of the world very comfortably and safely; but it is scarcely suited to the capacity of the southerner who has been brought up only to gallop loosely over the flat. There are many fine country places scattered over this picturesque district—instances being Eslington (Lord Ravenswater's) and Callaly Castle (Mr. H. Brown's). Beyond Biddleston and Alwinton a hill-pack carries the sport of foxhunting into the heart of the mountains—its title being the Redewater, under the Mastership of Mr. Robson.

Section E is the new territory bequeathed by the Northumberland—and, Berwick, with a still further uppermost corner hunted conjointly by three packs.

Some leading meets in the different parts of Lord Percy's country are as under—the days of meeting being subject to arrangements scarcely concluded at the date of writing. Monday, Wednesday, and Friday have hitherto been Lord Percy's days; but at least one more per week will now be taken in.

Along the coast (which will probably still continue to be Monday ground) are, among others, Bamburgh Castle (once the residence of Lord Crewe, Bishop of Durham). There are various gorse coverts to be drawn near, and other fixtures may be selected for the same programme of work. Ellingham (Sir John Haggerston's) comes next, with woods round it, and a fine gorse (The Hagg, associated with many great runs) close by. Doxford is the residence of Major Brown, the late Master; and there is a good gorse at Brunton (Sir G. Grey's). About Lord Grey's seat at Howick are woods on every side. At Ratcheugh again there are rocky crags to be drawn; and almost in the same district is Craster (the property of a gentleman of that name) where the seabanks are covered with gorse. From the kennels (at Green Rig, close to Bilton station) or from Lesbury they draw a long wooded glen called Callasies; and Bank House is for the banks of the Coquet—Newton Hall being another meet.

In the district we have denominated Section B, Belford is advertised with the word *west* after it, to denote the way hounds will "gang" to draw—after coming by train to Belford. With this index subjoined, it is understood that the adjacent moorland, with its gorses and young plantations, will be visited. Chatton is a meet from which it may happen that Lord Tankerville's park at Chillingham may be run through —in which case hounds must "ware" wild cattle and deer, and you, as an unprotected horseman in a red coat, should keep well on the look-out for the patriarch-of-the-herd. Common Flat is another meet; and so is the great rocky fastness of Hebron Wood. From Eglingham they draw Beanley Wood, etc.; and at Leamington Branch are good plantations.

In section C is Fowberry Park, the principal covert from which is a rough damp place, in Northumberland yclept a *moss*. Thence they get on to Lilburn (Mr. Collingwood's), Ilderton Decoy, and Percy's Cross (a fine gorse). By the way, the Northumberland gorses were as completely nipped, and rendered useless, by the frost last winter as were those of the Midland Counties.

Section D comes into most notice in the spring, and gives Lord Percy the chance of making a later—and an earlier—season than falls to the lot of most masters. Ilderton is a favourite meet, for which hounds come overnight to the kennels at Powburn, and from which they have whins and hills to draw, as well as the dell of Roddam Dean. From Ingram they look for a fox among the " glitters " (*Anglicé*, stones and boulders), and may draw on to Percy's Cross or go to Glanton Pike (a fine large gorse on the hillside). There are good coverts at Burton—the meet being there, or at Trewitt (Sir W. Armstrong's) where many new plantations have been made. Thrunton Crag is a place that might fairly be drawn every day of the week— being some miles of wooded rocky hill.

Lord Percy's newly acquired country (Section E in our classification) is of a somewhat rough description. Here they may meet at Belford, to draw north—by Middleton Hall, Detchant, and Kyloe. These are all large woods, composing the only real woodland in that part of the country. On the other hand, they may meet at Beal, with a view to working homewards. Speaking generally, the whole of this district is made up of woodland and moorland. Doddington is a likely meet—or Ford, for Lady Waterford's home coverts. A good deal of whin grows here, as also on Fenton Hill (Mr. F. Lambton's property and place of residence). At Horton Hill are plantations and gorses, belonging to Mr. G. Culley of Fowberry.

All that now remains to be mentioned of Lord Percy's territory is the uppermost part of the country, which he is to visit once a month (the Duke of Buccleuch and Major Baillie-Hamilton—of the Berwickshire—engaging to do the same). To do this hounds will have to be brought overnight, or by train—in the latter case probably to Beal station. The principal meets on Lord Percy's side have hitherto been Haggerston (Capt. Leyland's)—drawing on to Bowsden Whin (Mr. Gregson's) and Berrington Dean (the property of Lord Grey). Woodend Wood (Mr. Sitwell's) lies in the centre of this neutral ground—and is full of foxes. Round Berrington Dean is a great deal of nice grass. Longridge and Cheswick are the points marking a good district which may be drawn from either.

Good and long runs as so often take place in Northumberland, it seldom happens but that a single horse will do the day's work. In fact, second horses have never been made an institution of the north. A sturdy well-bred one is the horse of the country; and it is expected of him that he should be equal to as many hours in the field as a foxhound. In most of the county of Northumberland he travels on the top of the ground—though that ground may often be hilly, and at times even rocky. It is probably his native soil; for horse breeding is much in vogue on the border, whether with a view to profit or to pastime. The fences, though intricate, fail to puzzle or distress him; while they seldom possess breadth or height enough to call for great effort. Thus, if his shoulders be good and his back strong, he is likely to reach home again at night without undue exhaustion of frame or limb—though his stature may not approach the standard that the same burden he had been carrying all day would demand in a heavier country.

I am told—as a peculiarity of North Northumberland—that it has the effect of making all hounds run mute, and that, however much cry they possess on first introduction to the country, they invariably lose it after a short experience there. The scent may possibly have some curious property, leading to such a result; but why that result should be universal it is difficult indeed to understand. That hounds already naturally inclined to silence (in their case deserving any other epithet than golden) should be encouraged and confirmed in it by the nature of the country, is intelligible enough; for the wide open inclosures and thin straggling fences offer no check whatever to their direct progress. Their fox is not led to deviate much as he goes; while they can carry a head all the time, and keep moving as quick as the scent will carry them.

Lord Percy resides at Alnwick Castle; his Kennels being, as above mentioned, at Green Rig. His hounds were purchased from Major Brown, who had previously bought them at an almost unprecedented price from Lord Poltimore. Alnwick and Rothbury are the points a visitor might select as posts of observation, for hunting intended. And, finally, it may be noted that, for spring and autumn hunting, no better sphere than that of Lord Percy's exists.

THE MORPETH.*

MID-NORTHUMBERLAND has for the last three years been hunted by Mr. J. B. Cookson—his father, Mr. John Cookson, having, for many years previously, also presided over the fortunes of the Morpeth. The River Coquet separates his country from Lord Percy's on the north; he touches the Tynedale on the south-west, and goes southward as near Newcastle as coal-pits and coal-railways and colonies of pitmen will let him. The sea limits him on the east; while, as he only hunts two days a week, he is not called upon to go farther west than the country is tempting. For, beyond the westward line coloured on the map, hill and moor become so confirmed that foxhunting is virtually discontinued. And below the town of Morpeth, again, the ground becomes almost at once a broken network of railway and coalmine; and the chase has no longer any status.

But between Morpeth—or, rather, its river the Wansbeck—and the Coquet a great deal of pretty hunting ground is to be found, less hilly on the whole than Lord Percy's, and varying from flat clay, grass,

---

* *Vide* Stanford's "Hunting Map," Sheet 2, and Hobson's Foxhunting Atlas.

and plough in the east to rough moor on the west. All the country carries a steady, seldom a flying, scent; and the foxes are of the stout hill-bred sort common to Northumberland generally. It may be noted of the hills and moors respectively that a scent is generally to be found on the former when damp from recent rain; but when the rocky surface is dry hounds have much difficulty. The moorlands, on the other hand, being more consistently wet, seldom fail to hold a workable scent. A fox found in the immediate neighbourhood of the hills is pretty sure to strike upward at first, run the upper ground for a time, and come down again as he feels himself getting distressed. Thus, when a whin on a hillside is to be drawn, men generally post themselves above to view the fox away and to be in a position to follow him. A start being effected, they will then spread out—assisting each other by voice and signal to keep the chase in view as it winds along the ridges and twisting slopes.

Mr. Cookson not only finds foxes in fair numbers; but has the reputation of being able to kill them quite as readily as his neighbours—his score being more than up to the average for two days a week. His pack are excellent workers, and well in hand. His Kennels are at Newminster, near Morpeth; and he himself lives with his father at Melton Park on the Wansbeck.

As with Lord Percy's country, the Morpeth runs down from north to south in strips that differ considerably one from the other. The Morpeth must be divided into three, to give any idea of its composition—the three divisions being the east (or coast), the centre, and the west.

I. Parallel with the sea is a stiff clay country, with rough hedges, planted on earth banks—old ragged hedges that have never been cut or trimmed, and where necessary have been strongly mended up with dead thorns. Most of this eastern country is under cultivation; though a good deal of grass is to be seen alongside the line of railway—as you run from Newcastle to Berwick-on-Tweed — and may give the traveller a scarcely justifiable idea that he is in a second Vale of Aylesbury.

II. Down the middle of the country runs a district, for the most part under tillage but with some grass. It has less of clay in its soil, and is not so stiffly fenced as the east. It is much intersected by small wooded glens, puzzling to hounds, baulking to horsemen, and leading foxes to turn. All the Morpeth country, in fact, is much cut up by burns — the accepted distinction in the north between brooks and burns being that the latter run between trees and are to be scrambled through, while a brook is held to be a stream with steep banks and to be jumped at a fly. From the presence of these, and from other causes, the Morpeth may be spoken of rather as a hunting than a riding country. And though, as above mentioned, its foxes are stout and strong, they are by no means invariably straight runners.

III. The West portion has in it a great deal of rough moor grass land, with woods of considerable size (plantations and small woods being the general coverts of the rest of the country). But it is not till

The Morpeth.

you reach the extreme west of all—south of Rothbury —that you meet with hills of any severity. Touching the Tynedale, again, is lighter, better-going ground, merging into what that Hunt consider their best territory—and foxes are continually passing from the one country into the other.

The horse to show you sport with the Morpeth needs to be such as you might usually denominate an "useful sort"—meaning thereby an animal blessed with no special high qualities, but endowed with substance, endurance, and a good constitution. If his skin is a trifle thick, and the hair on his legs somewhat robust in texture and exuberant in growth, he will be none the less capable of forcing his way harmlessly through thick thorn fences. An excitable blood horse would run considerable risk of knocking himself about, both here and in Lord Percy's country. One of sturdier limbs and more stolid temperament will be likely not only to keep his value together, but to carry you in comfort from day to day. Unlike those of the Duke of Buccleuch's country the fallows cannot be galloped at all times as they come; and a fast horse is therefore not so much wanted. The Morpeth days of hunting are Tuesday and Saturday, with an occasional bye-day, and some of their chief meets are as follows :

In their Eastern district they go, by train, to Acklington Station, to draw the Duke of Northumberland's plantations near at hand, and probably those of Lord Grey at Chevington Wood. By the same means they reach Widdrington Station, for Mr. Cresswell's woods close by. These are a certain find; and then come a number of other large woods, to wit, Ulgham (which no southerner would suppose to be pronounced Ufham !), The Blubbery, etc. The meet of Cresswell or of Seaton Delaval means the coverts in the neighbourhood—these, like most of the Morpeth, being wood-plantations, as against the more frequent whin-coverts of the extreme north. From Morpeth-Quarry-Banks, however, besides the extensive overgrown banks of the Wansbeck, they have Middlemoor Whins (the property of Mr. Lawson of Longhurst and the Duke of Portland) to draw. The Wansbeck, like the greater number of the Northumberland rivers, is prettily wooded for many miles of its length. Below this point are soon found coalpits with their yawning mouths and busy populace.

In the middle portion of the country are Blagden Park (Sir Matthew White-Ridley's) Benridge, Kirkley Hall, Whalton Village—all of which are meets in turn, for their adjacent coverts (chiefly plantations of inconsiderable size). In the neighbourhood of Whalton is a very fine gorse, Edington by name; and not far from it are Lord Carlisle's woods at Morpeth Common. Another meet is Meldon Park Corner, commonly called Meldon Dyke Nuke—a *dyke* being a roughly built wall, without mortar, or of alternate layers of stones and turf, in contradistinction to a *stonewall*, by which is meant a wall built by masons with lime; a *nuke* being a corner, or a bend in a fence. From this fixture the Banks of the Wansbeck, as far up as Hartburn, may be drawn, or else they may go to the woods of Nunriding and on to Pigdon. Further north are Horsley and Lindon, where there are woods, and at Bywell a gorse; and a little to the west are Todburn Gill (a little wooded glen) and Wingates, with young plantations and some more grass.

In the Western district are Nunnykirk, with woodlands amid a grassy country. West of these come the Tomboy Plantations, called after a racehorse of Mr. Orde's—who was also the owner of Beeswing. Every pitman was wont to put his money on the latter mare; and, fortunately for them, she won all her races—except on one hapless occasion, when each pitman in Northumberland had to sell his pig or proclaim himself a defaulter. The present Mr. Orde is great nephew of that celebrated sportsman, and a great patron of foxes and hunting. Nether Witton and Rothley are meets, in the midst of rough well-wooded country, which carries a good scent and is very useful for spring-hunting. Finally, Wallington (Sir C. Trevelyan's) is close upon the edge of the Tynedale—the plantations being within half a mile of the dividing river.

The town of Morpeth would be found the best central point from which you could see the Morpeth hounds in the field; and it lies on the main line of railway along the east coast to North Britain. Rothbury and Newcastle also give access to the country from its north and south margin respectively.

THE RUFFORD.*

THE County of Nottingham, though a next-door neighbour of Leicestershire, is where the great northern area of plough begins, and grass comes to an end. As you cross the Trent, in fact, you leave "The Shires" and embark upon The Provinces. You may wander northwards, and find first-rate foxhunting everywhere as you go. But it is foxhunting of a less elastic, perhaps less gaudy type than you left behind. Hounds are as good—in some instances even better. Foxes may be ditto; horses very nearly so. Huntsmen are quite as clever; and Masters just as fond of the game. The falling-off is found in the ground, the scent, the dash, and the go. The gain (?) is the freedom from a crowd of good company. All the world does not care about coffeehousing. No, but foxhunters are a sociable race, whether at work or play. Rigorous sport, alas, does not go on all day and every day; and pleasant companions at your elbow are very often a godsend.

The South Notts, as their name implies, take all the lower part of Nottinghamshire. The Rufford follow

---

* *Vide* Stanford's "Hunting Map," Sheet 9, and Hobson's Foxhunting Atlas.

The Rufford.

along their northern border, and hunt its centre, leaving the north of the county to the Grove. Plough and big woods are the portion of the Rufford: but, if dealt out to them with a lavish, it is not altogether with an even hand. They take in a strip of Derbyshire on the west. This is also plough; but a much lighter plough than where they near Lincolnshire and the Blankney on the east—the Trent running between the two Hunts. Sherwood Forest is their great playground in spring and autumn; and this is a vast extent of light covert and open glade. Eastward they have deep dense woodlands amid stiff clay, where when hounds run they can leave horses out of sight. In short, Sherwood Forest and the Derbyshire strip form the lighter side of the country; "The Clays" (as the east is aptly termed) the heavy side.

Sherwood Forest, whether as existing woodland or as reclaimed forest, occupies an immense breadth of the Rufford Country, and spreads even into the Grove and the South Notts dominions. Much of it, of course, has been disforested since the days of Robin Hood and his merry men. But the green woods still flourish in all their old magnificence over thousands of acres; and the Dukeries are masses of woodland beauty such as England can show nowhere else. Clumber (the Duke of Newcastle's), Welbeck (the Duke of Portland's), Thoresby (Lord Manvers'), and Rufford (Mr. Henry Saville's) compose the Dukeries— the two former being in Grove territory, and the whole being kept up by their owners with the greatest pride and care. The broad grass rides are tended so unremittingly, that the mossy turf will bear a carriage wheel—yet is so firm that a horse's hoof sinks to no great depth even in the wettest winter. Radiating from various central points these beautiful green cuttings throw the view in every direction through the masses of rich old timber. At the foot of the spreading oaks is a carpet of low bracken covert, which scarcely hinders fox or hounds, and altogether fails to hide the latter in their work. Thus, as you gallop the rides from point to point, your eye may follow the chase almost as freely as in open ground. It may indeed be said, without fear of contradiction, that no more lovely site for cubhunting exists than the Dukeries. To move through its grassy glades, and mark its bubbling trout streams, your heart goes back at once to sympathy with the bold outlaw, whose life was sport and whose food was the forest game, though he drew bow with a halter round his neck. The fat fallow-buck was guarded by penalty of death in those days. If Reynard were but as well cared for by the paternal government of modern times, sport would be more plentiful than it is in the forest of Shirewood.

Here and there in the forest is a patch of strong covert—possibly willow growth by a brookside—where a fox is most likely to be found. But the bulk of the great area that comes under the denomination of The Forest is either such as described above, or else has been broken up for cultivation, having detached woods scattered over its extent. An immense proportion of the Rufford Country—whether the Forest or the Clays—is, in fact, taken up with covert of one description or another. The Forest occupies the heart

The Rufford.

of the country; and deep strong woodlands figure largely amid the Clays.

The latter district, again, apart from its covert, is a totally different sort of country. The light soil of the Forest and Derbyshire side is replaced by a stiff holding clay of the most absolute type—cloggy, sticky and tenacious as wax. And yet field is separated from field by strong stake-and-bound fences that *must* be jumped, and with ditches that are only too ready to take in exhausted horseflesh. When the ground is at its wettest and deepest hounds can run best; and only a light man on a very high-class horse can hope to live with them then. Mr. Percy Williams, the most successful huntsman and horseman in the history of the Rufford, could skim like a swallow over the Clays. But then he was comparatively a feather in the scales, and rode horses that would have carried a welter weight over Leicestershire. He hunted the Rufford for fully twenty years, showing great sport. As a rider he had few superiors; and as a quick clever huntsman he could overcome many difficulties. He gave up the country about a dozen years ago; since which it has been in various hands, and Mr. Algernon Legard has now been succeeded by Mr. Harvey Bayly.

It will be seen that two distinct classes of horse are required to hunt with the Rufford. For the Forest side the best conveyance is a thoroughbred that can gallop the rides and jump a small fence outside; while for the Clays you must have a powerful horse that can go through the deepest dirt and jump a strong fence out of it. The one side entails easy work upon horses;

the other is not only tiring but is as difficult to live over, with hounds when they really run, as is to be found in any Hunt in the three kingdoms.

Very small fields attend the Rufford in any part of their country. There are no towns of any magnitude within range, unless we except Chesterfield on the western border—and that is not a very sporting place. Again, the number of resident gentry is but small— the Dukeries and other large properties usurping so much of the ground. The farmers have usually turned out in some strength; but the "bad times" have affected them, and limited their hunting, as much in Nottinghamshire as elsewhere. If you were minded to run down from a distance to see the Rufford, you might come to Mansfield or Tuxford (each about four hours from London). But a visit to Ollerton in spring or autumn would repay you best. You would see the Forest under its best conditions, and the Rufford in their prettiest sphere. Ollerton is quite in the centre of the Hunt, and touches upon the thick of the Forest.

The kennels are the property of Mr. Henry Savile (one of the strongest supporters of the Hunt), and occupy a charming situation in his park at Rufford Abbey. Four days a week see hounds in the field— Monday, Tuesday, Thursday, and Saturday being the days chosen.

For the Forest some of the chief meets are Thoresby Park, Rufford Abbey, Clipstone, Edwinstowe (the residence of Mr. Harvey Bayly, Master of the Rufford), Langwith Lodge (Col. Welfitt's, a former master), Mansfield-Wodehouse, &c.; while further west, in a

The Rufford.

more open country of light plough and some grass, are Sutton Scarsdale, Hardwick Hall, &c. In the extreme south, where the Forest runs down to Newstead Abbey, some small portion of it is drawn neutrally by the Rufford and the South Notts.

Turning to the Clays, we find woods too frequent to enumerate, and plough of one sample everywhere outside, excepting the meadows alongside the Trent, which foxes seldom touch. It is more than a fair scenting country, however; and foxes are as plentiful as they need be. The most notable woods, perhaps, are Wellow Park Woods, Ossington Woods (Lady Ossington's), Winkburn Woods (Col. Burnell's), Kelham Woods (Mr. Manners Sutton's), and Kirklington (Mrs. Boddam-Whetham's). With these, Kneesall Green, Laxton, and Walesby may be mentioned as chief meets on this side of the country.

www.ingramcontent.com/pod-product-compliance
Lightning Source LLC
Chambersburg PA
CBHW022104300426
44117CB00007B/582